"There is no gathering darkness in these reports from the evening of an active lifetime. International anecdotage, yes—anywhere from one to five stories per meditation, but mental dotage, no. Spiritual lessons that should be familiar come in fresh language sprinkled with ironic humor. This, implies the author, is what he has lived by. Memories of adventurous youth interweave with grandfatherly sentiments. Grave subjects are underlined with Scripture or other telling quotes, and sealed with prayer. Readers of any age who join the veteran author's outlook of faith will find self-pity irrelevant. Here we have matter for meditation, stories for opening a meeting, or thoughts to spark a Sunday school lesson."
—*John L. Ruth, author of* The Earth Is the Lord's

"In this book a beloved elder and skillful storyteller looks back over eighty-five years and shares wisdom he has gleaned from a lifetime of Christian service. As illustrations of spiritual truths, he uses his own experiences in Russia, Canada, England, Paraguay, Kansas, and Pennsylvania. The book, though interesting to all ages, is especially helpful to persons facing the last decades of life."
—*Elaine Sommers Rich, author of* Pondered in Her Heart

"Time and again I had wished I could attend a meeting where Peter Dyck would tell his stories. Now they are in this book, with all their color, pathos, and gripping, nourishing Bible truth! The stories are preserved for me, for many others, and for our progeny."
—*Ruth Brunk Stoltzfus, founder of* Heart to Heart *broadcast, and pastor*

1·57

Other Books by Peter J. Dyck

A Leap of Faith

The Great Shalom
Shalom at Last
Storytime Jamboree

Up from the Rubble
(with his wife, Elfrieda Dyck)

Getting Home Before Dark

Stories of Wisdom for All Ages

Peter J. Dyck

Herald
Press

Scottdale, Pennsylvania
Waterloo, Ontario

Library of Congress Cataloging-in-Publication Data
Dyck, Peter J., 1914-
  Getting home before dark : stories of wisdom for all ages /
Peter J. Dyck
    p. cm.
  Includes bibliographical references.
  ISBN 0-8361-9135-8 (alk. paper)
    1. Christian life—Meditations. 2. Christian aged—Religious
  life. 3. Christian life—Mennonite authors. I. Title.

  BV4580.D93 2000
  242—dc21
                                                    00-038842

The paper used in this publication is recycled and meets the minimum require-
ments of American National Standard for Information Sciences—Permanence of
Paper for Printed Library materials, ANSI Z39.48-1984.

To order or request information,
please call 1-800-759-4447 (individuals);
1-800-245-7894 (trade). Website: www.mph.org

To our daughters,

Ruth and Rebecca

Whatever you do, in word or deed,
do everything in the name of the Lord Jesus,
giving thanks to God the Father through him.
—Paul, in Colossians 3:17

Contents

Foreword

If you worry that growing old necessarily means growing inactive and useless, then you need to read this book. At age eighty-five, Peter Dyck passes on to us a rare resource that is both a summing up of his life and a call to others to a spiritually active elderhood.

Woven in with inspirational stories about his ministry are many valuable lessons, often tailored to seniors, about everything from how to travel as a gracious visitor to how to find happiness through the practice of forgiveness.

Through his tenacious belief in God and his untiring life of helping others, Dyck has fought the fight of faith and won. He wants to show others the way to the same victory.

Dyck's greatest contribution is his advice on spiritual agility, how to stay in good religious shape in spite of advancing age. He shows us a way to keep one foot on earth while reaching out to eternity with the other, a spiritual balancing act of extraordinary finesse, strength, and beauty.

Reading this book is like sitting with a spiritual sage, a mature mentor, who gently prods our conscience, pushes our commitment, and nudges our compassion toward greater holiness, virtue, and caregiving.

Dyck will not allow us to excuse ourselves from active discipleship because we think we are too old. Rather, he invites us to use all our senior years to more and more become the "new creation" God intends us to be.

—*Jerry K. Robbins, Morgantown, West Virginia*
Retired after thirty-five years of service in campus ministry

1

For God's Sake, Do Something!

For God's sake, do something!
—Martin Luther

Sometimes I find it extremely difficult to get started on a new writing project. Writing this book is a good example. I piled up articles, books, and notes in my "incubation box" for two years, but nothing hatched. One day my wife, Elfrieda, was in the hospital, and I had a clean desk, with all correspondence answered and no excuse for further procrastination. So I simply took that leap and plunged in, just to get started. I know from experience that once I am started, my juices will begin to flow. I will actually enjoy writing.

Retirement is like that. I don't mean just stopping the work; that's not retirement. Successful retirement is a deliberate process with a conscious and more or less clear beginning, starting long before age sixty-five.

At all ages we need to be aware of our life now, in the past, and in the future. Then we will be like the ideal poet whom Matthew Arnold commends "To a Friend":

> From first youth tested up to extreme old age,
> Business could not make dull, nor passion wild:
> Who saw life steadily and saw it whole.

With a steady and whole vision of life, we will be able to make wise choices and live with purpose.

Martin Luther didn't like the slow pace of the Reformation and the halfhearted attitude of many of the German people. He was so frustrated that he cried out in one of his public meetings, "Um Gottes-willen, tut etwas! (for God's sake, do something!)." So I'm going to do something. But what? What would I really like to do during my retirement, remembering that I may be retired for five, ten, twenty, or more years?

I heard of a man in Ontario who looked forward to his retirement with great longing and expectation. How wonderful it would be when that day came. He would sleep late, have a leisurely breakfast, put on his slippers, and read the morning paper.

The man dreamed of sitting by the window and watching the children go to school, then sipping a second cup of coffee and watching men and women hurrying off to work. He had been working and waiting for that bit of heaven for many years. At last he would be in a successful retirement.

He lived to see that day. He did just as he had planned it: with slippers, coffee, and the recliner. It felt so good. He really enjoyed it—for a few months. His wife was the first to notice small changes in his behavior and moods. He became restless. He seemed frustrated. He didn't know what it was. Then he developed physical symptoms of something wrong.

He went to the doctor. You guessed it. The diagnosis: "Your idleness is going to kill you." The prescription: "Get off that recliner and do something!"

Dear Lord, for my own good, for the good of others, and for the sake of your kingdom, keep me out of that recliner and show me what I can do now that I am retired.

2
I Can Do Everything!

*I can do all things through [Christ,] who
strengthens me.*
—Paul, in Philippians 4:13

If I say I can do everything, people will take it as a joke, an exaggeration, or a ploy to get their attention. However, I didn't say that; the apostle Paul did. He would have made a good American.

When other countries were (and still are) drawing borders around ethnic, religious, and cultural traditions, the United States formed a pluralistic society with a government of the people, by the people, and for the people. When others thought it was impossible to have a viable economy without cheap slave labor, England and then the United States abolished slavery. Though some discrimination and unfairly low wages remain, the country is still striving to achieve these ideals.

When nobody believed it could be done, Americans sent a man to the moon. Now the Hubble space telescope is 380 miles away from earth, searching the universe for clues of what's out there. Perhaps Hubble will let us know when our cosmos is going to end and whether it will be with a whimper or a bang.

Don't tell Americans that they can't do everything. Someone saw the inscription, "What is past is prologue," on the cornerstone of the National Archives building in Washington. He asked a taxi driver what it meant. The cabbie replied, "That's government talk. It means, 'Brother, you ain't seen nothin' yet!' "

When Paul writes to the Philippians that he can do everything, however, he isn't boasting about technological progress or merely being optimistic. He means that for Christ he can endure hardships, such as floggings, jail, hunger, and thirst (2 Cor. 11:24-27). Paul admits that he cannot do this in his own strength, but only "through [Christ,] who strengthens me."

Here is a message for young and old alike. The young people can say that with Christ's help they can kick bad habits, resist temptations, and control their tempers. The older people can say that with Christ's help they can overcome the fear of aging, frustration about their loss of energy, and resentment when told to move into a retirement community.

Yes, indeed, with Christ we can do all these things—and more! Jesus says, "I tell you, the one who believes in me will also do the works that I do and, in fact, will do greater works than these" (John 14:12).

Like Jesus, we all can reach out to the needy world around us. Younger people can serve others with their enthusiasm and vigor. Older people offer more experience and perhaps a bit more wisdom.

Paul says he can endure hunger. We say that in a world where every morning there are three hundred thousand more mouths to feed, we can share and give. We can resist the temptation to waste; we can practice good stewardship of God's resources.

Paul says he can endure thirst. We say that in a world where 40 percent of the people do not have enough water or safe water, we can make it possible for Mennonite Central Committee (MCC, Akron, Pa.) to help them get water. MCC can send out experts who dig wells, build dams and cisterns, and conserve runoff water from hills and roofs.

Paul says that he has endured thirty-nine lashings five different times, countless floggings, and has been "beaten with rods" three times (2 Cor. 11:23-25). We say no to the violence all around us, in streets and schools, on the screen, and in more than twenty countries where there is open warfare. We send parcels to war victims and peacemakers to help people resolve their conflicts. We say no to capital punishment and yes to rehabilitation. We say no to killing and yes to life.

We can do all this through Christ, who strengthens us. Indeed, when we act together in harmony, with clear vision and determination, it is not a boast to say that we are doing more than Jesus did, as he said we would. At least we reach more people than he did in his life on earth.

The same is true in education. With 40 percent of the world's population illiterate, our churches are doing a fantastic job in development, not teaching little children to read, but training teachers to teach the children. These new teachers act as multipliers, reaching more people, not only with the alphabet, but also with the Word of God. This is true with the printed page, the radio, and television. The younger generation is making videos with Christian messages in many languages for people who have never heard the gospel.

It is an encouraging and wonderful experience to see how some Christian young people are resisting the pressures of the world (consumerism, nationalism, and militarism) and are actually marching to a different drummer. With good education under their belts, far better than their parents and grandparents, they are determined to make a difference in the world. With Christ's help, they will.

For the younger as well as the older generation, we need to remember that, as Paul says, we can do everything *if* (1) our thinking is changed, and (2) we let Christ help us.

Let us look first at thinking. It all starts in our heads. Paul knows that and tells Romans, "Do not be conformed to this world, but be transformed by the renewing of your minds" (12:2). Another translation (TEV) says, God can give "a complete change of your mind." To the Philippians, Paul urges, "Let the same mind be in you that was in Christ Jesus" (2:5).

These fascinating statements reveal a profound insight into human behavior. Paul is saying, "Change your thinking that has been formed by your teachers, the media, and the culture surrounding you." Our security is not in military strength. Our happiness does not depend on money, possessions, or good looks.

Real living does not come by looking out for ourselves first. Fulfillment is not achieved by being a workaholic. Youth is not the time to indulge our every whim and wish, and old age is not the time to behave as if the end has come.

Now comes the second step, letting Christ help us. We seem to be able to do a good bit on our own, especially if we have strong wills and have received good training. However, sooner or later we have to confess with Paul, "I do not do what I want, but I do the very thing I hate. . . . I can will what is right, but I cannot do it" (Rom. 7:15, 18).

At first I thought that in this insight, we older people are a step ahead of the younger generation. We have lived long enough to know that we need help, while the youth may still think they can do it on their own. On second thought, that may be wishful thinking. If turning to Christ actually comes from experiencing our weakness, if it comes with age, then many older people would turn to Christ. But that has not happened. Most commitments are made early in life rather than late.

Perhaps young people have an advantage because they are more flexible and open to change than we seniors are. Youth as much as seniors can discover the truth of David's statement, "By my God I can leap over a wall" (2 Sam. 22:30). Our inability to do that has nothing to do with arthritis and stiff knees.

With Christ we can do even better than leaping over a wall—we can tear down that wall! (Eph. 2:14). Our world is full of walls that need to be torn down—walls of fear and distrust, walls of pride and hate, walls of suspicion and envy, walls of racism and nationalism, walls of intolerance and bigotry, walls of ignorance and prejudice.

Instead of building walls, let's build bridges. Tear down the wall that society has built between the youth and older people, and build a bridge from the one to the other. We can start at both ends and meet in the middle, as is sometimes done when building bridges over natural divides.

Being bridge builders is so much fun, so rewarding and satisfying. We can begin in the family, move on to the neighbors, to the church, and into society. It will take deliberate thought and effort, and it will work best if we enlist others to help us. Once we recognize the urgent need for bridge building, and once we call on the Lord to help us, we can do it. We can build bridges of love and understanding, tolerance and respect, trust and cooperation.

It can be done if we do two things: change our thinking and let Christ empower us. We can be quite confident, whether young or old, that with God's power, we can make great progress in doing everything that God wants us to do.

Lord, there is so much in our world that needs to be changed.
If my thinking needs to be changed, then let me change it.
Thank you for the promise that you will help me become an
agent of change.

3
Redeeming the Time

Be careful then how you live,
not as unwise people but as wise,
making the most of the time.
—Paul, in Ephesians 5:15

For my sixty-fifth birthday, the MCC staff gave me a suitcase and a book. I laughed at the suitcase because I thought my traveling days were over. That was twenty years ago. Now the suitcase is worn out, and I still travel.

I randomly opened the book *Passages,* by Gail Sheehy (see Bibliography), and spotted this statement: "When men retire, they soon die; when women retire, they keep right on cooking." There's likely a lot of truth in that. Statistics have often shown that women outlive men by at least four years, on average.

Americans are quite time conscious. We say that time is money. Our MCC International Visitor Exchange Program provides orientation for young people from thirty or more countries. We have to explain that Americans regard time very differently from many African and South American countries.

MCC tells these young people that when they get to a meeting five minutes late, it is enough to simply excuse themselves. If they arrive twenty minutes late, it is better to add a brief explanation, to say they had car trouble or whatever. If they are late by half an hour or more, which is common and doesn't mean a thing in their home countries, they need to give more of an explanation than just to say, "We had car trouble."

Most of them accept this with a smile, though we can tell that they are amused by it. In their assignments, they soon learn that it is not acceptable in North America to consistently arrive late for breakfast, work, or church.

The apostle Paul, an avid traveler who must have worn out many pairs of sandals in his church-planting efforts, urges the Ephesians to make the most of their time. That echoes what the psalmist said hundreds of years earlier: "So teach us to count our days / that we may gain a wise heart" (Ps. 90:12).

What does it mean to gain a wise heart, to make the most of our time? The Chinese philosopher Yutang Lin says, "Besides the noble art of getting things done, there is the noble art of leaving things undone. The wisdom of life consists in the elimination of nonessentials."

This modern person talks about the "wisdom of life" much the same as the psalmist prayed long ago for a "wise heart." Both are related to the wise use of our time.

During a life span of 70 years, the average American spends 17 years sleeping, 28 working, nine relaxing, five eating, five traveling, three being sick, two dressing, and one year on religion. How much of this is wise use of time? How much is wasted time? Most of us spend time foolishly and even kill time. *Poor Richard's Almanac* exhorts, "Dost thou value life? Then do not squander time, for time is the stuff life is made up of."

When we still held jobs, we attended time seminars. We tried to make the best use of our time. We got up with the alarm clock. We turned off the TV. We worked hard. But when we are in retirement, we have time, perhaps too much time. We may not know what to do with all our time.

That brings us to a significant detail about time. In the Greek New Testament, the word *time* is used in two ways:

chronos means days and hours, chronological time; *kairos* means opportunities. Time is nothing without content. When Paul urges the Ephesians to be wise, "making the most of the time," he adds a reason: "because the days are evil." He is not using *time* in the common sense of length. Instead, he means, "Seize the opportunities to be a witness for Christ."

Hence, instead of filling each hour with frantic activity, we need to ask ourselves the basic question: What is the purpose of our life as a whole? If we are clear on that, we have likely conquered 90 percent of our temptation to waste or kill time.

If a grandchild asked me what the purpose of my life is, I would likely answer, "The purpose of my life is that by faith and struggle, by joy and sorrow, by slipping back and going forward, I become more like Christ." If I fail in that, no matter how well I have succeeded in using my time otherwise, I have failed.

Today is always commonplace. Yesterday was beautiful, and tomorrow is full of promise. The challenge for the Christian is to carry into each moment the greatness and solemnity of the purpose of life. That will be redeeming the time, putting meaningful content into time, and seizing the opportunities.

I thank you, Lord, for life. Help me in my closing years to make good use of my time by focusing more on the ultimate purpose of living. As I seek to become more like you, grant that some of this may be passed on to the younger people in my life.

4
Pegs and Ropes

Sing, O barren one who did not bear;
burst into song and shout, you who have not been
*   in labor!*
For the children of the desolate woman will be more
*   than the children of her that is married,*
*   says the LORD.*
Enlarge the site of your tent,
*   and let the curtains of your habitations*
*   be stretched out;*
do not hold back;
*   lengthen your cords and strengthen your stakes.*
—Isaiah 54:1-2

In these pages, I often refer to children and grandchildren, though not all seniors have such offspring. For some, this was a personal choice; for others, it was a "gift," desired or not (1 Cor. 7:7). It has always been like that.

Today couples feel bad when they want children and cannot have them. In the days of Isaiah, it must have been ten times harder. When a married woman did not have children, it was a personal disappointment, a social disgrace, and even counted as God's punishment.

Isaiah uses this image of a barren woman to describe Israel's experience. The people took the prophet to be saying, "God has punished you for your disobedience. Now he has forgiven you, and your days of suffering are over. Like the barren woman, you were disappointed and disgraced; but now that's past." The woman is going to have children, lots of them!

Lengthen your cords and strengthen your stakes. Enlarge your tents. Good days of peace and plenty are ahead. Hardships and disappointments are over. A new chapter is beginning. There will be a rich harvest.

Many older people have testified that in retirement they experienced living a new chapter, being unexpectedly fruitful. Some people, such as Wilma Rudolph, are shining examples of overcoming handicaps and difficulties and winning.

Wilma was born prematurely, contracted double pneumonia, and then had scarlet fever. Even worse, polio left one leg and foot twisted inward. What chance would the world offer a black girl from Nashville, shuffling about with metal braces on her legs? However, Wilma had a dream. Her Christian mother kept saying, "Honey, the most important thing in life is for you to believe in your dream and to keep on trying."

That's what she did. At age twelve, Wilma discovered to her great joy that girls could run, jump, and play ball. Soon she realized that disciplined practice was the secret to success. Wilma ran every day. She got on a basketball team, and the team won. She competed in track and won. She beat every girl in the Tennessee high schools.

Wilma entered the Olympics. In 1956 at Melbourne, she won a bronze medal in the 400-meter relay. At the 1960 Olympics in Rome, 80,000 fans chanted, "Wilma! Wilma! Wilma!" as she entered the arena. Wilma, once a little crippled girl with leg braces, won the 100-meter dash and the 200-meter dash. Her team won the 400-meter relay. She was the first woman in history to win three gold medals in track-and-field Olympic events.

Edna Ruth Byler lived in her husband's shadow, but she had a vision. She was a homemaker, taking care of their two children. Joe was sent to Europe to do relief work during

World War II, leaving his family in Pennsylvania for over a year. Edna was caring for the children. In addition, she started to do a few extra things for other people.

In 1947, Edna accompanied Joe on an administrative trip to Puerto Rico. While Joe went about his business, Edna watched the women do beautiful embroidery. She was fascinated. Many of the women were desperately poor, living in miserable shacks, hardly able to feed their families. Edna's heart went out to them. She wondered what they could do to supplement their family income.

As Edna thought and prayed about it, one strategy became clear to her. She decided to buy some embroidery, pay them cash for it, take it home, and try to sell it. That's what she did.

Back in Akron, Edna tried to interest MCC in starting a self-help program for poor Puerto Rican families. MCC was still mostly a man's world and declined this well-intentioned proposal as not being businesslike.

Edna had something the men lacked: imagination! She kept ordering embroidered material and other handcrafted goods and selling them in churches. By 1958, the Byler's basement looked like a store, with materials spread around. It was a warehouse and a gift shop. Before long, she was giving employment to women, not only in Puerto Rico, but also in Jordan and other countries. She bought their handcrafted materials, sold them in North America, and turned the net proceeds over to MCC for relief.

Eventually, MCC caught on and took over the project, first calling it Self-Help and then renaming it Ten Thousand Villages. In 1998, poor women and men in 35 countries were supplementing their incomes by making 2,300 different handcrafted items. These products were retailed in Canada and the United States through some 190 stores, netting about 15 million dollars for MCC.

We do not know how many people have benefited from

this project. A conservative figure would be at least the 50 thousand who actually have produced the items. If we count the children who now can eat better and go to school because father or mother is working, then the figure is between 60 and 100 thousand. With the proceeds, MCC was also able to help many others.

Don't let anybody say one person can't make a difference! When Edna Byler died on July 6, 1978, we recognized her initiative and enterprise by planting a tree in her memory at the Akron (Pa.) Mennonite Church.

Another example is the Canadian Foodgrains Bank. In 1975, a group of people who had served overseas with MCC were concerned about continued famines in many countries, frequently because of revolutions and wars. As many as 20 million people were dying every year from hunger. On the other hand, farmers in Canada had lots of grain, sometimes more than they could sell.

These MCC veterans put their heads together and urged farmers to give wheat to feed starving people, especially in Asia and Africa. They called it the Canadian Foodgrains Bank (CFB). My brother John R. Dyck was the executive director.

At first, it was a small operation, a load here and a load there. Within a few years, word spread and farmers contributed generously and willingly. Then the Canadian government supported this good cause by donating three bushels whenever the farmers contributed one.

The CFB faced initial opposition because it seemed contrary to MCC's basic philosophy of helping people help themselves. Some feared that giving relief would inhibit long-term agricultural development in areas where the wheat would be consumed.

On the other hand, should we not feed people when they are starving? Furthermore, much of the grain was used as an incentive for work.

In Ethiopia, five thousand workers are busy from January

through June, the dry season, building dams to catch rainwater for irrigation. For their labors, they are paid with wheat. Ethiopia is only one of the twelve countries in which CFB is involved. Thus, about 150 thousand people receive such direct help in a year. In addition, a single dam will provide water to irrigate vegetables that will feed another 100 thousand people.

In 1983, MCC invited other Canadian churches to join CFB; nine other denominations and agencies became members. In one year, more than 40 thousand metric tons of grain valued at over 20 million dollars are shipped overseas.

In 1998, to demonstrate the joy of working together in CFB, 65 farmers in the Westlock area of Alberta rolled out their combines to see how fast they could harvest 160 acres of wheat—a large field! They set a world record by doing it in 15 minutes and 43 seconds.

A notice in a Saskatchewan newspaper read: "If you're not afraid of hard work for a good cause, call us at CFB." No one knows how many millions of hungry people receive food because of the Canadian Foodgrains Bank.

Pegs and ropes. Yes, indeed, strengthen your pegs and lengthen your ropes. Never think that one person can't make a difference. That's why we recycle the newspapers at our retirement center. We take them to a dairy farmer. Our newspapers serve at least three purposes: news for readers, bedding for cows, and fertilizer for the soil.

Heavenly Father, I may feel that I have no special gift to offer. Show me today what I can do to brighten the corner where I live. Help me to encourage someone with a smile, a word, or some deed, however small it may be. With your blessing, it can multiply and grow.

5
Sharing Our Joy

I am glad and rejoice with all of you—
and in the same way you also must be glad
and rejoice with me.
—Paul, in Philippians 2:17-18

The New English Bible translates this verse, "Rejoice, you no less than I, and let us share our joy!" I like that. It sounds like the familiar saying that shared joy is doubled, and shared sorrow is halved.

We were on board the steamship *Volendam* with 1,693 passengers going to South America. They all were refugees, some planning to pioneer in Paraguay and others in Uruguay. Among them was Ernst Regehr, a farmer and a minister from Prussia. Like all the others, he had endured World War II (WW II). When the Russians occupied Poland and Prussia, he lost his farm, all his possessions, most of his relatives, and the church with the cemetery where his parents lay buried. He lost everything, even his country—but not his faith in God.

We boarded the ship on October 7, 1948, and twenty-one days later we arrived at our destination. Every evening we had devotions on the open top deck, the only place large enough for so many people to gather. The choir would sing, there might be a recitation by a young person, someone would read the Scripture, and then one of the lay ministers or I would preach. People looked forward to this time of worship and fellowship.

When it was Ernst Regehr's turn to bring the message, he read from Philippians, one joy passage after another. He touched on almost all sixteen of them: "Rejoice in the Lord always; again I will say, Rejoice!" (4:4). "I rejoice in the Lord greatly" (4:10). "Make my joy complete: be of the same mind" (2:2). "I remember you, constantly praying with joy in every one of my prayers for all of you" (1:3). "Finally, my brothers and sisters, rejoice in the Lord" (3:1).

The people got the message. Or did they? They understood that we should be thankful and rejoice in the knowledge that we have a loving and caring God. That was no problem. We don't always understand God, but the Bible says God loves us, and that's what we have believed from childhood.

They also understood that this life of pain and suffering is not the end, even though they lost all their possessions and were refugees. There is life after death, when God will wipe away all the tears from our eyes. We rejoice, Regehr said, because our ultimate destination is heaven, not merely Uruguay.

Oh, yes, Brother Regehr, we understand, the refugees thought. In some spiritual way, we do rejoice. But what are you saying? Should we be thankful and rejoice that we have lost all our possessions? Our houses and lands? Our horses and cows? Our gardens and orchards? Our schools and churches?

Brother Regehr, what are you saying? You can't be serious! Surely you're going too far! How can we be thankful for the Russians brutally invading our country, taking everything we had, and then driving us out of our homeland with nothing but the clothes on our backs? Brother Regehr, surely you don't mean that!

But he did mean it! It was so quiet you could hear subdued crying. Over a thousand people listened to him explain that Paul was in chains in prison when he wrote that joyful letter to the Philippians. What did he have to rejoice about? He was sitting in a dark dungeon, with cold irons around his ankles and rats running around. He faced an uncertain future, maybe death. His lot was much worse than ours. Yet no less than sixteen times in that letter, he says, "*Rejoice!*"

The waves splashed against the ship. A seagull glided silently above the masts. People reached for their handkerchiefs. Some shook their heads in disbelief at what they heard.

Still Brother Regehr went on quoting the apostle Paul, all the time showing by his body language, and especially by the expression on his face, that he meant every word he said. He certainly was not lecturing his people, and he wasn't really preaching to them either. He was just sharing his own joy. He never raised his voice. Often he smiled. He seemed so relaxed and happy. The people were stunned.

At last, he was finished. He concluded his message with a prayer. For some of his listeners, that was the last straw. With a cheerful voice, he thanked God that he had allowed everything to be taken away from them:

Our hands were always so full, and now they are empty. They are empty so that you can fill them with treasures more precious than anything we have ever possessed.

O Lord, thank you for giving us the opportunity to start all over again in Uruguay: in our schools and churches, in our families and marriages, in our community relations with one another, and in our own spiritual lives.

Lord, so many people wish that they could be given just one more chance, the once-in-a-lifetime opportunity to start all over again, but it is not granted to them. To us it is granted, Lord, to start all over again, and we thank you from the bottom of our hearts. Amen.

That night on the *Volendam* the refugees were discussing only one topic—Ernst Regehr's message. Many agreed, some were uncertain, and a few had the courage to disagree.

Two days later we had a funeral. The sea was calm, but my heart was troubled. How were we going to bury the body? I had never done anything like that before. Elfrieda and I talked about it. All we knew about funerals at sea was what we had seen in films. We agreed that we wanted nothing like that: sliding the body down into the water the way children in the park scoot down the sliding boards. Splash! That's it, now he's gone. Our reaction: No way!

I spoke with the captain, who was understanding and cooperative. His crew would make a casket. The same equipment used to lower lifeboats would lower the coffin into the water. For special effect, we would do it just after sunset. He would stop the engines, and the ship would glide silently through the waves.

Flood lamps would illuminate the coffin on its slow and quiet way downward; other lights would be turned off. The captain put the first officer in charge of everything. I was to lead the service.

What an unforgettable experience that became! Just as planned, the engines stopped and the ship slid silently through the water. The coffin went down ever so slowly. Over a thousand people were leaning on the railings, watching and praying.

At last the coffin reached the water. I heard the first officer command, "In God's name, let go!" The sailors above us released the ropes, which spiraled down in artistic coils until they reached the water. We could still see the coffin, which seemed to be gliding along on the surface. Then we saw it slightly submerged. For a brief moment, it was still there, and then it just faded away.

While all eyes were peering into the water, we suddenly heard a loud blast on the foghorn. The lights came on, and the ship began to vibrate as the motors started up again. We were full steam ahead to Uruguay.

Just as Ernst Regehr's message had been the topic of conversation after his evening devotions, so the day after the funeral, everybody on the ship talked only about being buried at sea. Many of the refugees were deeply moved. We began to entertain new thoughts about the resurrection. The body would be gone, dissolved, and disintegrated, but the Spirit would return to God. How could that be? It was another mystery that we could not understand but only believe.

Some years later we visited the former refugees, who became pioneers in Uruguay. Ernst Regehr gave me a copy of a catechism he had written for young people, to help prepare them for baptism and church membership. It had 250 questions and answers.

I was not surprised to see that the theme of gratitude and joy was dominant in the catechism, as shown in question 248:

We are no better than other people, but we are better off than many other people. We have the gospel, and we have Jesus Christ, and through him we have peace. But the best is yet to come, in eternity. Now listen carefully: Are we really a happy and thankful people? Do others notice our joy wherever we go and whatever we do?

Thank you, Brother Regehr, for calling us to be joyful in all situations. We do believe what Paul wrote to the Philippians: "God will fully satisfy every need of yours according to his riches in glory in Christ Jesus" (4:19).

Lord, make me a joyful person—not just happy on the surface, or because I have what I need, or because I can sing that "everything's going my way." Let me be truly joyful because I know and believe that you love me and will take me home at last to be with you forever.

6

Six Sources of Family Strength

Be subject to one another out of reverence for Christ.
Wives, be subject to your husbands. . . .
Husbands, love your wives. . . .
Children, obey your parents in the Lord. . . .
Honor your father and mother. . . .
Fathers, do not provoke your children to anger,
*   but bring them up in the discipline and*
*   instruction of the Lord.*
—Paul, in Ephesians 5:21-22; 6:1-4

As seniors, we have many advantages over our children and grandchildren. We have more time, experience, and perhaps money, at least a somewhat guaranteed income, though it may not always keep up with the outgo. With willingness to put these to good advantage for everyone, let us consider some basic factors that make for strong families. Many messages are long on describing symptoms and short on prescriptions, but not here.

The Symptoms

1. The American family is sick and in deep trouble. One study found that husbands and wives communicate with each other 17 minutes a day.
2. About 50 percent of marriages end in divorce.
3. In a divorce, everyone gets hurt, but the only truly innocent party, the child, gets hurt the most.
4. Premarital sex has become a teenage sport and adventure.

5. In 1998, firearms were used to kill 5,285 children in the United States, 153 in Canada, 109 in France, 57 in Germany, 19 in England, and none in Japan!
6. Since homosexuals have "come out of the closet," the issue has divided families and churches.

The Prescription

1. Recognizing and Admitting Our Interdependence

Equality of the sexes is great: equal rights, equal opportunities, and equal pay for equal work. However, men are not women, and women are not men. We are built differently, function and feel differently, and think differently. To say *different* is not a value judgment, not better nor worse, just different. We complement each other. We need each other.

The Creation story sheds light on this. First, there was only Adam and no women. According to Genesis 2:4b-24, it was truly a man's world. That should have made Adam happy, but he was lonely and likely yawning a lot. God saw his condition, knew what the problem was, and knew how to solve it.

So the LORD God caused a deep sleep to fall upon the man, and he slept; then he took one of his ribs and closed up its place with flesh. And the rib that the LORD God had taken away from the man he made into a woman and brought her to the man. Then the man said, "**WOW!** [okay, I added that]. This at last is bone of my bones and flesh of my flesh." (Gen. 2:21-23)

Some believe God didn't take Adam's rib, but took his backbone to make the woman. Seeing some of the spineless men around, that's an interesting thought. However it happened, men and women do complement and enhance each other.

All married couples know that it is by the grace of God that our marriages have not fallen apart. Another reason keeps Elfrieda and me from filing for divorce: we need each other. I don't remember people's names, but Elfrieda does. She doesn't remember directions, but I do. Separated, we are both lost; together, we make a good team.

We were invited to a farm in Kansas to have dinner with a family in our church. There were so many Stuckys, Waltners, and Krehbiels that I got them all mixed up. I could find the farm, but I couldn't remember the names of the people. On the other hand, Elfrieda knew all the 800 members of the church and their children by name. However, if she had to go to that farm alone, she'd never find the place. A cloverleaf is enough to confuse her.

I had no problem finding the farm. Once there, Elfrieda whispered the names of our host family into my ear, and all was well. So we decided long ago that we simply had to stay together. Divorce would be disastrous for both of us.

There is a serious point in such an experience and in the creation account: we need to recognize, admit, and frankly acknowledge our deep interdependence. We need each other in a hundred different ways—not just for remembering names or reading a map.

2. Respecting Each Other

Surprised? You probably thought that if love is not the first source of family strength, it surely ought to be the second. No way! Without respect, love doesn't have a chance. Respect first, then love.

Take the findings on premarital sex, for example. Studies show that engaged couples who indulged in premarital sex were far less likely to get married than couples who did not. The *Today* TV show interviewed young people about sexual relations and reported that at least 40 percent of teenagers had sex by age fourteen.

The host of the show asked one fourteen-year-old boy about his relationship with a girl after having sex with her.

He said he didn't want to have her around. The host pressed the point, and the boy became upset, repeating that he didn't want to have anything to do with the girl after sex. It was obvious that there had been no love, no intimate relationship, and no respect—just the biological experience of sex.

Respect for each other is the foundation of family strength. The opposite of respect is to despise. Respecting is looking at someone with esteem, always looking up, never looking down on someone, never just using someone for self-gratification. A husband and wife respect each other as real persons, as capable, and always as made in the image of God.

Respect shows in the tone of voice, in body language, in attitudes, and in everything, even in not opening the other's mail. When respect goes down the drain, the cement that holds the marriage together is gone.

That goes for the children as well. Children must be taught to respect their parents, their siblings, and other people. And parents must respect their children. However, respect has to be earned. Parents must behave in ways that encourage their children to respect them. In the climate of respect, love grows.

3. Submitting to Each Other

Paul wrote to the Ephesians, "Be subject to one another out of reverence for Christ" (5:21). In our efforts to achieve an egalitarian society, we play down the differences between men and women. But the big thing is learning how to get along with each other.

People bristle when they read, "Wives, be subject to your husbands as you are to the Lord" (5:22). In no text does Paul call for men to rule over women. He says that in marriage husband and wife should be "subject one to another" (5:21). This was a radical position to take in Paul's day. Half of this equation means that the husband is "subject" to the wife, and vice versa, one to the other (cf. 1 Cor. 7:3-4, 33-34). Such mutual subjection was unknown in a world where both Gentiles and Jews had a low view of women. Rabbis prayed, "I thank you, Lord, that I was not born a Gentile, a slave, or a woman." They seriously debated whether women had souls. Rabbinical law seemed to treat a woman as a thing rather than a person.

Ancient Semitic custom let the husband divorce his wife by simply declaring, "You are not my wife" (cf. Hos. 2:2). The Mosaic law ruled that he had to (have a scribe, likely) write a document (cf. Jer. 3:8), yet divorce was still easy: "Suppose a man enters into marriage with a woman, but she does not please him because he finds something objectionable about her, and so he writes her a certificate of divorce, puts it in her hand, and sends her out of his house" (Deut. 24:1).

Later some rabbis trivialized what could be counted as "objectionable." Thus Hillel said that if a wife spoiled her husband's dinner by putting too much salt on it, that was enough cause for divorce. If she talked with another man in the street or went out without covering her head, he could send her out of his house.

This Ephesians 5 passage is not about subordination of the wife to her husband, as claimed so often; it is about love (see below). Here Paul expressly describes the kind of love that the husband must have for his wife:

• It must be a *sacrificial* love. "Husbands, love your wives, just as Christ loved the church and gave himself up for her" (5:25).

• It must be a *caring* love. "Husbands should love their wives as they do their own bodies. . . . He nourishes and tenderly cares for it" (5:28-29).

• It must be a *permanent* love. "For this reason a man will leave his father and mother and be joined to his wife, and the two will become one flesh" (5:31).

Paul makes it clear that in a Christian marriage there are not just two partners, but three: the third is Christ.

4. Loving Each Other

It is a tall order for husbands to love their wives as Christ loved the church. This means sacrificial, caring, and permanent love, not merely romantic love. The term *romantic* comes from translated Latin stories. In German, a novel is called a *Roman*, an imaginative and unreal life, where people live happily ever after.

A young man feels romantic love when he writes to his ladylove, "I will climb the highest mountain, cross the hottest desert, and swim the widest ocean to come to you." He spins out a whole page on how nothing in the world can keep him from her. Then he adds, "P.S. I'll see you on Saturday, if it doesn't rain."

Once MCC placed a young German exchange visitor in the Mennonite Publishing House. He was so happy, learning new things every day and enjoying his relationships with the people working there. Every week, however, he received a letter from his girlfriend in Germany: "Ohne dich, sterbe ich! (without you, I die!)."

It finally got to him. He had been in the program only a couple of months when he needed counseling. The people at the Publishing House tried their best but accomplished nothing. He was going to break his agreement and go back to Germany. That's when I stepped into the act at Frankfurt. "Easy," I told myself. "I'll just have the girl come to my office. She'll realize that if she really loves him, she should encourage him to stay and finish his year. He's happy in America, and she will be brave and wait."

What an unforgettable, utterly frustrating evening! After two hours, she still kept repeating that stupid ditty, "Ohne dich, sterbe ich," and saying she would keep writing that to him. We had one more lever to pull, one that should bring them both to their senses: I pointed out that, according to the contract, if he did not finish his twelve months in the assignment, he would have to pay for his travel and other expenses.

I can still see him coming to our Frankfurt office every payday for nine months, to pay his debt. Even worse, within weeks of his return to Germany, his girlfriend left him and married another man.

In his book *The Art of Loving*, Erich Fromm says, "The romanticizer fashions his object in the image of his own imagination, worships the image, and ignores the real person." Romantic love is not enough to sustain marriage for a lifetime. How different is Paul's image of husbands loving their wives as Christ loved the church and gave himself up for her.

That beautiful 1 Corinthian 13 passage comes to mind. Say it aloud, and meditate on it:

Love is patient; love is kind;
love is not envious or boastful or arrogant or rude.
It does not insist on its own way;
it is not irritable or resentful;
it does not rejoice in wrongdoing,
but rejoices in the truth. (13:4-6)

Somebody said, "Repeating that text is just a crutch. If I don't love my wife, reading that passage a thousand times won't change anything." Maybe not; but Paul urges us to build our character by thinking about things that are true and pure (Phil. 4:8-9). Do you have a better suggestion? Marriages are in such bad shape that we can use all the help we can get.

Here's something we can learn from the Russians. At their wedding palaces, the bride and groom step onto a cute little rug to take their marriage vows. When they step back, the attendant rolls up the rug and hands it to the groom. They take it home. This is an impressive marriage ceremony.

That little rug cannot save a marriage. But suppose after some time, they have a misunderstanding. They talk, argue, and raise their voices until one remembers that little wedding rug. It is not just a souvenir to be taken out on their anniversaries and admired. It is a tool to use in situations of conflict.

They bring out the wedding rug, and toss it on the living room floor. Both husband and wife stand on it. There is one problem: the rug is small, and they don't feel like standing that close to each other. It was just wonderful on their wedding day—but not now! If, however, they have the courage or the humor to stand on it together, what do you suppose is going to happen?

A man in Pennsylvania called me not long ago to report that he had heard me tell about the wedding rug in Russia. He said that he had just gotten married as he stood with his bride on a small wedding rug. He laughed heartily, then got serious and said, "I hope it works."

Marriages cannot be saved simply by repeating 1 Corinthians 13 or standing on wedding rugs. Unless we work at our marriages, they will fall apart. Show me a happily married couple, and I will show you two people who work at their marriage. Love needs to be nurtured in a hundred different ways: a kind word, a smile, a gesture, doing the extra things, saying "please" and "thank you," and above all often saying and meaning, "I'm sorry," and "I love you."

Like birds, we must keep the nest warm. Watch how they do it when they are hatching their eggs. They never leave it for long. Even if one or the other of us must travel, we can use the telephone, letters, or e-mail to help us keep the nest warm.

5. Having Clarity and Agreement on Financial Matters

First, money itself is neither good nor bad. It is "the love of money" that is a root of evil (1 Tim. 6:10).

Second, muddled or unfair finances can lead to more squabbles than two pups fighting over the same bone. A wife was unhappy and explained to her husband that it wasn't the money but the principle of the thing that aggravated her. Since he controlled the money, he had what money represents: power and control. He made all the decisions. She resented him running the family affairs as he wished without her participation.

There are many different ways for husband and wife to handle their finances, and one way may be as good as another, depending on the couple. The important thing is to have full clarity and agreement. Elfrieda and I have had some differences in our years of marriage, but we have always been able to talk out the money issues. Money has never been a problem. Not even once!

6. Having a Sense of Permanence

Young people today are reluctant to make commitments. Many prefer just living together for a while to see whether they are compatible before making a commitment for life. Some move from one trial relationship to another, leaving confused and disoriented children in their wake.

When Communism in Russia threw out God, it also threw out the idea of family permanence. In 1920, Lenin reported great success in setting up a new society not based on old-fashioned bourgeois capitalist concepts. He said, "We are establishing communal kitchens and public eating places, laundries and repair shops, infant asylums, kindergartens, children's homes, educational institutes of all kinds."

The state was largely taking over the functions of the family. Divorces were obtained by signing a document obtained at any post office.

A year later, Lenin had second thoughts about all this. He saw what happened when people had children but were not responsible for them, when the basic family unit was virtually dissolved. Groups of young people, whom the media called "wolf packs," were terrorizing neighborhoods. Lenin called for restraint and urged parents to discipline their children. After a few years, it became difficult to obtain a legal divorce.

One of the great bulwarks of the family is a sense of permanence. We Christians believe that, with few exceptions, the marriage relationship is sacred and binding for life. That permanence can be destroyed through neglect, indifference, or distractions. It takes firm resolve, careful planning, and faithful persistence to build permanence into the family.

Children desperately need that sense of permanence. When they ask for stories about when their parents were children, they are instinctively reaching out to discover roots, identity, and belonging. They want a sense of permanence. When parents wisely and lovingly nurture such reaching out, one day they will likely hear their children say, "In our family, we do it this way," or "In our family, we don't do that."

As parents and grandparents, we are concerned about our children and grandchildren. We must be sure where our own strength comes from if we are to be a positive influence in our families. Sometimes our lives are flooded with demands, with too many activities. We feel sapped.

It is well to remember that Jesus had the same experience. We can follow the advice he gave his disciples: "Come away to a deserted place all by yourselves and rest a while" (Mark 6:31). Likewise, Isaiah affirms, "In quietness and in trust shall be your strength" (30:15b).

Family solidarity, history, and roots are great sources of family strength. When I was a student in Chicago, our class assignment took us to skid row. We saw alcoholics and human derelicts who had fallen so low that social workers could not reach them. The law with its punishments had no effect on them. The appeals and admonitions of ministers fell on deaf ears.

We were told that occasionally when someone mentioned family and home, they listened, became thoughtful, and sometimes cried. Likewise, when the prodigal son in Luke 15 hit bottom and "came to himself," his first thought was about home. That became the turning point in his life. He went home.

Planted deep in our hearts is the longing to be at home, to belong, and to be secure. Can it be God's will that street people and refugees lack homes? I believe God wants us all to have three homes: In one, a family unit lives in peace, often husband and wife with children. In the church, we gather as a larger family. A third home awaits us when this earthly pilgrimage is over; we hope to enter the dwelling prepared for us (John 14:2), to be "at home with the Lord" (2 Cor. 5:8).

So there they are, the six sources of family strength: interdependence, respect, submission, love, agreement on financial matters, and a sense of permanence.

In my yearning for love and peace, Lord, grant me strength to do my part in making them realities in our families. Help me to give and not just receive, to care and share when it is not expected, and to forgive as you have forgiven me.

7

A Message for Old and Young

Remember your creator in the days of your youth,
before the days of trouble come,
and the years draw near when you will say,
"I have no pleasure in them."
—The Teacher, in Ecclesiastes 12:1

Professor Mathews came into the English classroom at the University of Saskatchewan with a Bible in his hand. Showing a Bible was unusual at that sophisticated institution. He said he was going to read us one of the most beautiful, poetic, and imaginative pieces of literature ever written.

I knew it was going to be Psalm 23 or 1 Corinthians 13. Instead, he read the first seven verses of Ecclesiastes 12, without comment or explanation. When he was finished, we all sat there, looking at each other with puzzled expressions on our faces, wondering what that had been all about. We hadn't understood a thing. It was all a riddle and meant nothing to us.

Twenty years later, I discovered the key to unlock that riddle. Let us examine that "beautiful, poetic, and imaginative" writing and see what sense it makes, if any. The Teacher/Preacher tells us to remember our Creator

> before the sun and the light and the moon and the stars
> are darkened and the clouds return with the rain; in the
> day when the guards of the house tremble, and the strong
> men are bent, and the women who grind cease working
> because they are few, and those who look through the win-

dows see dimly; when the doors on the street are shut, and the sound of the grinding is low, and one rises up at the sound of a bird, and all the daughters of song are brought low; when one is afraid of heights, and terrors are in the road; the almond tree blossoms, the grasshopper drags itself along and desire fails; because all must go to their eternal home, and the mourners will go about the streets; before the silver cord is snapped, and the golden bowl is broken, and the pitcher is broken at the fountain, and the wheel broken at the cistern, and the dust returns to the earth as it was, and the breath returns to God who gave it. (Eccles. 12:1-7)

Let us look at a few of these crisp word pictures, given in terse phrases:

Before the sun and the light and the moon and the stars are darkened. We should remember our Creator before that happens. No problem, we think. We have lots of time. The sun and the moon are not going dark for another 5.5 billion years, astronomers say. So we're in good shape. We decide we don't have to think about our Creator or worry about the judgment.

I remember walking across the farmyard in Russia one evening, holding my grandfather's hand. He looked up and said, "I see that there is somebody upstairs with a lamp." I looked at the upstairs windows and could see no light, but the moon was coming up over the house roof. I said, "Grandpa, the light you see is not upstairs; it's the moon just coming up." I was about six or seven years old, and suddenly I realized for the first time that grandpa was going blind. Soon the sun and moon would be "darkened"—for him.

Before . . . the clouds return with/after the rain. Enjoy the sunny days of youth before the rainy days of age. When it stops raining, the sun comes out. Except when we are old and things look bleak all the time. How different from the days of childhood! When we were children, we'd fall and hurt ourselves, but after mother had wiped away the tears (rain) and kissed the sore spot, we were happy again. Clouds and tears were momentary; sunshine and laugher prevailed. That is not the way it is now. We are hurting. Our bodies ache. Our minds are in pain, too. One would think that after all these "clouds" and "rain," the sun would shine, but no! The mail just brought a letter announcing the death of a close friend. The next day my brother called to say that he had returned from the doctor and the news was not good. He has cancer. Yes, indeed, the clouds return. Instead of sunshine, there's going to be more rain and pain, a winter of life.

When the guards of the house tremble. Now what is that supposed to mean? Who are the guards or keepers of the house? Why do they tremble? Paul said we live in these houses of clay, our bodies, until the day of resurrection, when we are given new resurrection bodies (2 Cor. 4:7; 5:1-5). The "guards" or "keepers" of our bodies are our hands. Without our hands, there would be no houses, no chairs, no shoes, and no computers to drive us crazy. Human hands have made so many things around us. But what if these hands tremble?

My sister was a nurse. She left nursing and became a teacher; her "keepers" trembled so much that she couldn't function as a nurse any more. She could pick up a needle to give the patient a shot, but she could not hold her hands still. Imagine a nurse coming at you with that needle shaking like a straw in the wind.

When . . . the women who grind cease working because they are few. These grinding "women" are our teeth. Other translations say the "grinders" stop working because so few are left. Before modern dentistry, the common thing to do with an aching tooth was to pull it out. I saw my first toothbrush at age 12, when we came to Canada. We often see pictures of people in Africa with only three or four teeth. The message is clear: remember your Creator before all your teeth have fallen out. Think about God before you are that old.

When . . . one rises up at the sound of a bird. That was not I as a teenager. I could sleep soundly even if a freight train was rattling past my window. Imagine our surprise when our father told us that in recent years, not the "sound of a bird" but the ticking of the clock kept him awake. We respected him too much to laugh. For his next birthday, we nine children pooled our dimes and quarters and bought him a battery-operated clock that didn't tick, since we had no electricity on the farm.

When one is afraid of heights, and terrors are in the road. When I was young, I'd climb to the top of the windmill on our farm and wave to the little people below. Not now! When an old person falls and breaks a hip, that is not the same as when a child falls. The healing takes much longer, and complications can set in so easily.

I remember visiting a retired church member in Kansas years ago. We had missed her in church for several Sundays. I asked her what the problem was. She said it was the steps: "They are so high, and I'm afraid I might fall." I almost asked, "What steps?" The next day, I looked at those "terrors" at the church entrance. I counted them: four. Four little steps made her afraid. There was no railing, and winter's snow and ice made those four steps dangerous. It was enough to keep her from church. These days we do more to overcome such terrors and make our buildings accessible for everyone.

The almond tree blossoms. How the Teacher jumps around from one thing to another: from going blind to light sleeping, from losing your teeth to being afraid of heights, and now this almond tree, whatever that is.

This metaphor is simple and beautiful. Come with me to an orchard in early spring. All is still gray, except the almond tree, which is beginning to blossom. At first the blossoms are pink, but after a week they turn white. Can you see them? Scattered among all those other fruit trees, there are half a dozen or more white-capped almond trees, blossoming. It's a lovely sight. Look around the next time you're in church, and you'll see them. Just like the snow-white blossoms fall off with the first stiff breeze, so also the white hairs of some older people fall off after a while.

The grasshopper drags itself along, perhaps like someone on crutches. Most seniors don't get around as far and as fast as earlier. Mobility is eventually curtailed.

And desire fails. Only three words this time. You're catching on, aren't you? Now you know why Professor Matthews was so excited about this "beautiful, poetic, and imaginative" passage in the Old Testament. Here we have nineteen pictures of an old person! It's like a slide show, one shot after another, each from a different perspective, but always about an aging person.

Of course, desire fails. Food doesn't taste like it used to, listening to music is no fun anymore with those stupid hearing aids, travel is out of the question, and sex? Some might almost ask, "What's that?"

The mourners will go about the streets. When someone died, it was an oriental custom to invite professional mourners to wail and lament. Members of the family or a caregiver tell the mourners that their grandfather is near death. The mourners *silently* wait outside. They walk up and down in front of the house, staying close to the window where the grandfather is in bed. They keep looking up to the second floor, waiting for someone to open the window and signal that the old man has died. Instantly, they begin their mournful wailing.

The writer is saying, "Remember your Creator before that moment comes. That's cutting it too close." There is such a thing as deathbed repentance, but that is too close for comfort.

You may be wondering who wrote this dramatic and realistic literature. Perhaps you are thinking that it was an underprivileged person, maybe poor, certainly someone who didn't have much fun in life. Otherwise, he wouldn't have written such morbid stuff.

Scholars believe the Teacher was King Solomon. He was so wise that three thousand years later, we say it requires "the wisdom of Solomon" to solve a difficult problem. He was said to be the richest king in the Middle East.

As for having fun, if he wanted something, he got it—food, wine, and women. He said, "I kept my heart from no pleasure!" (Eccles. 2:10). He ended up with about a thousand wives and concubines (1 Kings 11:3). If he made the rounds kissing a different one good-night each evening, it would take him almost three years to get back to the first one.

Solomon had seen and experienced it all, and he had tasted life to the full. He says, "Do you want to know what the bottom line is? I'll tell you: Remember your creator in the days of your youth, before the days of trouble come, and the years draw near when you will say, 'I have no pleasure in them'" (Eccles. 12:1).

Before the silver cord is snapped, and the golden bowl is broken. Solomon invites us into an oriental tent. It is night, but light is shining from a wick emerging from a bowl of oil. The lamp is hanging from the top of the tent by a cord. We know at once that we are in a rich man's tent because the bowl is made of gold and the cord holding the bowl is silver. But look what happens! The silver cord snaps; the golden bowl falls to the ground and breaks. The oil spills, and the light goes out.

There is no way to rekindle it. The end has come. Our lives, like that golden bowl, hang by a thread. When that thread snaps and breaks, that's it. Life in this world is over.

Before . . . the pitcher is broken at the fountain, and the wheel broken at the cistern. We are in the open, beside a fountain and a cistern. Both dispense water, so essential for life and a fit symbol of life. What will you do when the pitcher that dips life-giving water from the fountain is broken? When the wheel that hauls up water from the cistern has fallen apart from use and age?

There is nothing you can do. The water is still there, life on earth continues, but as far as you or I are concerned, that's the end. Now the author drops all metaphors and speaks in words everyone can understand: *The dust returns to the earth as it was, and the breath returns to God who gave it.*

It is surprising and unusual for an Old Testament writer to have such a clear concept of life after death. He says that the breath or spirit returns to God.

All this is so true. The Teacher has pounded into us the message that we should remember our Creator in our youth, before all these calamities of old age come upon us. What does this say to seniors?

1. Share this with young people. Don't hesitate to point out that youth is a time of choices. Choices rhymes with voices; our young people hear so many voices in schools, from friends, from the media, from surrounding culture. It can be confusing to know how to choose. We find help by remembering God in such situations and by praying about them. Temptation flees when we're on our knees.

2. Encourage youths to start living for others, to do something for someone else every day, to volunteer. We used to sing, "Give of your best to the Master; / Give of the strength of your youth" (Howard B. Grose). From your own experience, tell youths that the most difficult life is when you just live for yourself. Helping others makes this world a better place to live in and is gratifying to us.

3. Point out to them that youth is a time of forming habits. After age thirty, most of us don't change much; we just become more so. Habits can become our servants, but they can also become our slaves. When the youth pray

about life and remember their Creator, they find help in forming useful and liberating habits, not habits that lead to destruction and death.

4. There is a message here for all of us. When we reach the golden years, we realize they sometimes are not so golden after all, especially when calamities hit us. Then it is wonderful to know that our lives have not been wasted. We can sit back, relax with good consciences, and enjoy what is left of life.

I evacuated older people from Birmingham to safety in the English countryside during WW II. As The Woodlands, the haven of rest and safety, filled up, I noticed one old woman who always looked so sad. I thought I should interrupt my usual schedule to talk to her, but I didn't know what I could say to cheer her up.

I didn't want her to start crying; then I, young and inexperienced, wouldn't know what to do. One day I sat down beside her and began a conversation:

"Grandma Wiggins, you seem so sad. What's troubling you?"

She shook her head and reached for her handkerchief.

I thought, *Oh, no, not that!* So I quickly continued: "Are you worried about your house? I remember where you lived. I'll be glad to go and see whether it has been bombed or not. Would you like me to do that?"

She said, "No, young man; it's not the house."

"Perhaps you have a son in the military and are worried about him."

"No, young man, that's not what troubles me."

"But why are you so sad, Grandma? This is a nice place, and you're safe here."

Sobbing pitifully, she said, "All my life I have lived just for myself. I never did anybody any good."

I don't know if she had fairly taken stock of her life. Perhaps she had overlooked how she had helped others, and this was false guilt. Yet how sad to think that in the evening of her life, when she should have been sitting in her rocker, relaxing and enjoying what was left, her conscience gave her no peace. It kept whispering, "You blew it, didn't you? You only had this one life to live, and you blew it!"

It is not too late to avoid that kind of a situation. We can remember our Creator, even in retirement, and live for others.

5. Finally, along with the young people, we want to remember our Creator because before long we are going to meet him face-to-face. It would be so wonderful to meet him as a friend, not as a judge to be feared; to meet him as one whom we have known for a long time, our Savior and our Lord; to meet him and to say thank you, ten thousand times ten thousand thank-yous.

O Creator, we remember you in youth, midlife, and old age.

8
When Do I Move?

Very truly, I tell you, when you were younger, you used to fasten your own belt and go wherever you wished. But when you grow old, you will stretch out your hands, and someone else will fasten a belt around you and take you where you do not wish to go.
—Jesus, in John 21:18

It was a pitiful sight. She was crying, and her husband was lying helpless on a mattress on the floor of an empty room, watching the children carry out the furniture. At last they were going to move into a retirement community.

Right then I decided that this would not happen to Elfrieda and me. We would move when I could still give instructions to our friends who would come help us move, when I could still carry boxes and furniture myself.

The August 29, 1996, issue of the *Mennonite Weekly Review* reports that ours was "A Move at the Right Time to the Right Place." The brief article quotes me saying, "The move was easy. The decision to move was difficult. We had lived in Akron, Pennsylvania, for twenty-seven years. The heart said stay. The head said go."

There is much to be said for staying in your own home as long as possible. The government even encourages it. A lot of voluntary and professional help is available, from Meals on Wheels and visiting nurses to the American Association of Retired Persons.

For many of us, however, the day will come when we need to move into a retirement community. It is extremely difficult for most seniors to decide when to move and where to move.

We are not alone in making these decisions: God is with us, our families are ready to help, and we have church friends with whom we can and should discuss a change in all candor.

We moved to Scottdale because we have children and grandchildren living here; also, two Mennonite churches are in town, and a new retirement facility had just been opened. Since we relocated, I have learned of other couples who moved to a new place to be close to their families.

It is a sobering fact that after retirement, our world shrinks. There is less travel for business or church and fewer committee meetings; those things soon belong to the past. We focus more and more on the family.

Blessed are those seniors who have loving and caring children and grandchildren. Like retirement itself, this is something that needs to be valued and nurtured long before we reach retirement age. Though we moved because of family, there are many other good reasons for moving.

Some people work with companies that locate them far from longtime friends. It is not surprising that when retirement comes and they are no longer tied to places of employment, they tend to move back to their home communities. When at last they are free, others move so they can be near the church of their choice or a college community or because of special interests such as sports or hobbies. Some move because of the climate.

Whatever the reason for the move, sooner or later the time will come, however, when we experience the truth of John 21:18. When young, we chose our own paths; but when we grow older, someone else chooses them for us.

However, this does not necessarily mean going to a place

where you do not wish to go. Sometimes that happens, but many older people have happily moved into retirement communities for reasons listed above. They are content, especially if they feel that the move was God's will.

In his hymn "Lead, Kindly Light," John Henry Newman says it so well: "I was not ever thus, nor prayed that Thou / Shouldst lead me on; / I loved to choose and see my path, but now / Lead Thou me on!"

Thank you, Lord, for loving and leading us, especially in this important step of retirement.

9

Learning to Let God

When I look at your heavens, the work
of your fingers,
the moon and the stars that you have
established;
what are human beings that you are mindful
of them,
mortals that you care for them?
—David, in Psalm 8:3-4

I was preaching in an old church in Switzerland. The lighting was poor and the print in my Bible suddenly seemed small and blurred. My arm was too short to hold the Bible far enough away. I asked if anyone in the audience started wearing glasses after forty. Several hands went up. Then I asked if I could borrow a set of glasses. People laughed; they thought I was joking, but it worked.

All I needed was a magnifying glass. Nothing else was wrong with my eyes nor with theirs. We simply had *presbyopia*, the fancy word for the hardening of the eye lenses. When we were young, they were soft and flexible. As we aged, the lenses hardened. As a result, we couldn't focus quite so well or could focus only at a greater distance from the eyes.

It's quite harmless. Yet it came to me as a shock that I could no longer see as well as I had before. I started to wear glasses. Later, I began to wear a hearing aid. Then some teeth were replaced with a partial plate. I was learning to let go. Nevertheless, there were always compensations or aids available.

When our friends had to surrender their car keys because of age and the safety factor, they saw no compensation for that. A year after they had to give up driving, they had not yet recovered from that shock and the enormous loss of their independence.

Aging means letting go—letting go of a job, of responsibility, of authority. It's a dominant theme among seniors. The more we let go, the more dependent we become on others. Some find this extremely difficult to accept. I suspect that it is primarily because they only see what they are giving up, like the car keys, and do not see what they are gaining in exchange.

In *Life After 50*, Katie Funk Wiebe lists three gains:

• Finding meaning through being rather than doing.

• Discovering freedom from competition at work and in the world in general.

• Welcoming the opportunity to give back to society the lessons we have learned over a lifetime by mentoring younger persons (73-74).

ESTHER BENDER

The potter molding the clay

For successful retirement, we need to put *giving up* into proper perspective. It is not only giving up health and freedom, power, and authority, but ultimately it is surrendering our will and life itself. With the hymn writer, Adelaide A. Pollard, we sing,

Have thine own way, Lord!
Have thine own way!
Thou art the Potter, I am the clay.
Mold me and make me after thy will,
While I am waiting, yielded and still.

As I get older, Lord, help me to see that for every surrender of something I hold dear, there is a compensation, a new gift, a new opportunity. I thank you that when I give up this life itself, you will give me a new life with you for all eternity. I thank you, Lord, that you are mindful of me, that you care for me, and that you love me.

10
How Old Is Old?

Today I am eighty years old; can I discern what is pleasant and what is not? Can your servant taste what he eats or what he drinks? Can I still listen to the voice of singing men and singing women? Why then should your servant be an added burden to my lord the king?
—Barzillai, in 2 Samuel 19:35

We asked the people in church to tell us when a person is old. A ten-year-old boy said 20, a 20-year-old college student said about 30, and a 60-year-old grandmother said about 70. They all thought that old was about ten years older than they were. Even at 85, I do not feel old. Sometimes I wonder how I ever came to live here among these "old people."

However, age is beginning to show. Seeing, hearing, and tasting are not the same. Running, climbing, and even sitting up straight are problems. Nevertheless, with a bit of thought and discipline, we can slow the aging process. Doing so is good stewardship. We can exercise and watch our diets. We can think positive and happy thoughts. Both the physical and the mental activity will help to slow down our aging processes.

I am thankful that while still young, I came across a book that had a profound influence on my thinking process. Ralph Waldo Trine said we can control our thinking. That had me sitting up and taking note.

Trine said that we don't have to think bad thoughts; it is in our power to switch to thinking good thoughts. We don't have to think the worst of other people; we can think well of them. We don't have to dwell on problems; we can think positive and dwell on the solutions. That had a tremendous influence on my life.

I had never heard or read about the place and the importance of our wills. I had never thought I could just *will* to do something or *will* not to do it. Later I learned to modify this expectation, especially when I read Paul's lament: "I can will what is right, but I cannot do it. For I do not do the good I want, but the evil I do not want is what I do" (Rom. 7:19).

However, at that formative stage in my life, Trine's book was a tremendous boost to my moral and spiritual growth. It meshed with Paul telling us to "take every thought captive to obey Christ" (2 Cor. 10:5). Paul also calls on believers to deliberately think about things that are true, honorable, just, pure, pleasing, commendable, excellent, and worthy of praise (Phil. 4:8).

I discovered that I had a *will*. I could not make others do what I wanted them to do, but I could make myself do it. Even today, I still think we often fail to appreciate the fact that we can do many things, if we really want to. We underestimate the place, the value, and the power of the will.

Up to a certain point, we are in control of slowing down our aging process. We can *will* to slow it down. The advantages are at least twofold. First, we can be productive longer and enjoy more of life. Second, by keeping ourselves in shape and prolonging self-support, we may delay the onset of disability. Thus, we may shorten the last stage of life, when we are senile, dependent on others, and running up medical bills.

If we take proper action now, we won't have to be like one broken-down fellow telling another, "If I had known I was going to live this long, I would have taken better care of myself" (anon.).

There are other advantages. Our loved ones will be relieved of some caregiving for us. They come to visit, and we spend happy hours together. They are concerned about our health and ask how we feel. However, while we are still capable, they do not have to help us dress or shop, or take us to the doctor. If we really love our children, we will do everything possible to take the best care of ourselves—for *their* sake, as well as for ours.

We can enliven our days by volunteering in the community or away from home with dozens of organizations. Hospitals and Meals on Wheels are always glad for help. The Mennonite Association of Retired Persons (MARP) has 3,600 members in six states and programs Service Opportunities for Older People (SOOP). Over 130 volunteers serve with SOOP in 51 locations in the United States and Canada. Ten Thousand Villages, Mennonite Disaster Service (MDS), and MCC can always use retirees, sometimes abroad, more often near home.

Then there are the grandchildren. What a blessing we can be to them and they to us. At this stage in our lives, we at last have time. We still have enough physical and mental energy to relate to them. We have marvelous opportunities to encourage them with stories, by sharing experiences from our own lives, and by modeling the values we believe are worth passing on.

Children beg, "Daddy (or Grandpa), tell me about when you were a boy." "Mommy (or Grandma), tell me about when you were a girl." All children love stories. Psychologists explain that children instinctively say, "Tell me who you are, and then I will know who I am."

When young parents are busy, likely both employed, you might do some driving for them. You could take your grandchildren to a ball game or a swimming pool and stay to watch. You could carefully select a video, see it with your grandchildren, and discuss it afterward. Depending on their ages, you could take them on longer trips, with their parents' permission, of course.

You could invite grandchildren into the kitchen for a cooking party. Elfrieda has enjoyed baking peppernuts with her grandchildren. Grandfathers can work with the grandchildren in a workshop or garage, or in other activities they both find interesting.

In the summertime, the yard and the garden beckon. How about doing some gardening together? That is a marvelous opportunity to show them the mystery and the majesty of God's creation.

Boys are fascinated by cars. They dream of the day when they will be able to sit behind the wheel and drive. If they have learner's permits, why not teach them to drive? I took my two grandsons to nearby empty parking lots for practice. What excitement and fun that was! They never tired of it. As soon as they arrived, they would ask whether they could have more lessons. It is hard to say who enjoyed it more, they or I.

A piece of paper was lying on the pavement. I asked a grandson to straddle it with the car, then to turn around and run over it with the left wheel. As the car neared the paper, he raised himself up in the seat so he could still see it. Suddenly he braked. "I can't see the paper anymore," he said. He missed the paper because he was not experienced enough to know where the wheel was. Similarly, he hit the curb with his right front tire when he tried to park. He had to learn where the front tires are without seeing them. What fun!

I learned that a child has to be old enough and interested enough to do a particular activity. When Peter Scott, our oldest grandson, was still quite a lad, I suggested that perhaps he would like to learn how to ride a bicycle. He was a polite child and wanted to please his Opa (grandfather), so he agreed.

I went to a great deal of trouble to get a bicycle his size. We put it in the trunk of the car and drove to the church-yard. There we practiced, or more accurately, there I ran alongside, holding the bicycle. He sat on it, wondering how long this was going to last. After a bit he said, "Maybe you ought to have some rest. Why don't we sit in the shade of a tree for a while?" We did. I thanked him for being so thoughtful of me.

After running and holding the bicycle another ten or fifteen minutes, he wondered whether he should perhaps learn to ride it in stages, not all at once. We talked about that for a while. For the third time, I ran with him when, sure enough, he had another thought: "Perhaps Oma [El-frieda] doesn't know where we are and is worried about us. Maybe we ought to go home."

I must confess that teaching Peter how to ride a bicycle had been totally my idea. What I planned to do was so fixed in my mind that it took me a while out there in the heat to realize what was going on. Peter didn't want to ride. Period. He wasn't ready.

A couple years later, Peter proudly told me that he had his own bike: "Do you want to see me ride it?" His parents told me, "He learned to ride in no time flat, without coaxing or much help"—when he was ready.

Another opportunity grandparents ought not to miss is to help their grandchildren see the larger world. They need to be prepared for a global economy and a world community. A baby's world is no bigger than to the end of its fingers and toes. Kindergarten and school help expand the child's world. However, it is sad how many teenagers have never had the opportunity to leave their city or state, let alone go to another country.

The other day we were talking with our daughter Ruth

about the time we sent her to Paris for a summer. We thought it would be good for her to experience another culture and learn to speak French like the French do rather than like her teachers in Frankfurt, Germany, where we lived. She was about twelve. Her host family expected her to care for two children and do some cooking and other household chores.

Looking back on that experience thirty-five years later, Elfrieda and I wondered whether she had been ready for it. Ruth admitted that it had been tough; she was often stretched to the limit. Then she broke out laughing. We wondered what was funny. "Now Jack and I are letting our sixteen-year-old daughter go to Austria as an exchange student for a whole school year, not just for a summer vacation!" she said.

It may not fit everyone to expose their children this way to another culture, language, and religion. Yet, there are endless variations. The important thing is to be concerned, imaginative, courageous, and willing to take risks and spend a little money. There is no substitute for that kind of experience. Classrooms, books, and films cannot take the place of personal experiences and involvement with people who think, talk, and act differently than we do. Being provincial in the twenty-first century will be a real handicap.

How old is old? In *I Don't Know What Old Is, but Old Is Older Than Me,* Sherwood Eliot Wirt agrees largely with Paul Tournier in *Learn to Grow Old.* They advise seniors to launch a second career (Tournier) or follow a calling (Wirt). This must be more than a hobby. It should be something deeply satisfying and useful to others. "Find your calling," says Wirt, and you will reap joy and deep satisfaction in your retirement years.

Wirt's chapter on "Enjoyment" begins with the joy children and grandchildren bring into our lives and the joy we bring into theirs. He says seniors need "to *enjoy* the family relationship," not for what we wish our family members were or what we hope they will become, but for what they are right now.

Once more, Lord, I thank you for life and all the joys you provide for me. Help me never to take one day, one person, or one event for granted.

11

Power Through Gratitude

May you be made strong with all the strength that comes from his glorious power, . . . while joyfully giving thanks to the Father.
—Paul, in Colossians 1:11

Does the title look backward? Perhaps you expected "Gratitude for Power." That is a valid point, but we won't pursue it just now. We want to think about receiving power through gratitude and about being ungrateful and thus having no real power in life.

The first three or so years after retirement can be quite difficult. Since the average retirement period is now about thirty years, we must consider how to get through these first crucial years without impairing the remaining years. As retirement years have increased, there also are many more seniors. During the 1980s, the number of older Americans increased by 5.7 million (22 percent).

Well over half of these seniors are women; 70 percent of nursing home residents today are women. Demographers predict that when the wave of 75 million baby boomers reaches retirement age, our society and its Social Security (U.S.) or Social Insurance (Canada) is going to be in deep trouble.

Even today, coping with retirement requires all the inward strength we possess, plus a heap of help from the outside. In addition to doctors, nurses, social workers, pastors, and other skilled people, there are the children and grandchildren. They are perhaps the first to notice mental and behavioral changes in their parents and grandparents, and the first to offer help.

If the elderly parents seem to be depressed, they need to talk about it. Why are they not interested in daily and routine matters? Why do they have sleeping and eating problems? Why does their energy level seem so low that they are always tired? Why do they have difficulty concentrating? Why do they feel so useless and worthless?

Depression is closely related to anxiety. In her book *As We Grow Old*, Ruth Fowler says, "The simplest solution when confronted with anxiety is for [adult] children to ask questions in a nonjudgmental way." Find the cause, then work toward a solution.

Here is one solution that sometimes works wonders, especially if the parents are committed Christians. Simply recall and thus relive earlier years when the children were still at home, when father and mother had secure and satisfying work at home or away, and they all enjoyed family and church life. Families can reminisce together, page through picture albums, or see old family videos or slides. They can share and laugh together, strengthening their sense of being family.

The grown children might draw attention to the fact that their parents have always been so thankful, and how they appreciated that. This gratitude was not merely expressed in daily prayers or on Thanksgiving Day. It was always there, sweetening all of life like a spoonful of sugar sweetens all the tea in the cup. Their consistent *gratitude is an attitude*. That's my first point.

There is much to be said for not dwelling on the past, especially on our disappointments or failures. With Paul, we mostly need to be "forgetting what lies behind and straining forward to what lies ahead" (Phil. 3:13). Yet there are times when looking back can bring the encouragement we need for facing the future. It can be a way of putting things into proper perspective, of making our peace with life and its experiences.

For example, the family can recognize that outwardly there have been changes since the parents' retirement. The parents may have moved into smaller quarters, and the children may be taking more responsibility as decision makers and caretakers. Yet the family members still love each other as much as before.

The parents' basic attitudes toward life have not changed with retirement. They are still thankful, still trust God to see them through, and still have the church and their friends to encourage and support them in whatever way possible. This could lead to fruitful discussion that may be quite therapeutic.

The children and grandchildren keep visiting their parents and grandparents and reminiscing about the good times they had together. They need to emphasize that these good times will continue into the retirement years, although differently expressed and experienced. In so doing, they make a discovery: *gratitude facilitates problem solving.* That's my second point.

As they look at problems together, whether financial or work related, personal or interpersonal, they need to be seen against the backdrop of the fact that the parents are alive and coping with their health situations, good or bad. They still have family and church, and probably many years ahead of them. It is important to put things in perspective. As this happens, the problems diminish as the good things of life take center stage.

In Paul's letter to the Colossians, we find an example of gratitude being an attitude that permeates all of life and helps solve problems. The congregation at Colossae was made up of Jewish and Gentile believers. They hit upon something they thought was a brilliant idea: a plan to launch the most perfect and all-inclusive super religion. They were going to take the best from all of the backgrounds and traditions and blend them into one. They set out to choose the best from Judaism and Greek philosophers like Plato and Aristotle, and then to add Jesus and his teachings to this ersatz mixture. Presto, there you would have it—the perfect religion, they thought.

When Paul became aware of this syncretism, he knew he had a problem of major proportions on his hands. His first reaction may have been to tell them that what they had brewing in their religious pot was heresy, a denial of revealed truth. He might have been tempted to lecture or scold them. Whatever his temptations, we know he finally wrote them a brief letter of four chapters—but what a letter! What a model of problem solving!

Paul begins by addressing them as "faithful brothers and sisters in Christ in Colossae." Then he says, "In our prayers for you we always thank God, the Father of our Lord Jesus Christ, for we have heard of your faith in Christ Jesus and of the love that you have for all the saints."

I remember asking a professor in seminary whether this was flattery and an attempt to soften the blows that were to follow. Was it authentic? Did Paul mean what he wrote? The answer was instant and clear: absolutely authentic. Paul was not playing political games. He meant every word he wrote.

That is only the beginning. Paul says as clearly as it can be said that Jesus Christ must "have first place in everything" (1:18). As we read that letter, we are struck by the fact that it is sprinkled throughout with words like "thankful," "giving thanks," and "grateful." Paul says, "I rejoice to see your morale and the firmness of your faith in Christ" (2:5). I count eleven such expressions! This is in a letter of correction and reproof.

If we had been there and pointed this out to Paul, I imagine he might have replied, "Oh, did I really say it that often? I didn't notice. I guess those words and phrases of thanksgiving just slipped in because I really am grateful for the Colossian church." Gratitude was an attitude. Thus the problem was solved. Paul's gratitude, which was a basic attitude, helped to solve the problem.

Here is a third factor to notice: *gratitude facilitates communication*. We all know how important communication is at any stage in life, but certainly during the first three or so years of retirement. Seniors need to be able to talk freely about their problems. We live in an age of communication, and sometimes I think I can express myself well enough to communicate what is on my mind.

Nevertheless, there are barriers to communication. One day in Brazil, I discovered that when I thought I was communicating, I was merely talking. That kind of thing happens in church and in our prayers more often than we realize. Words, words, and more words, and yet we are not heard (Matt. 6:7). In Shakespeare we read: "My words go up, my thoughts remain below; / words without thoughts never to heaven go!" (*Hamlet*, act 3, scene 3).

While in Brazil, I was asked to speak at chapel in a school where I expected everybody to understand German. I spoke of hunger. How terrible not to have food, to die of hunger! I told the students about my experience of hunger in Russia after the revolution. Then I turned to a lad of about twelve in the front row and asked, "If you had more food than you needed and other boys and girls had none, wouldn't you share it with them?" He shook his head and made a motion with his hands that I thought meant he was undecided.

A bit disturbed by this response, I turned away from him and addressed the larger group. But the reaction of that little boy bothered me. I returned to him and repeated the question, this time saying that surely he would share his food if the starving boy happened to be his best friend. Again he shook his head and made those shaky motions with his hands that I thought meant "maybe yes, maybe no."

As soon as chapel was over, a teacher said, "Peter, we forgot to tell you that among all these German-speaking Mennonite children, we also have a few native Brazilians who only speak Portuguese. That boy didn't understand a word you were saying."

In that case, ignorance kept me from communicating with the boy. For seniors, it frequently is fear, worry, anxiety, or a host of other problems that clog the channels of communication. Whatever the cause of the difficulty, one of the most effective ways of opening and unclogging channels of communication is through the expression of gratitude.

Thankful and thoughtful people communicate more quickly and better than ungrateful people—unless they are griping about a product or service. That is partly because people are more ready to listen to a person saying positive things and expressing gratitude.

We had a young volunteer at MCC headquarters who always had a group standing around her during coffee break. A few times I stepped up closer to discover the secret of her popularity. It wasn't that she was such a great storyteller, or that she had important news to share. It was simply that when she talked, whether about her family, school, church, or friends, whatever the subject, she always had something good to say about everybody and everything. She was authentically grateful, and it attracted the other workers like blossoms attract bees.

How different from a mother I recently heard in a television interview. She talked about the tragedy in 1970 when four students at Kent State University in Ohio were shot and killed during demonstrations against the Vietnam War. Her son was one of the victims. She said, "I don't want to forget what happened here. I am bitter. I cannot forgive."

I can't imagine many mothers crowding around to hear what she has to say. Suffering people do need to be heard so they can work through their grief and anger. This woman, however, has cultivated her bitterness for thirty years. She has built her life around it. Poor woman! She not only lost her son; she still has not had closure. Still bitter. Still no peace.

So there you have it! Gratitude is an attitude, it helps in problem solving, and it certainly facilitates communication.

Thank you, Lord, for so many people, young and old, who have encouraged me in this time of transition into retirement. You have given us so much, Lord. I ask for one thing more: a truly grateful heart.

12

Getting Home Before Dark

O LORD, heal me, for my bones are shaking
with terror.
My soul also is struck with terror,
while you, O LORD—how long?
—David, in Psalm 6:2b-3

As I get older, one of my favorite poems is "Let Me Get Home Before Dark," by J. Robertson McQuilkin (see the Appendix). It begins with a positive statement of not being afraid of death because death means entering life eternal. Sundown and longer shadows alone do not frighten me.

Still, the possibility of slipping morally, of making a fool of myself, or of becoming lukewarm spiritually—those things frighten me. After all, "there is no fool like an old fool" (John Lyly). Thus McQuilkin admits,

> But I do fear.
> I fear the Dark Specter may come too soon—
> or do I mean too late?
> That I should end before I finish or finish, but not well.
> That I should stain your honor, shame your name,
> grieve your loving heart.
> For, they tell me, few finish well. . . .
> *Lord, let me get home before dark.*

McQuilkin talks about the darkness we see in every personal care unit of retirement homes. Grouchy old men and women make life difficult for others and themselves. Once they were young and strong, kind and loving, but something happened. Their generous spirits shriveled, their minds became suspicious, and they became something we thought existed only in horror stories, not in reality.

The children don't know their own parents; emphatically they say that he or she was never like that before. O Lord, please, don't let that happen to me. Let me get home before a darkness like that overtakes me. McQuilkin describes this so eloquently:

> The darkness of a spirit
> grown mean and small,
> fruit shriveled on the vine,
> bitter to the taste of my companions,
> burden to be borne by those brave few who love me still.
> No, Lord. Let the fruit grow lush and sweet,
> a joy to all who taste;
> Spirit-sign of God at work,
> stronger, fuller, brighter at the end.
> *Lord, let me get home before dark.*

I heard wonderful reports of a professor who was brilliant, stimulating, and always ready to help others. He was a great leader among our people. I enjoyed reading his writings, always positive and hopeful.

Years later, when he was an old man, I met him and we worked together. At his funeral, I spoke by his grave. But where was the man of whom I had heard such glowing reports when I was a youth? This man had become distrustful of others, mean and small in spirit, and suspicious of what I was doing. He didn't have a good word to say about anyone. What had happened? How sad that he could not get home before dark.

There is another kind of darkness, not so much of the spirit as of the mind. Webster defines *dementia* as "a condition of deteriorated mentality." Nature has turned the lights off. Yesterday he was president of the United States; today he doesn't even recognize his own wife. Alzheimer's disease is the most common expression of this dementia. Huntington's disease, Parkinson's disease, Lou Gehrig's disease (ALS), and multiple sclerosis might lead to other forms of dementia.

When I think even for a moment that my thinking and behavior could be impaired like that, I pray with all my heart, *Lord, let me get home before dark.*

Our bodies are naturally getting weaker and more frail. Our minds slow down. Memory is not what it used to be. That is normal as we age, and I will accept it gladly. It all shows that "our outer nature is wasting away, . . . preparing us for an eternal weight of glory" (2 Cor. 4:16-17). I am ready.

I'm not afraid of death. I have peace with God. I can say with Paul, "I have fought the good fight, I have finished the race, I have kept the faith" (2 Tim. 4:7). Nevertheless, I am afraid of what might happen before the end comes. That is why Elfrieda and I resonate so strongly with the closing thoughts of this wonderful poem:

The outer me decays–
I do not fret or ask reprieve.
The ebbing strength but weans me from mother earth
and grows me up for heaven.
I do not cling to shadows cast by immortality. . . .

But will I reach the gate
in lingering pain, body distorted, grotesque?
Or will it be a mind
wandering untethered among light fantasies or grim terrors?
Of your grace, Father, I humbly ask . . .
Let me get home before dark.

13

The Greatest Joy of All

Then Peter came and said to him, "Lord, if another member of the church sins against me, how often should I forgive? As many as seven times?" Jesus said to him, "Not seven times, but I tell you, seventy-seven times."
—Matthew 18:21-22

Yesterday's evening news reported a hit-and-run car accident. A man was killed. The police knew the hit-and-run driver was a woman. The widow said emphatically, "I want her to hurt. I want her to feel what it's like to have a broken heart."

That seems to be the common attitude: get even, punish them. That's why our jails are overcrowded. It's the old eye-for-an-eye and tooth-for-a-tooth mentality. Some seniors bear grudges for something that happened years ago. They have not forgiven.

The old saying "forgive and forget" is nonsense, of course. We can't forget, and God doesn't forget either. However, when there is forgiveness, every time we think about the hurt, the old feeling of paying back is gone. There is no more pain.

A man came to me after a meeting. He was sobbing and kept saying, "I can't do it! I can't do it!" As I put my arms around his shaking body, I asked, "Is it that hard?" He just nodded his head. After a while, he said, "It's my father." After another long silence and sobbing, he said, "This will be the hardest thing I've ever done in my life, but I'm going to do it. Please pray for me."

Forgiving is serious business because it is basically for our own spiritual, emotional, and physical benefit. We may or may not establish a new relationship with the person who injured us; that is not the heart of forgiveness. When we forgive, we finally stop hurting ourselves, hand the whole matter over to God, and believe what he says: "Vengeance is mine, I will repay, says the Lord" (Rom. 12:19).

Forgiving means to have closure, to experience freedom, and to regain spiritual power. Forgiving and forgiveness bring healing and restoration of a right relationship with God.

I thought and prayed for years that God would reveal to me the greatest joy of all. I knew that it was not money and possessions. I thought it might be good health, a loving family, good friends, the birth of a child, or many other meaningful happenings. At last it became clear that it was none of these things.

Jesus and the gospel have showed me that the greatest joy of all is to know that I am forgiven and that I have forgiven every person who has hurt me. Heaven and earth rejoice with me over such repentance, says Jesus repeatedly in Luke 15.

Today I am convinced there is no greater joy than that. There is no more important lesson to learn than how to be forgiven and how to become a forgiving person.

Lord, too long I have waited for the person who wronged me to repent. I know now that all this time, I have been his captive. Give me the power and the grace to forgive and to hand it all over to you, asking you to deal with him. Set me free at last, Lord, free from the thought of getting even, free from the bondage of the unforgiving spirit within me, and free to forgive as you have forgiven me.

14
What Time Is It?

It is not for you to know the times or periods that the Father has set by his own authority.
—Jesus, in Acts 1:7

We were at the end of our tour in the Soviet Union. Because I had been there numerous times, the group of four men and one woman from Canada and the United States had asked me to be their leader. It was a good experience. We spoke in many meetings, sharing the Word and encouraging the believers on their spiritual pilgrimages. We met with government officials, especially with members of the Council of Religious Affairs, learning from them but also witnessing to them.

Christians in the Soviet Union had a hard time during the seventy years of Communism, especially during the beginning of the Stalin era. They had problems in dealings with the atheist government and within their own ranks, the churches. Some felt that the best way to survive was to cooperate with the government, always praying that they would not go so far as to compromise their faith.

Others felt that the government had no business interfering in church matters, so they went underground. They met secretly for worship in homes, caves, and forests; they published articles and portions of the Bible in secret; they would have nothing to do with the government. They also shunned their brothers and sisters in the aboveground or registered churches. These indeed were difficult times.

The twenty-one-day tour was ending. We were being hosted by members of the Baptist church in Moscow and the All-Union Council of Evangelical Christian-Baptists (AUCECB). With some twenty people around the table, we had enjoyed a wonderful dinner when Alexei Bychkov, the general secretary of the AUCECB, rose from his seat to make a speech. John Lapp, sitting beside me, promptly whispered, "Peter, as leader of our group, you make the response."

What was I to say? So many thoughts were swirling through my head. I had to think fast. In a few minutes, I would need to be on my feet and speaking. As I often do in situations like this, when there is no time for reflective prayer, I just shot up a short and fervent petition: "Lord, help me!" The Germans call that a *Stoszgebet,* a "bumper-prayer"—the bumper on the car is called a *Stoszstange.*

In Mark's Gospel, Jesus says that believers are not to worry about what to say when they are persecuted: "When they bring you to trial and hand you over, do not worry beforehand about what you are to say; but say whatever is given you at that time" (Mark 13:11). Even though my situation hardly qualified as persecution, I still needed help.

At the end of his brief speech, Bychkov presented each of us with a wristwatch made in Russia. Then he sat down.

Thanking him for the watches, I asked, "What time is it?" They all looked at their watches and told me the correct time. I set my new watch. Then I asked again, "What time is it?" One or two at the table called out the time again. I thanked them. Then for the third time, I asked, "What time is it?" By then, they all knew I was not asking for the time of day but probably had something else in mind.

I surely had their attention, so I said that the time for healing had come. It was time for the registered and the underground churches to come together again. It was time for Christians in Canada and the United States to break out of their nations' cold-war mentality and to build bridges of understanding and friendship to the churches in the Soviet Union. It was time for all of us to be more united and bolder in presenting the good news of the gospel of Jesus Christ to unbelievers.

What time was it? It was time for us to make concrete plans for publishing a Bible commentary in the Russian language. This would help the 35,000 Baptist ordained but untrained preachers and other church leaders.

That speech was spontaneous, triggered by the gift of the watches moments before, yet also growing out of our extensive traveling and visiting in Russia. It was one of the times when I felt in a real sense the leading of the Holy Spirit. After all, Jesus tells believers not to worry about what they are to say. "It is not you who speak, but the Holy Spirit" (Mark 13:11). When that happens, you know it, and you won't forget it.

What time is it? No, I am not looking at the clock, but I ask again, What time is it? This time I am not looking at the churches in Russia. I am thinking of the older people in North America, in Mennonite, Brethren in Christ, and other churches. So I ask for the third time, What time is it?

It is time for seniors to wake up and recognize that we have started new chapters in our lives. New opportunities are ahead of us. We no longer get up with alarm clocks; we're retired or on different schedules. We take care of our physical needs: brush our teeth, eat with discretion, exercise, and take naps.

What about our mental and spiritual needs? What about our families, the church, and the needs in society? Perhaps now is a good time to take inventory and decide what we are going to do with our time, with the rest of our lives.

The big temptation for seniors is to drift along. They putter around in houses or gardens, doing useful things or just entertaining themselves. Perhaps they have workshops and make crafts to sell at MCC relief sales. They may go golfing and fishing; but who wants to golf or fish every day? A widower friend of mine has no children. During the summer, he goes fishing several times a week. He has only one problem: he doesn't know what to do with the fish he catches. He has no family to eat them; his meals are provided in the seniors' home where he lives.

"So what do you do with the fish?" I asked him.

"Throw them back!" he replied.

How would you like to do that, catch fish only to throw them back so you can catch them again the next day? Poor fish! Poor fisherman!

Yes, it's time we started thinking about what we are going to do in retirement. One of the challenges confronting seniors is to stay intellectually alive and alert. Someone said that the wisdom of life is to die young, but as late as possible.

We all know how sad it is to meet a person who is relatively young but already old in thinking patterns. One student told me his major concern was economic security. A good job, a house, a car, a family, and vacations—that's all he wanted. How sad! In his mind, he was already an old man.

To stay mentally young, we need to exercise our minds. My wife's sister-in-law Katie took courses at the university in Winnipeg when she was in her eighties. There was so much she wanted to learn while she was able. She was as curious as a three-year-old child.

Years ago we placed two Canadian teachers in the international Bienenberg Bible school near Liestal, Switzerland. One was a retired pastor, and the other was a young man just out of college. The younger man's German was poor, and he had no teaching experience. The older man's German was good, and he had been preaching for forty or more years. It certainly was an uneven start.

The pastor had a barrelful of sermons that he modified a

bit to fit the classroom lectures. The younger teacher regularly stayed up till midnight preparing his lectures.

All went well the first year. The students liked and appreciated both teachers. However, something happened halfway through the third year that surprised everyone. The older man ran out of teaching material and energy. His barrel was dry. Students noticed that he began to repeat himself. He was less focused in his presentations and seemed less relaxed. Sometimes he even appeared to be tense and uncomfortable facing the class.

One morning during chapel, he stood in the pulpit, cried, and admitted to the students and faculty that he had run out of steam. He said he had taught everything he knew and had nothing more to say.

The old man was worn out and had the good sense to resign and go home. The younger teacher kept up his studies, diligently preparing each day's lectures. He kept on learning and growing as he shared with his students. A few years later, he left the Bible school and worked on his doctor's degree. He was a disciplined and hard-working student.

One might say he ran on a generator powered by a giant windmill (the Spirit), while the older man ran on a battery. The battery is charged once, then just gives up its power till it is drained and dead. The generator keeps on producing electricity, powered by the wind (Spirit).

This is true both intellectually and spiritually. We need to grow or we stagnate and die. It is not important that we constantly check our spiritual pulse, but it is important that we stay close to Jesus. In the image of John 15, we are grafted onto him to produce fruit.

When our connection to Christ becomes a reality, growth will be inevitable. We will be given new insights. Our awareness of personal and world needs will increase. Relationships will change. Joy and peace will abound. Gratitude will become an attitude.

Problem solving will be enhanced. Cares and worries will no longer be the burden that they used to be. Resentments will evaporate. We will also realize that the spiritual growth is never finished. It is a process that continues to the end.

What time is it? It is time for us to stop being suspicious of other Christians, especially members of another conference or denomination. Suspicion is like cancer in the body; it spreads from one organ to another. As surely as cancer kills the body, suspicion kills the spirit. It robs us of all joys and friendships, laughter and love. As seniors we are in the best position to stop the cancer of suspicion from spreading and instead to release a flow of trust and goodwill.

What time is it? It's time to speak up for peace and become more active in peace efforts, like Atlee Beechey's organization of Seniors for Peace. Many of our young people have only vague ideas about our biblically based Anabaptist peace teaching. They need us.

Someone gave me the manuscript of a novel for evaluation. In this story, supposedly based on facts, a young man asks who the Mennonites are. The answer is that they are followers of a Dutchman called Menno Simons, who taught Christianity with something extra—pacifism.

That erroneous and misleading answer matches what some people actually believe. They think nonresistance is a peculiar Mennonite teaching, tacked onto the gospel, something extra that other Christians don't have. They don't see peacemaking as firmly rooted in the teachings of Jesus and the Gospels. We know better.

Then there is the government adding billions of dollars to the military budget, even though the Soviet Union is gone and Communism is no longer a threat. President Dwight Eisenhower unmasked this evil in his speech to the American Society of Newspaper Editors on April 16, 1953:

Every gun that is made, every warship launched, every rocket fired signifies, in the final sense, a theft from those who hunger and are not fed, those who are cold and are not clothed. This world in arms is not spending money alone. It is spending the sweat of its laborers, the genius of its scientists, the hopes of its children. . . . This is not a way of life at all in any true sense. Under the cloud of threatening war, it is humanity hanging from a cross of iron.

The United States passed a $280 billion military budget for 1999. Even without airplanes, one aircraft carrier costs $3 billion. It staggers the imagination to think what that small amount of the total military budget could do if diverted toward feeding the hungry, clothing the naked, promoting education (40% of the world's people are illiterate), and improving health care.

As seniors, we need to get the facts and then share our peace convictions and the clear teachings of Jesus with our families and communities. That is the least we can do. We can dare to speak out and take the risk. At our age, what do we have to lose? We have the world to gain.

What time is it? Time to volunteer and help others. This can be done on a one-to-one basis, like reading to a blind person, or it can be done with any number of organizations and agencies in the community. There is something within reach of each of us if we are still physically and mentally able. We can help those who no longer can help themselves, and it certainly will be a blessing for us. In "The Parting of the Ways," Jeanette B. Gilder spoke so well: "Wouldst thou thy godlike power preserve, / be godlike in the will to serve."

What time is it? Time to sit back and take a long look at our marriages. Half the marriages celebrated in our time are dissolved. Young people are hesitant to make commitments for life; some just live together to see how it "feels." If it feels right, they might get married later. Yet many of them lose respect for each other and drift apart.

One-parent families are an accepted norm; children are sadly neglected and confused. "As the family goes, so goes the nation." No wonder the nation is in trouble with alcohol and drug abuse, violence on the screen and in the streets, school dropouts, teen pregnancies, and overcrowded prisons.

It is time to ask what message our marriages are giving to our children and grandchildren. If you still have a spouse, how caring and loving is your relationship? Have you discarded bad habits? Have you stopped giving the silent treatment? Are the tensions and misunderstandings gone? Do you respect each other? Do you talk about these things with your grandchildren? Do you tell them that respect always has to precede love, that without respect, love doesn't have a chance?

What time is it? Time to take another look at our churches and see whether we measure up to the New Testament understanding of the church. Are we gathered communities of believers who encourage, support, and correct each other?

For millions of Christians, church used to be a building, as Luther said, *a place* where the Word is rightly preached and the sacraments are rightly handled. For many Christians today, the church or congregation is simply a casual gathering, a social club of converted people who have a right relationship with God. They think chiefly of a vertical relationship, "my God and I."

The true church, however, has a horizontal dimension of new relationships, not only with God, but also with each other. Paul wrote to the Corinthians:

> For just as the body is one and has many members, and all the members of the body, though many, are one body, so it is with Christ. For in the one Spirit we were all baptized into one body—Jews or Greeks, slaves or free—and we were all made to drink of one Spirit. (1 Cor. 12:12-13)

Does that describe your congregation? If not, what can we as seniors do about it?

One Sunday I was in a Frankfurt church, listening to the pastor preach on this text. He told his audience that their congregation had nine thousand members, with about two hundred present that morning. Then he stated that those present hardly knew each other, just enough for a greeting.

Yet Paul says, "If one member suffers, all suffer together with it; if one member is honored, all rejoice together with it" (1 Cor. 12:26). The pastor challenged those present: "How can we do what Paul says?"

As seniors, we can do a great deal to make our churches real New Testament congregations. Church needs to be a place where people hurt and rejoice with each other, where strangers are welcome, and where children and young people feel accepted.

What time is it? Time for a new beginning. Each of us must determine just where this new beginning will be. It depends largely on the roads we have traveled thus far. For some, the change will be slight; for others, enormous. Fifteen years ago, I was in an enviable position; I was able to move from my active work with MCC into retirement without major problems of adjustment or change.

Pastors, teachers, social workers, and others have enjoyed daily direct contact with people; they may be blessed with a relatively smooth transition into retirement. They can do for others so many things that are both necessary and satisfying.

For others, like farmers or factory workers, retirement may be more difficult. Not much in their daily occupations has prepared them for a sudden transition into retirement. Yet retired farmers often do assist the next generation taking over their farms. Many retired workers use their skills in helping others keep up their houses or cars, or in volunteering to clean up and rebuild after disasters. Retired busi-

nesspersons provide valuable counsel to start-up business-
es. And so on.

Paul Tournier talks about doing in retirement something
that "is neither a job nor a hobby." In other words, take the
best of both worlds. That is exactly what Tournier himself
did. As a doctor and psychologist, he spent his retirement
time privately counseling people, writing, lecturing, and
harvesting his training, but doing it at his own pace and his
own discretion.

What time is it? It is time to share our stories with our
grandchildren. That will be our next chapter.

*I thank you, Lord, for the precious gift of time, for opportuni-
ties and new challenges. Grant me the wisdom to know what
to do with the rest of my life, and give me the courage to do it.*

15

Sharing Our Stories

You shall love the LORD your God with all your
heart, and with all your soul, and with all your
might. Keep these words that I am commanding you
today in your heart. Recite them to your children and
talk about them when you are at home and when
you are away, when you lie down and when you rise.
Bind them as a sign on your hand, fix them as an
emblem on your forehead, and write them on the
doorposts of your house and on your gates.
—Moses, in Deuteronomy 6:5-9

The Hebrews were concerned about passing on their story, keeping salvation history alive. Moses lists perpetual instructions (above) to guide parents in passing on their experiences with God to their children. About the only thing Moses didn't mention was to proclaim it through bumper stickers on chariots.

Today we have tape recorders, video cameras, movies, and the ease of writing with typewriters or computers. I believe in using any or all of them, but I draw the line at bumper stickers. That's not my style.

My parents lived through turbulent times: the revolution and civil war in Russia, the resulting famine, and the birth of the MCC in 1920 to feed the starving people. They migrated to Canada when they both were forty-two years of age, taking all nine of us children with them. They struggled through a new beginning in Canada, learning the English language, surviving the Great Depression, and much more.

We children asked our father to put some of these experiences in a book. So he wrote his *Autobiography* (372 pages) and printed about twenty copies. We can never thank him enough. His opening sentence was written on December 19, 1929, when we had been in Canada for two years: "These days I have been reading the diaries of my grandfather; finished today. I believe this is the third time that I have read them."

My own grandchildren, for whom I write, are five generations removed from my father's grandfather who made those daily journal entries! When I realized how we pass our stories on from one generation to the next, it became clear to me what I should write in our family story, *A Pilgrim People*. That is what I want our children and grandchildren to know:

If you are to make sense of life,
  you need to have a sense of history.
If you are to know who you are,
  you have to know who your parents and grandparents
  were.
We hope this book will help you discover your true self
  and also contribute to giving you a sense of direction.

In one of Leo Tolstoy's novels, someone comments about a man who had gone bad: he had lost the distinction between right and wrong because he had lost touch with his family. When my siblings and I wrote *A Pilgrim People*, it was our sincere attempt to help our children and grandchildren stay in touch with their families and their faith. We left it entirely up to each one of us what to write, how to write, or how much to write. The book contains many pictures.

The response was so positive that we produced a second volume. In it we presented the diaries of my great-grandfather. He was a forty-niner (of 1849), and for ten years he dug and panned for gold in Oregon before returning to Europe. We also included my father's diaries and *Autobiography* (translated from German to English).

This is one way of passing on our heritage, experiences, faith, and values. As the psalmist put it,

> We have heard with our ears, O God,
> our ancestors have told us,
> what deeds you performed in their days,
> in the days of old. (Ps. 44:1)

In these diaries and the autobiography, we read about our ancestors' faith and their struggle with nature as well as with human nature. Pioneering in Russia was tough. My great-grandfather's entry on March 13, 1879, is brief as always, but it says volumes:

> Mar. 13, 1879: Storm in the house. Yesterday Cornelius Froese was here; discussion about nonresistance.
> Dec. 23, 1887: Mayor Bergmann has forbidden the playing of cards. This is, of course, carrying out what the ministers decided. Time will tell what kind of fruit this tree will bear.
> May 11, 1892: Today we started fighting grasshoppers on the main road, crushing them with seven rollers.
> May 12: Destroyed grasshoppers with squashers.
> May 28: The grasshoppers are winning.
> May 29: Killed 160 pounds of grasshoppers.
> June 12: Four men caught grasshoppers with canvases.

On September 5, 1894, my grandparents had five children; two weeks later they had only one. An epidemic swept through our colony, situated on the banks of the Volga River. Two girls died the week of September 6 and were buried in the same casket. The following week a boy and girl died and were buried in the same coffin. That left only one son, my father.

He spoke and wrote three languages: Russian, German, and English. In Canada, shortly before his death, he wrote a poem in German. On the back of the sheet, he added, "This is probably my only poetic attempt, and so imperfect; but I wrote it because, 'Love compelled me to do it.' " His poem is beautiful in the original German. The translation is also so imperfect:

> For my dearly beloved Renate [his wife, our mother] as a remembrance of my last birthday on earth. Written April 13, 1948, on a quiet morning in the hospital:

> The ring is broken,
> And silent is the song
> of love, joy, and good fortune.

> Has the hour now come for parting?
> Then let us stand firm—
> Once more let us look back.

> We experienced so much,
> in the years past,
> of delightful marital bliss.

> Keep that in your memory;
> it is my bequest
> for your future pilgrimage.

> Alas, we must confess
> that we also failed;
> Which we regret so very, very much.

Yet:

> *We are reconciled to God,*
> *And will soon be crowned*
> *Through our Lord Jesus Christ.*

This poem, his autobiography, his diaries, and those of my

great-grandfather, all create a mood and atmosphere. One can almost sense "so great a cloud of witnesses" surrounding us (Heb.12:1). Reading them, we cannot avoid feeling enveloped in an environment, in a certain climate. Just as plants are affected in their growth and fruit bearing by their climate, so are people.

When Prime Minister Yitzhak Rabin of Israel was assassinated, his widow, Leah Rabin, blamed the killing on right-wing Jewish extremists. On public TV, she pointed a finger at Benjamin Netanyahu, the right-wing opposition leader, and said, "I blame him for creating a [political and social] climate that makes this kind of thing happen. . . . It's a pity that my husband had to die to change people's minds and attitudes. But I do believe that now the *climate* will change. The silent majority was silent too long."

My parents must have understood the importance of raising their family in a certain social *climate*. I remember many of our dinner conversations, the guests who visited us, the missionaries who were invited, the books we received for Christmas, the friends we were encouraged to bring to our house, and much more.

However, one event was the biggest proof of how my parents recognized the importance of the right environment in raising a family: they actually sold the farm and moved to another location that was more socially and spiritually desirable.

On arriving in Canada, my father had bought a farm in a culturally mixed and spiritually lukewarm community. Neighbors cheated us and lied to us. There were tensions and conflicts. Gossip and unfounded rumors filled the atmosphere. But that didn't matter because my father had a dream.

In the not-too-distant future, all or most of the Mennonites from our community in Russia would come to Canada, buy up these farms as they were put on the market, and be our neighbors. We would change everything and become a different community. We would have a church, and support and help each other; it would be something like it had been in Russia. He dreamed of us living in a healthy climate again.

It didn't happen. In 1930, Russia closed its doors to all emigration. The Iron Curtain, as Winston Churchill called it, shut off the East from West. My parents were crushed. They had spent their last savings on buying this farm. They had worked hard for five years to improve it. Then they saw their dream collapse.

I remember hearing them say more than once that the main reason they had left the Soviet Union was because of their children. They did not want us to grow up under atheistic Communism. The fact that our current community was not desirable had not bothered them much because all that would change when the others from Russia joined us.

Now what? It must have taken a great deal of courage and a firm conviction about the importance of the *climate* for them to decide to sell the farm and move again. This time we went to Laird and the Tiefengrund area north of Saskatoon.

They were so right. We were teenagers, and we reached out into our neighborhood for companions and friends. It is not surprising that most of my siblings married people within easy driving distance of our farm. All are members of the church. All of us are profoundly thankful for the wisdom and courage of our parents when they moved. The climate in which we had been living was not likely to build good character and foster spiritual growth.

The well-known eighteenth-century frontier preacher and his wife, Jonathan and Sarah Edwards, are bright examples of the importance of raising a family in a positive spiritual climate. The Edwards had eleven children. Biographers credit especially Sarah with raising them and making sure that the family climate was right. She was patient and kind, but firm. She treated her children with love and courtesy, but she could also be strict. The children responded with love and courtesy.

A. E. Winship made a study of 1,400 descendants of the Edwards family. He identified their professions and reported that many of them became "nation builders":

13 college presidents	1 dean of a medical school
80 public officials	65 college professors
100 lawyers	3 U.S. senators
3 state governors	1 dean of a law school
30 judges	1 U.S. vice-president
66 physicians	1 controller of the U.S. treasury

What an impressive record! What a family!

To show just how much the *climate* influences the kind of people we become, Winship also tells the results of another study that was different. Many of the 480 descendants of a Martin Kallikak became nation-destroying people. For example, 33 were sexually immoral, 36 were illegitimate, three were criminals, three were brothel keepers, and so on.

I used to have problems with Numbers 14:18: "The LORD is slow to anger, and abounding in steadfast love, forgiving iniquity and transgression, *but* by no means clearing the guilty, visiting the iniquity of the parents upon the children to the third and the fourth generation."

I used to think that if God is fair and just, he won't do that. If he is indeed "slow to anger" and "forgiving iniquity and transgression," then why zap the third and fourth generation for something they didn't do? Why punish the innocent? Okay, I thought, sock it to the father or mother who sinned; punish the first generation. They are the guilty ones; but leave the children and grandchildren alone.

Today I no longer think or talk like that. I have seen first-hand how attitudes, values, and lifestyles are passed from one generation to another by osmosis. Children absorb it from parents without knowing what is going on. What chance do they have? They grow up in an unhealthy climate and reap the consequences, just like the descendants of Martin Kallikak.

When I was pastoring, a young woman came to our church from time to time. One day she asked whether I could help her with a relational problem. I listened to her side of the story. Her husband was going to bed with her mother, his mother-in-law.

As I probed into their family situation, she told me that her parents were divorced. I asked about her grandparents and learned that her grandfather was an alcoholic. He had left his wife; she didn't know whether they were divorced or not.

The room in which we met was a mess, the TV was showing garbage, her little girl cried, and the mother shouted at her while talking to me. That's when the proverbial penny dropped. I understood why this moral pigsty was bound to pass on its lifestyle to the innocent little girl crying for love and attention.

How could that little girl, growing up in that climate, ever break the cycle? Yes, indeed, iniquity is passed unto the third and fourth generation, as the two studies above show—unless the cycle is broken. The good news (the gospel) is that it can be broken with God's help, through the church, professional counselors, friends, and concerned people with love and common sense.

As seniors, we have a wonderful opportunity to do something about climate and atmosphere in homes, churches, and communities. We have the time, and we have the experience. We know it takes listening and patience, courage to become involved, resisting the temptation to give orders and to take control of other people's lives, and a heap of love.

I remember listening to a retired pastor, who was so upset about conditions in his church that he was ready to leave. He talked about individuals with wrong attitudes and about long-standing problems that nobody tackled. On and on he went, lamenting the fact that his people just weren't very spiritual. It hurt him to think that this was their condition after so many years of his devoted ministry.

At last he ran down and stopped. I asked him one question: "Do you love your people?" He was silent a long time. I waited. He shifted his position in the chair. At last he got up and said he'd better be going.

Loving his people wouldn't solve all the problems quickly, but it would be a good start. That brings us to our next meditation, the need to name it.

Lord, I have so much to be thankful for! And so much to ask for, Lord. I need you today as much as when I was a child or even more. I see how life rushes on, how opportunities for contributing to a wholesome climate in family, church, and community come and go, like doors that open and shut. Give me a nudge, Lord, when I am too slow to enter, too cautious, or afraid of making mistakes. Spare me, Lord, from making the bigger mistake of doing nothing.

16
Why Not Name It?

So out of the ground the LORD God formed every animal of the field and every bird of the air, and brought them to the man; . . . whatever the man called every living creature, that was its name.
—Genesis 2:19-20

When God asked Adam to name all the animals, the assignment was not simply to say, "This is a *horse* and that a *cow*," or "I'll call this one a *monkey* and that one a *donkey*." That's just giving them labels, like people wearing name tags at a conference. It doesn't say anything about the animal.

In the biblical sense, to name something is *to know, understand, and reveal its character.* When we say a town has a bad name, we know of undesirable things going on in that town. A person like Mother Teresa makes a name for herself. We know about her efforts to alleviate suffering, help the poor, and care for the dying. The late King Hussein of Jordan made a name for himself with his national and international peacemaking efforts.

We cannot truly name cancer because there are still too many unknowns; hence, we cannot get rid of it. When the World Health Organization (WHO) named smallpox as a target disease, they knew all about it: what caused it, how it spread, and how to combat it. With a budget lower than the cost of one strategic bomber, they eradicated smallpox from the earth in ten years, by late 1977. Today there is not one case of smallpox.

If medical science could name AIDS, it would do the same thing—get rid of it. But until and unless it can actually name it and explain it, there will be AIDS.

One agency recommends writing down your financial goals, how much and when: "If you never set your goals, how will you know when you have reached them?" It is the same in all walks of life: unless you are able to name a goal, you're just drifting. The ability to name something means we're hot on the trail to understanding it.

Sometimes we are *unable* to name something, but often we are *unwilling* to name it or talk about it. We play games in the family, in church, and in politics. We avoid naming an issue; we talk around it in euphemisms to obscure and hide the real problem.

When the Swissair jet crashed off the coast of Nova Scotia in September 1998, a memorial service was held for the 229 victims. Participating pastors were forbidden to read from the New Testament or mention Jesus Christ. When they asked why this restriction was placed on them, they received no clear answers.

One response was that local organizers had gone too far. Later, it appeared that the instructions had come from higher up. The Canadian prime minister, Jean Crétien, expressed regret for the incident but would say no more. Not satisfied with this restriction and beating around the bush, one of the pastors perceptively said, "Let's name it and talk about it."

Henri Nouwen has published many books, such as *The Return of the Prodigal Son* and *Our Greatest Gift: A Meditation on Dying and Caring.* He says, "Aging does not need to be hidden or denied, but can be understood, affirmed, and experienced as a process of growth by which the mystery of life is slowly revealed to us."

It is extremely important to name something. In his autobiography, *To Dwell in Peace,* the activist priest Daniel

Berrigan says that if we are going to have peace, we must name the euphemisms standing in the way, values called up to be defended and fought for:

> Once the Beast was named, one noted with relief how the mind was cleansed of false names, those by which the Beast "deceived all." The masks came down: normalcy, security, national interest, family values, legitimate defense, just war, flag, mother, democracy, leadership, religion. The Beast stood there. He was naked and known. More: once named, he was also in chains.

Name it and then you can deal with it. If the Beast works for death, let's recognize that. We cannot deal with something as long as we have it on the tip of our tongue but use substitute words to conceal the true meaning of the thing. That's what happened to the word *sin.* It just faded away so that today we seldom hear it mentioned. Sin is scarcely recognized for what it is, as Karl Menninger claimed in *Whatever Became of Sin?*

A friend from France was studying at an American seminary for a year. Before she went home, we asked her to tell us about her experience at the seminary. She was quite positive: "I learned a lot and enjoyed it. But I'm puzzled that nobody ever talked about sin." We asked, "What did they call it?" She replied in her French accent, still puzzled but also slightly amused: "Mostly they just talked about hang-ups."

Seniors also need to name things in their relationships with doctors, families, financial counselors, and lawyers. It is the way to deal with misunderstandings and problems. Name it. Once it is named, we begin to understand it and can deal with it.

One night Elfrieda and I were packed into a car with children we couldn't count, partly because it was too dark but also because there were so many. The father was at the wheel, and his wife was beside him, with a baby on her lap. There must have been at least two more children in the front seat. We were in the back, with children on all sides, and each of us held one.

As we rolled along the highway, the mother introduced the children to us, naming them and telling their ages. We promptly forgot the names of the first few, names that were strange to us. After about five children, she said, "And the one on your lap, Elfrieda, is Mary. The one on your lap, Peter, is James. The baby in my lap is Elizabeth."

We thanked her and said we were pleased to meet them all. Then we admitted that we had already forgotten the names of the first ones, but we had noticed a change about half way through from unusual names to familiar Bible names. Both the husband and wife were pleased we had noticed that.

They eagerly explained that when they were married, they were not Christians but thought they were happy. They had one child after another, but life was a bit of a drag, without real luster. Then they had accepted Christ as their Savior and Lord. That had brought such a change into their lives, so much joy and satisfaction. So they decided that this freshness should be reflected in the choice of names for their children.

A profound change had taken place in their life, affecting outlook and values, attitudes and lifestyle, relationships, and even the naming of their children. The first children had to put meaning into their own names. The names of the last children came with a wealth of meaning from their association with the lives of important people of the early church.

Let us take three words that are prominent in seniors' lives and see whether we can name and understand them: *security, health,* and *peace.*

Security. At our residence for seniors, Elfrieda and I have just heard that outside doors will be locked for security reasons. Will the residents feel more secure? From a dinner conversation, I sensed that the most-vocal woman feels insecure because of her financial situation. One couple left a week ago because they had miscalculated their financial assets before they came.

Finances and locked doors are important. When we have those, will the residents feel secure? One women fell in her shower. She complained that there was nothing to hold on to. She hesitates to take a shower because she feels so insecure. The administration has announced plans to have secure bars placed in all the showers. Will we feel secure then?

Let's have the shower bars, to prevent accidents. Three people have fallen here in six months. Will we feel secure when the shower bars are in place?

What about the old man who cannot live with his children or without them? He needs them for transportation, for lifting things, and for helping him with his shopping and bookkeeping. But as soon as they are together, the atmosphere becomes stifled. He is close to tears when he talks about his family. He wishes he could feel assured of their love, and they wouldn't be so sensitive to every word he says. They also have their side of the story. Security? Nothing bothers the father and his children as much as their insecure relationship.

King Hezekiah said, "Like a swallow or a crane I clamor, I moan like a dove. My eyes are weary with looking upward. O Lord, I am oppressed; be my security!" (Isa. 38:14). When we install one security measure after another and still do not feel secure, we can cry out with Hezekiah: "O Lord, be my security!"

The psalmist was able to say, "He drew me up from the desolate pit, out of the miry bog, and set my feet upon a rock, making my steps secure" (Ps. 40:2). He was able to affirm, "Therefore my heart is glad, and my soul rejoices; my body also rests secure" (Ps. 16:9).

Health. When we enjoy good health, we hardly think of our physical condition. When we are sick, we become health conscious. Good health is such a blessing. Our German friends say, "Aber die Hauptsache ist doch die Gesundheit! (but the main thing is your health)."

Yes, health is important. That's why we are careful about our diet and exercise. We visit the doctor regularly for checkups. We take our vitamins and medications. Being sick is no fun for us or for others. But is physical health really *everything?*

What about our spiritual health? Does it affect our physical health, and vice versa? John Wesley attributed his good health to daily devotions, regular exercise, managing stress, and sleeping enough. The Teacher adds the need to hear and speak encouraging words: "Pleasant words are like a honeycomb, / sweetness to the soul and health to the body" (Prov. 16:24).

Three thousand years ago, people knew about psychosomatic conditions, the connection between body and mind or spirit. Isaiah writes, "Surely it was for my welfare that I had great bitterness; but you have held back my life from the pit of destruction, for you have cast all my sins behind your back" (Isa. 38:17). The best medicine is the assurance that our sins are forgiven. A good conscience and peace of mind, with a sense of humor, can energize our bodies and help maintain our physical health far beyond usual expectations.

Peace. How we all long for peace—peace of mind, peace with our loved ones, peace in our churches, and peace in the world. So often peace eludes us. Jeremiah's words are still true: people say "'Peace, peace,' when there is no peace" (Jer. 6:14)

Peace of mind, meaning peace with God, is basic and most important. This is personal. The evangelist Billy Graham has written a book on that topic. First John 3:21-22 assures us, "Beloved, if our hearts do not condemn us, we have boldness before God; and we receive from him whatever we ask."

On the other hand, suppose the still small voice of our conscience keeps telling us that we have neglected to do something or we have a relationship with someone that is not as it ought to be. Then what? Jesus gives a simple, clear, and difficult answer:

> When you are offering your gift at the altar, if you remember that your brother or sister has something against you, leave your gift there before the altar and go: first be reconciled to your brother or sister, and then come and offer your gift. (Matt. 5:23-24)

The Vietnam War was over at last, and four of us MCC workers were meeting with members of the Gossner Mission in East Berlin. They asked our delegation how we felt after being involved, directly or indirectly, in the Vietnam War. We shared our views and feelings frankly with them.

Then we asked them how they felt after being part of the Hitler movement, particularly being involved, directly or indirectly, with the persecution and massacre of the Jews. To our amazement, they said they had not yet solved that problem or cleared their consciences. This was in November 1980, and their Third Reich experience was some thirty-five years earlier!

We expressed our surprise and recommended a four-point program for clearing one's conscience:
- Open and honest confession and sincere apology.
- Making amends and restitution when possible.
- Accepting forgiveness from God and humanity.
- Going on with your life, humbled but wiser, knowing that the slate is clear.

They said that was all nice and likely biblically based, but they could not accept it. At least, they would have no idea how to implement it since it involved the whole German nation and the deaths of some six million Jews plus five million "undesirables." However, they did agree that on a personal level, it would probably work.

Probably? Of course it works! What other way works for peace of mind? Paul wrote to the Colossians, "Bear with one another and, if anyone has a complaint against another, forgive each other; just as the Lord has forgiven you, so you also must forgive" (Col. 3:13).

Peter asked whether forgiving seven times was enough. I'm glad he asked that question; it would have been on my mind, too. "Yeah, how often?" Jesus answered, "Not seven times, but seventy times seven" (Matt. 18:22, RSV). He was suggesting that long before we get to 490, we lose track. So we just keep on forgiving and forget the counting.

That is fundamental in obtaining peace of mind and naming something: forgiving as God has forgiven us (Matt. 6:12). If we are truly reconciled with God, the next step, reconciliation with people, will be much easier. It is not enough to have peace with God in our hearts, only vertical peace, without also having horizontal peace, peace with those around us.

By the grace of God, we experience this wonderful peace that the world cannot give nor take away (John 14:27). Then we will most likely become advocates for peace, knowing that peace will do for others what it has done for us. Paul writes, "All this is from God, who reconciled us to himself through Christ, and has given us the ministry of reconciliation" (2 Cor. 5:18).

Lord, our hearts are filled with gratitude as we reflect on how you have provided security, health, and peace for us. Show us how we can pass these experiences on to others around us. Help us to see the open doors, and give us the courage to enter. But in our sharing, Lord, help us also to love with a sincere heart and to tread softly.

17
Becoming Kinder

Be kind to one another, tenderhearted.
—Paul, in Ephesians 4:32

Love is patient; love is kind;
love is not envious or boastful or arrogant or rude.
—Paul, in 1 Corinthians 13:4

I never tire of quoting the great missionary, Albert Schweitzer: "As you get older, if you don't become kinder, then what's the point of getting older?"

We all appreciate little acts of kindness. Sometimes they make our day. When our daughter Ruth was a small child, she would pick dandelions and bring the flowers to us, beaming and exuding happiness. An act of kindness can make our day even more when we are giving rather than receiving. At our age, we all know how that works.

After the war, we were in Berlin, working with refugees. Christmas came, and they wanted to show their gratitude to Elfrieda and me for the food, shelter, and safety that MCC provided for them. However, there was nothing to buy, and they had no money. Nevertheless, they were resourceful; they had keen imaginations.

To this day we treasure the tablecloth made out of MCC flour sacks and the calendar-book made out of scrap paper. These gifts are worth more to us than anything that money might have bought. It was a cooperative effort, with many refugees contributing their ideas and work. The gifts were beautiful. We were moved to tears. Such art! Such ingenuity! Such kindness!

The virtue of kindness is nourished in the family. When parents and grandparents practice kindness in their relationships, the children and grandchildren will follow their example. They will absorb this beautiful quality of life by osmosis, without knowing it. It will become second nature to them. Kindness will spill over to neighbors and even strangers, blessing everyone with whom they come into contact.

Let us practice purposeful acts of kindness:

• Do a kind deed every day. Say an encouraging word. Hold the hand of your spouse. Overlook someone's fault or verbal jab with a smile and a friendly nod.

• Accept every kindness offered to you; never reject it, even if it is just a bouquet of dandelions or an empty flour sack.

• Memorize Albert Schweitzer's saying (above) and ask God to increase your kindness as the years pile up.

One day I watched a nurse sticking Elfrieda's arm with a needle to administer antibiotics. She tried twice to locate a vein and called for help. The next nurse made three attempts, then called for the "expert," who came in looking confident. He smiled, took the needle, made three tries, and left shaking his head.

I could hardly stand it: each time, they injected the needle under the skin and moved it left and right, up and down, in search of a vein. Yet Elfrieda, also a nurse, didn't say one unkind word, not even "ouch!" She encouraged them to keep trying and suggested that they use the other arm. "If you don't have a body to stick," she said good-naturedly, "how can you ever learn?"

The fourth nurse succeeded on her first try. I was so proud of Elfrieda! She was patient and kind (1 Cor. 13:4). Even when the door was closed and we were alone, all she said was "They did it! But it hurt."

When we lived in Frankfurt, Germany, after World War II, we heard a story about an Austrian family named Schicklegruber. Alios and Klara had several children. Before the birth of one girl child, the doctor was able to tell that she would be severely handicapped. Friends advised the mother to have the child aborted. However, she could not bring herself to do that.

When Paula was born, the parents, especially the mother, loved the retarded child very much. Eventually the mother taught her to eat by herself, dress herself, and even lace her shoes. She never went to school, but through the years her mother taught her to help with the household chores.

Before Paula was a teenager, her mother became seriously ill and was bedfast for a year. During that time, her daughter took care of her many needs. She did the laundry, prepared the meals, and kept the house clean. She never grumbled or complained but cheerfully did what she could.

One older brother survived and went to school. He was a healthy and bright lad with an artistic bent, and he loved to draw and paint. The father, who was illegitimate and using his mother's name, Schicklegruber, managed to lay claim to the surname *Hitler* thirteen years before Adolf was born.

We all know what became of the boy, but we had never heard of his caring sister, and the kindness she showed to her bedfast mother. We know which of the two was the greater blessing on earth.

Lord, you know how I appreciate it when others are kind to me. Help me to cultivate kindness, to express it often, gladly, and spontaneously until it becomes my very nature.

18
A Second Career

Whatever you do, in word or deed,
do everything in the name of the Lord Jesus,
giving thanks to God the Father through him.
—Paul, in Colossians 3:17

My friend Eric Habegger worked in a furniture factory. When off work, he divided his time between orchard, family, and church. He loves his fruit trees and is a good horticulturist. Eric is a registered Master Gardener.

When he retired, everyone knew what he would do with his spare time. He would work in his orchard. One day each year, his orchard is filled with fifty to a hundred invited people, there to learn from him. He teaches others, including me, how to graft by inserting a scion into a stock. He volunteers his time and skill for the nearby orchard of the historic Herr House.

One Sunday he brought his knife, a scion, and a stock to church to talk about grafting. The adults learned as much as the children. Eric said that the scion is a little piece cut from one fruit tree, and the stock is the branch of another. In grafting, he cut a wedge in the stock and inserted the little scion into it.

Then he talked about the mystery and beauty of how the little scion would become a part of the stock. It would attach itself to the stock and become one with it, producing a new kind of fruit. The sap and nourishment would flow from the stock into the little scion, keeping it alive, making it grow and produce fruit. Eric told us that he has one tree in his orchard that produces about a dozen kinds of apples.

Then he laid his knife aside, took his Bible, and read from John 15. Jesus says, "I am the true vine, and my father is the vinegrower" (15:1). He explained the process of pruning, removing some branches from vine or tree so it will produce better fruit.

His story became exciting when he explained that the word "abide" means *menoh* in the Greek. Jesus says, "I am the vine, you are the branches. Those who *abide* (*ho menohn*) in me and I in them bear much fruit, because apart from me you can do nothing" (15:5).

Eric picked up the grafted piece again. He said that if the little scion did not attach itself to the stock and "abide," if the two did not grow together, the scion would fall off and die. However, if it did "abide" by firmly and permanently attaching itself to the stock, it would become one with it and bear much fruit.

In this passage, Jesus uses some form of *menoh* eleven times: "*Abide* in me" (15:4-7). "*Abide* in my love" (15:9-10). If "my words *abide* in you, ask for whatever you wish, . . . that you bear much fruit," like the flourishing branch of a vine or tree (15:7-8). "If you keep my commandments, you will *abide* in my love" (15:10), and you will "bear fruit . . . that will *last*" (15:16).

Listening to Eric, I remembered a saying of Paul Tournier, the Swiss doctor and author of *Learn to Grow Old:* "Society desperately needs the services which the old are better qualified than the young to provide." He firmly believes that an older person needs to find a second career, like Eric in his horticulture. This second career can be quite flexible, in fact, much more so than the first career, the job. It can be full-time or part-time, but it clearly must be more than a hobby.

Hobbies, like stamp collecting or fishing, are good and interesting diversions for a brief period of time, but they rarely sustain the needed interest over many years, often decades. Furthermore, hobbies are chiefly for personal pleasures; a second career is for the benefit of the larger society or even for financial survival. Therefore, the second career is also more lasting and satisfying to the retiree.

Atlee Beechey, retired professor of psychology and peace studies at Goshen College, is a strong advocate of peace. He served as director of relief and service programs for MCC in Europe after WW II and later in Vietnam for several years. Atlee was a Fulbright lecturer in India, wrote books, and finally retired again. Like Eric, his second career was started long before he reached retirement.

In an age of unprecedented violence, wars, and revolutions, it was a natural transition for Atlee to launch the organization of Seniors for Peace. This keeps him busy organizing new groups, writing letters, lecturing, witnessing in Washington, and many other peace-related activities.

Meet another retiree with a second career. A farming couple moved to a small house in Hillsboro, Kansas. While they hosted me for a week, she talked freely, but he seemed happier listening. I was curious about his use of time. He merely said that he occasionally went back to the farm to help his son, and several times a week, he met with friends for coffee in a restaurant.

About the third evening, I again asked about retirement. His wife spoke up: "Henry, why don't you just tell Peter what you do all day? You enjoy it, and talking about it isn't boasting."

He invited me to follow him to his workshop. What a surprise! The place was filled with the latest in woodworking tools and machinery, stacks of lumber, and pieces of miniature furniture in various stages of completion. I gradually pieced the story together.

He had always loved working with wood, like my friend Eric loved working with fruit trees. After retirement, he was able to give all his time to it. I asked him why he hesitated telling me about it. He said it was because he gave all the furniture to the annual MCC relief sale, to raise money for the poor. "That's something one doesn't brag about," he said.

He wouldn't give me a dollar amount. Nevertheless, I figured out that since his retirement, he must have contributed thirty to forty thousand dollars. I was so pleased with the quality of the furniture and excited about his project that I placed an order for several pieces for my grandchildren's playhouse.

A second career is obviously not just a leisure-time activity and not only for personal pleasure. A second career has a goal and a mission. It is for the love and benefit of others more than for self, unless one is burdened with financial needs. Because of this noble purpose, it is also deeply satisfying to the retiree. That is why we must emphasize that a second career is not merely an escape from boredom. In a true sense, it is an absorbing interest (see meditation 28).

A second career can be voluntary or paid, but it is definitely not a second job. Such persons are not employees in the sense that they were before. They are absolutely free, no longer part of the organization, not giving or taking orders, and in no way interfering with the running of the old organization. Most retirees are free to pursue personal interests and talents.

Like Eric in his orchard and Atlee in his peace ministry, each is contributing according to their interests, training, gifts, and ability. They are serving "the common good" (1 Cor. 12:7).

Lord, there is so much need in the world, so much need right here at home. Open my eyes to see it, strengthen my will to do something about it, and give me the grace to relate to others with patience and love. Thank you for the assurance that you will lead me and sustain me in whatever it is that you want me to do.

19

Can You Imagine That?

I will pour out my Spirit upon all flesh,
and your sons and your daughters shall prophesy,
and your young men shall see visions,
and your old men shall dream dreams.
—Peter, in Acts 2:17, quoting Joel 2:28

The Wright brothers saw birds gliding smoothly through the air and had visions of making a machine so people could do the same thing. The World Health Organization (WHO) had a vision of eradicating the dreaded disease of smallpox. In 1920, Mennonites imagined that if they collected food for the starving people in Russia, they could save many lives.

Albert Einstein said, "Imagination is more important than knowledge." Today at airports all over the world, people board airplanes that fly like birds. The WHO launched its program to stamp out smallpox, which the *Encyclopedia Britannica* calls "one of the world's most dreaded plagues," and succeeded in less than ten years.

Today Mennonites through their relief agency, MCC, are feeding hundreds of thousands of people in many countries. I should know. I received such food after WW I and I was a distributor of it after WW II.

When famine swept over Russia after WW I, followed by the Communist Revolution, people were dying by the thousands. My father wrote in his journal, "Little Peter won't be with us much longer." I had typhus, was malnourished, and was expected to die. But MCC food arrived just in time. Here I am, eighty-five years old!

I am convinced that imagination is more important than knowledge. Everything has its beginning in someone's head, including the airplane, the smallpox vaccine, and the MCC relief program. Imagining something is always the first step to making something concrete happen.

In 1922, while MCC was feeding 43,000 hungry people every day in Russia, John Epp was on his tractor in Whitewater, Kansas. As he went around the field and thought about that feeding program, the idea of shipping food so far seemed ridiculous. John knew the soil in Russia was good, and Mennonites were good farmers. With rain, they could grow their own crops. But most draft animals—horses, oxen, and camels—had been eaten during the famine or had died.

Then John Epp had an idea. He imagined farmers in Russia going around their fields, not with horse-drawn implements, but sitting on tractors as he did, plowing their fields. Why wouldn't that work? John proposed that MCC send tractors and plows. The MCC executive committee liked the idea, bought fifty Fordson tractors and fifty Oliver plows in Detroit, and shipped them to Russia. One of them came to our community near Saratov, along the Volga River.

What a sight the day the tractor arrived and started plowing! One man was on the tractor, one ran ahead of it, one followed behind, and twenty or more were shaking hands with each other, making little dances, and thanking God for the gift from America.

"Imagination is more important than knowledge" is not an overstatement. It is a profound truth. Just before John Epp died on April 16, 1943, he imagined that even in his last hour he could help some poor person. He asked to be buried in a plain wooden coffin and in shirtsleeves. His suit was a gift for some needy person.

Ted and Justina Friesen lived in California, a major fruit-producing state. Every harvesttime they saw much good fruit rotting under the trees. The orchard owners would shrug and say, "That's just one of those things. Nothing can be done about it."

One evening as the Friesens were driving by the orchards, they had an idea: why not gather up some of that fruit, take it home, dry it, and sell it to help the needy? So that's what they did.

At first, they did it alone and only in the evenings, but soon friends and people from the church joined them. Within a few years, more than 250 volunteers were gathering fruit and taking it to a center for washing and drying. Some local folks still only come in the evenings, but others come from a distance, stay for a week or two, and work all day. They wash the fruit with an ordinary washing machine. People often smile when the Friesens tell them to set it on "spin dry."

The sale of this dried fruit brings in more than $50,000 each year. All of it goes to benefit the needy.

Then there is Jake Wiebe of Winnipeg. Since he retired 15 years ago, he has made more than 500 blankets. His son works at a clothing factory and salvages scraps and remnants for him. His wife, Helen, and other women have made about 50 quilts. All the blankets and quilts go to MCC for the poor.

One more story shows the power of imagination. Tornadoes and floods are powerful forces of nature. The day after a tornado destroyed much of Hesston, Kansas, a lady told me that she had seen a cow in the swirling funnel. Animals, houses, and cars were tossed about like toys. Water has the same destructive force.

In 1950, a Sunday school class in Hesston was brainstorming what they could do to help victims of disasters. That was the birth of Mennonite Disaster Service (MDS). Lowell Detweiler, longtime director of MDS, says in *The Hammer Rings Hope*, "Some suggest MDS stands for 'Mennonites Doing Something.' We are a doing organization: we shovel mud, we remove debris, we repair and rebuild homes, we listen, we eat, we tell stories, and we hammer out hope."

Through MDS, thousands of men, women, and young people bring help and hope to discouraged people. They give priority to the elderly, handicapped, widowed, low-income, uninsured, or otherwise disadvantaged people.

Wind and water are powerful, but the human heart and mind and the power of imagination are stronger. MDSers have seen the reconstruction of buildings and the restoration of relationships that had been broken and lives that were shattered.

As we age, imagine what we could do for others and for ourselves if we yielded ourselves fully to the Holy Spirit. I wonder what would happen if I were to dream of spending more time with my grandchildren, telling them stories, and traveling together. This might turn out to be a blessing for them and for me.

I wonder what would happen if I enrolled in a course of special interest at a nearby college or volunteered to work for Meals on Wheels or for Ten Thousand Villages. What would happen to me if I resolved to bury all grudges, to forgive everyone who wronged and hurt me, to turn my back on all these unhappy experiences of the past, and to turn my face fully to the future?

There is nothing wrong with dreaming, imagining some changes in me, and having visions of a brighter tomorrow. Jesus says that with God's help, "all things are possible" (Mark 10:27).

Lord, you have given me the capacity to imagine, to dream, and to have visions of myself and of the people around me. Thank you for that gift. Help me use it for the good of myself and others and for your glory.

20

Learning to Listen

This is my Son, the Beloved;
Listen to him!
—The Voice from the cloud, in Mark 9:7

We often hear parents say to children, "Now you listen to me!" Listening is not easy; it is a discipline and an art. Listening has to be learned. Few people are good listeners, but there are exceptions. William Alexander of the California Polytechnic State University participated in an MCC study tour to the Philippines. In an unsolicited letter to MCC, he commented:

> I have known Mennonites as a small religious community with a reputation for excellent farming. I expected the tour to consist of a number of demonstrations of improved farming practices—Mennonites patiently demonstrating their farming skills for the benefit of the Filipino men and women.
>
> At first, the tour baffled me; there wasn't any specific focus on farming at all, and then I was amazed. We visited poor Filipinos known to the Mennonite team. They were asked to tell us about their lives—the difficulties they encountered and how they survived.
>
> I found these Mennonites doing something very unusual; they were deliberately and carefully listening to the poor. No one listens to the poor, least of all the relatively rich development workers who have studied the problems of the poor and are anxious to offer their planned solutions.

When I was speaking in chapels and classes in a high school, students came to me for counsel. A fifteen-year-old girl cried as she poured out her heart. I asked whether she had told her mother about this problem. "Of course not," she replied. "My mom wouldn't listen!"

Later, I heard much the same from a boy; he couldn't talk to his father about something because his dad doesn't listen to him. Yet I'm sure these parents love their children. They want the best for them. That's why they sent them to this private school.

The first step is to make sure we are physically able to hear well enough. When I wanted help with hearing, I went to a medical specialist who recommended a certain hearing aid. He mentioned that a well-known public figure had one just like it. "If it works for him," he concluded, "it ought to be good enough for any of us."

"But he doesn't hear anything or anybody," I countered.

Instantly he shot back, "Oh, yes, he hears, but he doesn't listen!" The expert was right. What's the use of hearing if we don't listen?

Let us pay attention to Dietrich Bonhoeffer, the German theologian whom Hitler killed just before the end of WW II. "The first service we can perform for anyone is to listen." That call to listen surely goes out to parents, not only to pastors, relief workers, teachers, and national leaders.

Bonhoeffer's statement is weighty and worth memorizing. Active listening is something we seniors can do for and with each other. Sometimes that is about all we can do. Repeatedly we have had people thank us for listening to them.

Active listening means to *stop, look, listen,* and *respond.* Stop: let the other person know you are paying attention and count them as important. Make eye contact and look for nonverbal cues that may help you respond. Focus your attention on the words and the feelings or tone of what the person is saying or trying to say. Only then can you be ready to respond helpfully, by paraphrasing what you have just heard, or by asking a question that may lead to others working out their own solution to a problem.

Active listening is a service that retired people urgently need. Many of them have no one to talk to. They are lonely. They may be afraid—afraid a symptom could develop into something serious. They want to talk about it, but to whom?

Perhaps they received bad news of the death of a loved one and would like to share it with someone, but there is nobody. Maybe they just had a doctor's check-up and are coming back with a clean bill of health. With whom can they share this good news?

Who cares? Who will listen? Some people seem to be concerned only about their own lives. When you begin to share yours, that becomes an unspoken invitation for others to interrupt at the first opportunity and tell you about their own experiences. People want to share; they want to unload, but who is willing to listen?

Active listening is not only hearing what the other person is saying; it is also hearing what the other person is *not* saying. This is like reading between the lines. Such listening creates confidence, and confidence can lead to *intimacy,* which means "into me see."

While we ought to practice the art of actively listening to other people, we also need to be alert to the voice within us. We need to listen to our own conscience. Martin Luther said, "It is a dangerous thing to go against your conscience."

We believe that in addition to speaking to us through his Word, the Bible, God also speaks to us through the still small voice within us, our conscience. In 1 John 3:21-22, we read, "Beloved, if our hearts do not condemn us, we have boldness before God; and we receive from him whatever we ask."

God certainly speaks to us in many ways, through different channels, including the community of believers. I have never heard God speak directly to me in a voice that I could hear with my ears, like Samuel heard him (1 Sam. 8:7). However, I have often heard God speak to me through my brothers and sisters.

Elfrieda and I were happily serving the Eden Church in Moundridge, Kansas. We had been there for seven years when MCC called us to return to Europe. We faced a difficult decision: should we stay or go?

One day we felt the tug to stay because we thought our ministry at Eden was not finished. Those dear people of Swiss origins loved us, though our origins were Dutch-Prussian-Russian. The next day we realized the urgency of MCC's call, for which we were qualified partly because of our language facility and our earlier relief and service experiences in Europe.

We discussed the pros and cons and prayed about it. Then we consciously and deliberately sought the counsel of our brothers and sisters in the church. We wanted to hear them, to know what God was saying to us through them. When we finally decided to go, we were relaxed and at ease, knowing that we were doing God's will.

With many older people, the decision is not whether to stay in Kansas or go to Germany. The decision is whether to stay in your home or move into a retirement community. That decision can be extremely difficult.

Here is some good counsel: Use your head. Get all the information possible. Listen to your heart. Listen to your family and friends. God speaks to us. Do we hear him? Are we listening?

Lord, help me to become a better listener. Help me to pay attention to others and to you.

21

Passing on the Faith

I will utter dark sayings from of old,
*   things that we have heard and known,*
*   that our ancestors have told us.*
We will not hide them from their children;
*   we will tell the coming generation*
the glorious deeds of the LORD, and his might,
*   and the wonders that he has done.*
—Asaph, in Psalm 78:1-4

We know that Mennonites are losing many young people. Some join other churches; many join no church at all. What can we seniors do about this?

A great deal. First, we can model our faith. Just live it day by day. Walk with the Lord. Conduct devotions at home and attend church regularly. Contribute to worthy causes. Volunteer time and energy as possible. Our children and grandchildren, nieces and nephews, and other youths in the church—they're watching us.

Second, pray for them. Love them and pray for them. When my mother was a widow and old, she often had sleepless nights. After I told her how sorry I was for her, she laughed heartily: "There's no need to be sorry. The hours awake in the dark are a precious gift to me."

I was puzzled. Then she explained that when she couldn't sleep, she prayed for all nine of us children, beginning with the oldest, one by one. "Many times I go back to sleep again long before I have come to the youngest." I was glad to hear that, for her sake but also because I am in the middle and not the youngest.

Third, do what Psalm 78 says: talk to the younger set about your experience with the Lord. No need to get up in church, no need to be a missionary in Africa. Just tell the young people about your own spiritual pilgrimage. Try not to be preachy. As a young man of twenty-one in Russia, my father was unhappy. This is reflected in his *Autobiography*, which he wrote years later in Canada:

It was on a beautiful fall day, I think it was September. The workers were plowing. I was again having one of those miserable days in which I felt totally alone and abandoned. My innermost was in a shambles. After I had accompanied the workers to the field and returned, I had no desire to do anything. I tried reading, but that didn't go either. I knelt down again and again, but all I could pray was "Lord, help me." The anguish continued.

Then, I believe it was in the afternoon, I was helping the workers get the horses ready. I remember it so clearly; it was at the front corner of the barn where the big millstone lay. I was adjusting the reins of the horses when suddenly I felt myself completely overpowered, yet gently and mildly, but so holy and godly. I dropped the lines, went into my room and fell on my knees.

What was it? It was the Lord. I cannot describe the quiet, godly feeling that came over me. It flooded my being again and again. I felt and knew it was the Lord. "Come to me, all you who are weary and heavy laden, and I will refresh you."

Then it became quiet and peaceful in my heart. I could only continue to pray, "My Lord and my God." How long? I do not remember it any more. I believe it was several hours during which I knelt again and again before the majesty and holiness within my soul. And the Lord comforted and strengthened me so wonderfully, so gently and peaceably.

Finally I went outside, only hoping I would not meet anyone. . . . My heart wanted to say, "Lord, I am so unworthy," but the answer came, "Though your sins be as scarlet, they shall be as white as snow." And I went, flooded with the peace of God.

What a beautiful, open, and honest testimony of struggle and release! Listen to his next paragraph:

O world, laugh and make fun of this experience, if you can. I am not writing this for the world but for my dear children. Perhaps these imperfect words, which do not begin to describe the blessedness I felt, can one day strengthen you in your own pilgrimage. And another thing: If one or the other of you should not have this kind of experience, do not be discouraged. In those hours the foundation of my faith was laid. I am convinced that everyone must come to God in [their] own way and God will draw near [to us]. The only condition is that we come honestly and in childlike faith.

My father died many years ago. I am still deeply moved and inspired when I read this. What a testimony! What encouragement to us children! What an inspiration! How we do love and appreciate him for sharing this with us. If you cannot share your spiritual struggles and victories with your children and grandchildren in writing, then tell them your experiences or record them on tape or video. Perhaps you will never know how this may one day help to determine their choices and clear the murky path ahead for one of your loved ones.

Some of us seniors can pass on the faith by taking a young person on a trip. Not just any trip, not just as a tourist to see the world, but a trip with a purpose and goal clearly thought through.

My fourteen-year-old grandson Peter Scott and I went to Europe on the Anabaptist Trail. We started in the Menno Simons country of Friesland in northern Holland, went to France, Switzerland, Italy, and on to Germany. We recorded the twenty-one-day trip on video. It was a learning and bonding experience for both of us.

Recently Peter wrote, "To say that my relationship to you, Opa, has felt close is an understatement. . . . Our trip to Europe is still a highlight in my life."

Next in line was my granddaughter Deborah Scott. Again we went on the Anabaptist Trail, with the same positive experience of learning and bonding. Debby worried more than Peter when things didn't go right, as is bound to happen on a three-week trip. Later she wrote, "Looking back, I certainly could have saved a lot of energy worrying if I had just trusted God and really believed that 'there are no problems, only challenges.'"

When our next two grandchildren, Sasha Dyck and Cory Scott, were fourteen, the three of us went to South America. We began in Paraguay with a three-day celebration of fifty years of the Volendam Colony. Elfrieda and I had helped refugees move to that colony (see *Up from the Rubble*). We went to the magnificent Iguaçú Falls, which Eleanor Roosevelt compared to "poor Niagara Falls." We visited Mennonite colonies in Brazil and Uruguay. Twenty days later our last stop was at the statue *Christ the Redeemer* in Rio de Janeiro.

Two years later Cory wrote, "When people ask me what my most memorable event is, I always say my trip to South America with my Opa."

Like my father, and yet differently, I try to pass on the faith to our children and grandchildren. There are a hundred ways of doing it. These are only two examples. What is needed first is a concern to do something about it. Then we need the imagination and courage to actually do it. The rewards are gratifying.

Lord, we thank you for our precious heritage. Help me to understand that it is mine to keep only if I pass it on. Show me how to do it, Lord, and lead me every step of the way.

22
Life Before Death?

I came that they may have life,
and have it abundantly.
—Jesus, in John 10:10

I was preaching on John 10:10 in Karaganda, Kazakhstan (in the former USSR), when I asked, "Is there life before death?" A few minutes later, I repeated the question. The congregation was attentive but smiling. They saw their pastor come up behind me, place his hand on my shoulder, and whisper, "There's a slip of your tongue. You keep asking whether there is life before death. You mean, 'Is there life *after* death?' "

But I did mean life *before* death. Christians in the Soviet Union were being persecuted. Churches were being closed. Dictator Stalin was determined to stamp out religion. Pastors were afraid to mention conditions of life *before* death for fear of the midnight knocks on their doors, arrests by the KGB (the secret police), and exile in Siberian slave labor camps.

Preaching itself was dangerous; to mention needless suffering, pain, injustice, and untimely death would be downright foolish. It would mean a sure summons by the police, and everyone knew what would follow. So when Russians did preach in spite of threats, they at least tried to stay on relatively safe ground, such as life *after* death. In heaven, there would be no more tears. Yes, there is life after death.

At first, I had no idea how that audience in Karaganda had received my message. Then I discovered that at almost every place we visited later, the people asked me to preach on John 10:10. Word about life *before* death spread like wild-fire.

Maria Fast had been married less than a year when she was arrested. She was never told why, but she guesses it was because on Saturdays children came to her house to hear her tell Bible stories. When the people in charge of the slave labor camp in frigid Siberia found out that she was educated and a teacher, they gave her the daily job of counting and recording the dead.

She went from one miserable barrack to another, dragged the dead bodies out, left them lying outside the door, recorded the details on her notepad, and proceeded to the next barrack. The worst was when she wasn't sure whether the person was dead or still alive.

Years later, I asked Maria to write an article about these dehumanizing experiences, stressing especially how she had forgiven her persecutors. She said that she would write the article because it was true that she had forgiven all of them long ago. However, she asked for time to do something else first.

"Forgiving them is one thing," she wrote. "Praying for them is another." She wanted time to pray for them. Six months later, she wrote the article. Maria knew what Jesus meant when he said, "I came that they may have life, and have it abundantly." He meant *Life* with a capital *L*, not mere existence. Life here and now, *before* death. Hers was such a life. She had not only forgiven her persecutors; she also prayed for them.

While going to work in Russia, Henry Klassen passed a jail filled with hundreds of unhappy and mostly innocent prisoners. He was burdened to go inside and share the gospel with them. The prison warden said *nyet* (no). Higher authorities said *nyet*. He went clear to the top and heard, "*Nyet!* No preaching in prison!"

Some months later, he was summoned by the police and

ordered to stop preaching in his own church. He refused. He was arrested and sent to prison. When he told me about this later, he was as jubilant as a child at Christmas. At first, I couldn't understand why. Finally, I grasped that he was laughing about all those *nyets*.

There he was, inside the prison with all the other prisoners, sharing the good news about Jesus with them.

They said, "*Nyet*, you can't go inside that prison. Not even for a visit." And then they locked me up inside that same prison, gave me a place to sleep, gave me food that I didn't have to pay for, even if it wasn't much good, and kept me there for two years.

Seldom have I seen a more happy, relaxed, and thankful evangelist. He knew about life *before* death. His greatest joy was to share this Life with others.

Hans Rempel was thrown into the infamous Lubjanka prison in Moscow for no reason that he could imagine, except that he was a minister and preached. In the large holding room, prisoners jostled each other in shoulder-to-shoulder crowded conditions. It was almost impossible to eat the thin soup served without spilling most of it. Hans found refuge under the only piece of furniture in the room, a table.

One day he was under that table when a bearded Russian joined him. Hans gave him a smile, exchanged a greeting, and bowed his head. He was about to eat when the other man asked what he had just done in bowing his head and being silent for a little while. Hans explained that he was a Christian and that he had prayed, thanking God for the food.

To his surprise, the man extended his hand and said that he, too, was a believer, a member of the Orthodox Church. He suggested that they have communion together. "Here we are, all three of us, under the table," he said. "We have bread, even if it is stale and black, and we have the thin soup to drink instead of wine."

Hans didn't quite understand "all three of us." What did he mean? Cheerfully the man explained: "You and I and Jesus. All three of us are here under this table."

Often Hans had served communion in his church, always trying to have the service as authentic and meaningful as possible. However, he had never been more certain of Jesus' presence than the time when he had communion with an Orthodox Russian prisoner, eating stale bread and drinking thin vegetable soup under the table in the Lubjanka prison. Hans knew about Life *before* death.

As seniors in free and prosperous North America, we haven't experienced anything like the conditions described by Maria, Henry, and Hans. However, the question of *life before death* is just as vital for us as it was in Russia for them. Many older people feel neglected and pushed aside. They are lonely and afraid. If asked whether there is life before death, they might hesitate to answer. Some might even say yes, when they were younger, but not now. This isn't really living anymore.

The solution to this problem is found in our relationship to Jesus. He came to bring Life, and to bring it in abundance. Jesus meant that real joy and peace, real living, does not depend on outward circumstances.

Jesus still says, "I am the bread of life. . . . I am the light of the world. . . . I am the way, and the truth, and the life. . . . I am the resurrection and the life" (John 6:35; 8:12; 14:6; 11:25). If we come to Jesus, humbly believing and trusting him to do what he promises, we too can experience Life with a capital *L* before we die.

Thank you, Lord, that in spite of failing health and diminishing energy, we can grow and become strong inwardly. Thank you for the encouragement from our brothers and sisters around the world throughout the ages.

23

Humor: God's Gift to Us

For everything there is a season, . . .
a time to weep, and a time to laugh.
—The Teacher, in Ecclesiastes 3:1, 4

We didn't laugh much in our family, at least not when father was around. He was always serious. Life was hard in Russia and later in Canada. When I look at the family pictures taken back then, I can still hear my father telling us to close our mouths and look serious.

We children laughed among ourselves and sometimes with mother. Later I read that "a cheerful heart is good medicine, but a downcast spirit dries up the bones" (Prov. 17:22). "A cheerful heart has a continual feast" (15:15b).

Laughter or humor is frequently mentioned in the Bible; it is one of God's great gifts to us. I hadn't consciously observed or studied the fact that the Creator made us with an emotional scale ranging from tears and sadness to joy and laughter.

One of my favorite stories is about the older couple sitting on their porch. The wife said, "George, wouldn't it be nice to have some ice-cream?" The husband, a kind man, got up to get it from the corner store. "Wait," she said. "You know how forgetful you are. Write it down." He said he would remember, but she insisted he write it down. Finally, she gave in and repeated again what she wanted: "A little dish of vanilla ice-cream with chocolate syrup and a cherry on top."

Soon he was back and handed a brown paper bag to his wife. She opened it, looked inside, and there were two hamburgers. She examined them carefully and said, "You see, George, you should have written it down. You forgot the ketchup and the mustard."

There are many theories of laughter. In *Laughing Together: The Value of Humor in Family Life*, Dotsey Welliver lists four theories: incongruity or surprise, superiority or derision, relief or liberation, and pleasure. From this listing, we sense that laughter can be healthy and can be hurtful. We want to laugh *with* people, not *at* people. If we laugh *at* someone, we are making fun of others (derision) and looking down on them (superiority). However, when we laugh *with* someone, just for fun, it is wholesome for everyone concerned.

Laughter can be a relief and also a means of communication. One Sunday, Elfrieda and I had just returned from church. The young people had presented a brief skit to the congregation with the central message that church is where you can differ, but you still hold hands. I told her how much I liked that. She agreed.

While we were putting lunch on the table, I suggested modifying that message by substituting *marriage* for *church*. Marriage is where you can differ, but you still hold hands. Again she agreed. She usually is very agreeable.

Still I pressed the point. I didn't want her just to say the words; I wanted her to agree in her heart. I wanted her to agree that the next time we had a little misunderstanding, we would actually hold hands. As soon we realized we were arguing, we'd stop right there, move toward each other, hold hands, and continue to debate the point, whatever it might be.

Again, she agreed, though with a bit less enthusiasm. She's very clever that way; she can "see" things long before I can.

The day came, as it does in all marriages, when we had a difference in our recollection. I remember raising my voice and unconsciously moving away from her. Body language is so revealing.

The argument was far from its boiling point, but it was heating up when I remembered our agreement. The first thought flashing through my mind was that this could be an exception. Next time we'd hold hands, not now. However, I dismissed that thought as soon as it occurred to me. An agreement is an agreement!

I could have kicked myself for having been the one who had started this. How could I not have foreseen that it would be almost impossible to hold hands and argue at the same time? I'd have to move right up to her, real close, and touch her. I was in no mood for that. Stupid! Plain dumb! Nevertheless, it had been my idea, and she had agreed to it.

After a brief silence, I reminded her of our agreement. "Why not?" she said. "Here." She stretched out both hands to me. I moved closer, took her hands in mine, and—you can guess the rest. We both burst out laughing, embraced, and kissed. That was the end of that argument. Laughter had released the built-up tension and also facilitated communication. There was no need for words. We understood each other perfectly.

Humor is fine for defusing mild disagreements; yet we recognize that serious conflicts take more work.

Jesus used humor in his communications. He exaggerated, which is one expression of humor. He taught that we should be slow to judge others because we are not perfect ourselves: "First take the log out of your own eye, and then you will see clearly to take the speck out of your neighbor's eye" (Matt. 7:5). Why don't we laugh when that is read in church? Isn't it funny? A log or beam in my own eye and a tiny splinter in my brother's eye, and I want to take the splinter out?

Jesus also warned the disciples about the dangers of wealth: "Again I tell you, it is easier for a camel to go through the eye of a needle than for someone who is rich to enter the kingdom of God" (Matt. 19:24).

What would you say if your Sunday school teacher exaggerated like that? Would you think it was funny? Would you get the point, or would you think the teacher ought to stick closer to the truth? If all you're thinking about is the nonsense of a large camel going through a wee hole in the needle, you didn't get the message of the story.

Then there is the best joke of all—but nobody laughs anymore because we have heard it so often that we don't even see the humor in it. Jesus told the Pharisees that they were blind guides. "You strain out a gnat but swallow a camel!" (Matt. 23:24). Again the camel appears, that strange-looking animal that some say was made by a committee.

For over thirty years, this story was kept alive in the oral tradition till Matthew wrote it down. By that time, the story itself was lost; all we have is the punch line. The original story might have been something like this:

A man was traveling when he noticed it was lunchtime. He sat down on the grass beside the road, unwrapped his sandwich, poured soup into a bowl, and began to eat. Presently he noticed little specks in his soup. Tiny winged insects had flown out of the grass and landed in his bowl.

He was so preoccupied with flipping them out that he didn't notice a caravan of merchants, with their camels, coming up from Egypt, loaded with treasures. One of those huge two-humped animals with its crooked neck and wobbly legs left the road and walked along in the ditch. It came right up to where the man was eating his lunch, still concentrating on flipping out gnats. The man didn't notice that the camel had fallen into his soup, so he swallowed it.

Humor is for all ages. Children love it and seniors can benefit from it. Martin Luther said that if he wouldn't be allowed to laugh in heaven, he didn't want to go there. Isaiah said, "For you shall go out in joy, and be led back in peace;

the mountains and the hills before you shall burst into song, and all the trees of the field shall clap their hands" (55:12).

The case of Norman Cousins, longtime editor of the *Saturday Review*, is well known and a good example of how humor helps healing. He was diagnosed with a disease that breaks down the body's connecting tissue. The doctors treated Cousins with conventional medical wisdom, but eventually he was almost completely paralyzed and given only a few months to live.

Norman checked out of the hospital and chose an unconventional treatment: laughter and vitamin C. Every day he laughed hilariously as he watched *Candid Camera* and the Marx Brothers. After every show and his belly laugh, he was free of pain for at least two hours. He eventually was able to go back to writing and lecturing. Laughter was not the sole cure, but it certainly contributed to his recovery.

As seniors we can learn from that. Laughter facilitates communication. It can enhance relationships, contribute to physical healing, and make us easier to live with.

Lord, I have reached the evening of my life, when the shadows lengthen and the tears fall. Grant me the wisdom and the courage to also laugh at the many foibles of life, to laugh with others, and to laugh at myself.

24

A Second Pulpit

When you search me, you will find me;
if you seek me with all your heart,
I will let you find me, says the LORD.
—Jeremiah 29:13-14a

During the purges of the 1930s in the former Soviet Union, Stalin closed churches and silenced priests and ministers. Yet people kept gathering for worship. If there was no preacher or if the secret police was present and the minister was afraid to preach, the people would just sing. Soon they discovered that singing the songs Christians had sung through the centuries became their "second pulpit."

For North Americans, camping has become our second pulpit. I suggest that older people can be and are most helpful in carrying out this important mission. Let us pay brief visits to three camps.

The first is a children's camp. Suppose you are one of the resource people. You take your group outside to teach them Psalm 8 and meditate on it: "O LORD, our Sovereign, how majestic is your name in all the earth. You have set your glory above the heavens."

You tell the children that if they plant potatoes in their garden, they can expect to have potato bugs. These bugs hatch from eggs in seven days. A sparrow egg hatches in 14 days, chicken in 21 days, duck in 28 days, eagle in 35 days, parrot in 42 days, and snake in 49 days. Many eggs hatch in multiples of seven days. Every form of life in the animal and vegetable kingdom has a master plan that is perfect in every detail.

Consider this: "When I look at your heavens, the work of your fingers, the moon and the stars that you have established, what are human beings that you are mindful of them?" (Ps. 8:3-4). Look up to the sky. In 1984, there was a total eclipse of the sun in New Guinea and the Pacific. The moon got between the sun and the Earth. Here and there on Earth, there are two to five solar eclipses each year, some total, some annular (rim of sun showing around the moon), and some partial.

Astronomers can tell us when and where eclipses will happen. A swath of total solar eclipse, with a wider partial eclipse, will cross the United States on August 21, 2017. Owen Gingerich, a Mennonite astronomer, told me that it will not be early or late (the exact time depends on an observer's location). It will not miss the prediction by a hundred-thousandth of a second. "O Lord, our Lord. You are so great!"

The second camp is for teenagers. The lesson of the day is about trusting and cooperating. They are a wild and noisy bunch from Pittsburgh. Yet no one volunteers when you ask for someone to climb onto a platform eight feet high, be blindfolded, and fall backward into the arms of fellow campers. They don't trust each other. They bicker for over half an hour.

At last, one brave girl climbs up the platform and lets herself be blindfolded. She turns around and drops backward. They catch her. They all shout and clap their hands. Others follow her example. They are learning to trust each other.

Then there is the wall to scale. The challenge is for all to get over that ten-foot wall without a ladder or rope. This calls for cooperation. There is no way except all for one and one for all. It takes a while, but at last they accomplish it. They learn the meaning of Romans 12:5. "So we, who are many, are one body in Christ, and individually we are members one of another."

The third camp is for families. We like to think the word *solidarity* describes our family. A family retreat is a good time to reflect on what is holding your family together. If the Lord is doing it, you're in good shape.

Once we visited our daughter serving under MCC in Lesotho, in southern Africa. She was instructing and training nurses, so badly needed in this poor country. When we met her superior, the stern and unbending Sister had good words to say about Rebecca and her work. She also had one criticism: Rebecca receives too much mail, much of it from her home in America.

There was a brief moment of awkward silence. We were shocked. The Sister thought mail from home was a distraction for Rebecca, something that should be sacrificed on the altar of duty. I shot up a brief prayer, "O Lord, help!" Then I cleared my throat.

"With all due respect, Sister, permit me to say that we love our daughter very much. We want to do everything possible to make her stay here in Lesotho profitable for your people and for her. That is why we are visiting her, to be an encouragement. That is why we pray for her and write to her every week. With or without your permission, Sister, we plan to continue doing that: supporting her in our prayers and by our letters. It is our way of expressing family solidarity."

A family retreat is a relaxed time for communication, bonding, and securing solidarity. Parents and grandparents can plan carefully to make these things happen.

Thank you, Lord, for my family. Thank you for our campgrounds and retreats, our "second pulpits." Show me, Lord, how I can make a positive contribution to strengthen my own and other families.

25

What About Our Money?

For the love of money is a root of all kinds of evil.
—Paul, in 1 Timothy 6:10

Now here's a delicate subject that can easily lead to misunderstanding and tension between parents and children. As we grow older, how much should our children know about our financial situation? Shall we open the books and tell them everything? Nothing? What about insurance, savings, property, Medicare, wills, and other related matters?

Scholars tell us that Jesus talked about money and possessions in more than half of his messages. What does that mean for us?

Elfrieda and I have living wills; we also have our last will and testament. A few years ago, we decided that we should update our will. When that was finished, we sent copies to our daughters, Ruth and Rebecca. We assumed that they would keep them in a safe place until we died. Then they would open them and find out how much money their parents had and what they decided to do with it.

We have heard many stories of children gathering in the lawyer's office, silently watching as the will is opened, and holding their breath to hear what the parents left them, if anything. They wonder if it is fair and hope the scene will not erupt into family squabbles.

We were startled when Rebecca called us as soon as she had received her copy of our will. She said she liked it very much, but she had a suggestion or two to make. At our age and stage in life, we almost dropped our teeth. She had actually opened the will and read it before we died! She knew it all, and she had a few suggestions to make. Now how do you like that?

It didn't take us long to realize what had happened. Though unexpected and a big surprise, it was nevertheless a good thing, a real blessing. Since then we have talked and laughed about it many times. Of course, our children should know what is in that final document. It concerns them more than us, so why shouldn't they have a voice in drafting it? We were confident that they would not fight over our plans.

Slowly it dawned on us that we had unconsciously absorbed a worldly attitude about wills. What happened to us was God opening a window for insight, not only about money and possessions, but also about relating to our children.

Money is amoral, neither moral nor immoral. Paul did not say that money is the root of all evil, as we are often told. He said, "The *love* of money is a root of all kinds of evil" (1 Tim. 6:10). I have seen a lot of good done with money: feeding the hungry, clothing the naked, giving shelter to the homeless, educating young people, and many other helpful things.

Once a beer-brewing company offered the evangelist Dwight Moody a sizable sum of money for his good work. His co-workers knew that Moody was against drinking alcohol and wondered if he would reject the offer. That was not a problem for Moody. With a clear voice and conscience, he said: "Of course we'll take the money. The devil has had it long enough."

Money in itself is neither good nor bad. What we do with it makes it the one or the other.

In 1825, Robert Pollock, a young and gifted Scotsman, published a marvelous book on *The Course of Time*. He was inspired to write in blank verse, he said, because he thought it was the language of eternity. One of his topics was on money and gold and about a miser who held "strange communion" with his "yellow phantom," his gold.

Most for the luxuries it bought, the pomp,
The praise, the glitter, fashion, and renown,
This yellow phantom followed and adored.
But there was one in folly farther gone,
With eye awry, incurable, and wild,
The laughing-stock of devils and of men,
And by his guardian angel quite given up—
The Miser, who with dust inanimate
Held wedded intercourse. Ill guided wretch!
Thou mightst have seen him at the midnight hour,
When good men slept, and in light-winged dreams,
Ascended up to God—in wasteful hall,
With vigilance and fasting worn to skin
And bone, and wrapt in most debasing rags—
Thou mightst have seen him bending o'er his heaps,
And holding strange communion with his gold;
And as his thievish fancy seemed to hear
The night-man's foot approach, starting alarmed,
And in his old, decrepit, withered hand,
That palsy shook, grasping the yellow earth
To make it sure. Of all God made upright,
And in their nostrils breathed a living soul,
Most fallen, most prone, most earthy, most debased.
Of all that sold Eternity for Time,
None bargained on so easy terms with Death.
Illustrious fool! nay, most inhuman wretch!
He sat among his bags, and with a look
Which hell might be ashamed of, drove the poor
Away unalmsed; and 'midst abundance died—
Sorest of evils!—died of utter want.

What a graphic and horrible picture of a miser! There are many such in North America today. Something about money fascinates and enslaves; once you are in its grip, you never seem to get enough of it. On the other hand, many have discovered the joy of sharing and giving. It begins with nickels and dimes in kindergarten and continues through life. As we age and enter retirement, we are faced with a question: How much do we keep, and how much do we give away?

I am uneasy while watching the evening news and seeing the needs in the world—starving children, homes destroyed by floods and hurricanes, and innocent people suffering because of war and violence. I feel uncomfortable, knowing that we are secure in our home, with money to pay our bills, and some left over. Sometimes I feel like divesting ourselves of it all to benefit the many needy people.

One evening Elfrieda and I talked about that. She reminded me, "Giving it all away and going on welfare would not be right, and it wouldn't be God's answer to our dilemma."

Then we did some figuring. How much would we need in case one or both of us became helpless and needed personal care? We thought we had so much in our savings account, but with a little figuring, we discovered it was not even enough to pay for nine months in a nursing home. So we didn't give it all away. Yet the problem is real for many people: How much do I give? How much do I keep?

There is no easy answer or formula. Each must do as it seems right after careful reflection. Charles Wesley observed that as soon as people in England turned their lives over to Christ, they also became more prosperous. They stopped smoking, drinking, and gambling; they became better and more trusted workers and were promoted. He devised a formula that has become a slogan among Methodists and others.

Charles Wesley saw nothing wrong with earning more money. He soon realized, however, that there was something deceptive and wrong in accumulating money. So this is his three-step solution: earn all you can, save all you can, give all you can. Your own conscience must be your guide.

Conscience is the inner voice to obey. Yet we need to recognize that our consciences are informed and formed by what we observe, experience, hear, and read (as in the Bible and other trusted resources). It follows, therefore, that we may need to be more open about sharing our financial situations, questions, and problems with others, like family or friends, and possibly in small groups. That would be beneficial and enlightening for our consciences, making sure that they are trustworthy guides.

Like everyone else, we receive a flood of appeals for contributions. No doubt many of them are worthy causes. But how do I know when to give and when not to give? One noon a man with a kind voice called to ask me to contribute to MADD (Mothers Against Drunk Drivers). "Do you know about MADD?"

I told him I did and that it was a good organization. But before committing myself, I had a few questions.

He told me to go ahead. "Where are you calling from?" I asked.

He said Los Angeles. That was all the way across the nation in midday, a costly call.

I asked, "Are you a professional fundraiser?"

He said he was.

I asked how much of my contribution would actually go for MADD and how much for overhead—his salary, telephone bills, secretary, and so on.

He said he didn't know.

I pressed him. "You must be kidding. Just tell me."

He refused and finally asked me what percentage I thought might be reasonable.

I thought of MCC's overhead of about 10 percent, but I quickly realized that it is low because they have so many volunteers. So I replied that about 25 percent would seem fair to me.

There was a long silence. Finally he chuckled and said,

"You've got to be kidding!" and hung up the phone.

I had just read an article in *Reader's Digest* about the American Heart Association raising one million dollars. Not one dollar of that went for actual research and treatment of heart disease, the cause people thought they were supporting. It all went for advertising (education?), glossy prints, TV commercials, salaries of professional fundraisers, and so on.

Later I spoke at a conference in Ohio, concluding several days of messages with an address to the women. All that time the audience had been receptive but quiet. But then the women clapped. What did I say that made them clap? It was this:

"Elfrieda and I have decided that we are going to do our giving through our church. We will stop giving through our church channels when (1) we are told that they have enough money and can't use any more, or (2) we have lost confidence in our church and its organizations." They all applauded to show approval! Likely many of them were doing the same thing.

Another way we contribute is even closer home than the church; we give toward the education of our children and grandchildren. We decided long ago that we would assume responsibility for our daughters' college education.

It was understood that our daughters would be frugal, would take paying jobs while in college and work during vacation, but upon graduation they would have no debt. Too often we had seen young people wanting to volunteer with MCC but unable to do so because college debt had to be paid off first.

We contribute to the college fund for our five grandchildren from time to time as we are able, on the assumption that they will go to Mennonite colleges. They are free to choose. If they attend non-Mennonite colleges, that money will not be theirs but instead will go to one of our Mennonite colleges.

We know that might seem prejudiced, but we think we know what we are doing and why. We don't want simply more knowledge or more education for our grandchildren. We want an education in a Christian environment with a Christ-centered purpose.

I close with a quotation from Robert Jeffress in *Say Goodbye to Regret.*

> Saving, spending, and investing our money wisely are crucial to escaping regrets over our finances. But to paraphrase the words of one philosopher, "The best use of money is to spend it on something that will outlast it." For a Christian, that means investing in God's work.

Lord, I confess that I have problems with money. How much should I hold back for a rainy day? How much should I give away? I need your help. I don't want to feel guilty. Help me be a good steward.

26

What About Our Health?

*Moses was one hundred twenty years old
when he died;
his sight was unimpaired and his vigor
had not abated.*
—Deuteronomy 34:7

Say "health" and we think of food, exercise, and sleep. We blame the car, the TV, and the fast-food industry for some of our obesity. They are heavy contributors, but the problem is more complex than that.

Of the flood of better-health books, one heads my list: Kenneth Cooper's *It's Better to Believe.* Dr. Cooper coined the term *aerobics* in 1967 and is internationally known for contributing to better health and fitness. He says, "You must take what scientists have identified as your *intrinsic* beliefs and make them an integral part of your basic approach to health and fitness."

In other words, in addition to exercise, diet, regular sleep, and all the other fitness efforts, we need what some people probably never think about—a sincere faith, an authentic belief.

Dr. Cooper says *extrinsic* belief is a head faith that consists of going to church, observing rituals, and mechanically going through motions that don't touch the heart. *Intrinsic* belief is characterized by a "profound spiritual commitment, a sense of having found the ultimate meaning of life, a devotion to heartfelt prayer, and a quest for a truly transformed life."

Scientific studies have shown that there is a close relationship between honest and sincere religious faith involvement and reduced chances of depression and use of alcohol and drugs, says Dr. Cooper. There are fewer medical complications for maternity patients, less chances of contracting colon and rectal cancer, healthier emotional balance, reduced levels of stress, and stronger marriage ties. In other words, the strong link between faith and fitness is a demonstrated fact.

First, what about *food?* Obesity is not only a physical handicap; it is also emotionally discouraging and draining. An obese young woman came to work at our retirement center. We tactfully touched on the subject of weight. Elfrieda told her about her own experience with Weight Watchers. She seemed to be listening. We began to talk more frankly, offering to be her support group if she ever seriously decided to do something about her obesity.

One day she announced that she was going to start her weight-loss program, and she did, keeping us informed. Twenty pounds gone, 50, 100, then 110! She told us triumphantly that now she knew she could do it—and not go on a roller coaster, gaining it all back.

For some time, we had noticed a change in her mood and facial expressions. She was always courteous and friendly, but as she lost weight, she became radiant. She beamed when she announced that the experience had given her a whole new perspective on life, a new and better self-image. She was going to quit cleaning apartments and serving tables; she was going to college. And she did.

Some weeks later, she was back for a brief visit and to show us her new wardrobe. She was a different person. We rejoiced with her, especially that she had been able to lose the weight relatively early in life. Her secret was diet and exercise, coupled with a strong will.

During the war, I stumbled onto something in England

that stayed with me for more than forty years. I became a vegetarian. Food was rationed and meat was scarce. Three of us friends encouraged each other to cut meat out of our diet. We launched ourselves on this unconventional path, pledging to abstain from fish, flesh, and fowl. It wasn't for health reasons or a religious conviction. It was in response to the meat shortage and Albert Schweitzer's "reverence for life."

Years later, we learned that meat, especially red meat, wasn't all that good for us. Without knowing it, I had been on the right track. A doctor recently told me that he counseled his patients foodwise to spend a lot of time in the field and garden, and less time in the barn with the animals. I am still reaping health benefits from those four decades of "staying out of the barn," and even now I am still eating lean. I also learned many valuable lessons beyond the health area.

People reacted strangely when they learned of me being a vegetarian. The women almost always ran to the fridge for another carrot or lettuce leaf, as if I were a rabbit. Few ever questioned my source of protein or were concerned that I got it. I was always ready to share the fact that soybeans contain as much protein as meat, but I seldom had that opportunity.

Even more interesting was the reaction of men. Some examined my consistency, though often in a lighter vein. They asked whether my shoes or belt were made of plastic or leather. When I confessed to wearing leather, they gleefully pointed out my inconsistency. "Aha, an animal did die so you could have shoes!" Sometimes when I was weary of this, I replied in an equally flippant manner: "My shoes are made from the hide of a cow that died a natural death."

In such encounters, I often thought of Jesus meeting the Samaritan woman at the well. She used the same tactic, quizzing him for breaking the rules and seeming to be inconsistent. "How is it that you, a Jew, ask a drink of me, a woman of Samaria?" Aha, caught you, Jesus, didn't I? Caught you in a double inconsistency: First, as a Jew you shouldn't be talking to us Samaritans. Second, as a man you shouldn't be talking to me, a woman! (John 4).

We still play these games with each other. We are too quick to point out the supposed inconsistencies of others and too slow to see our own shortcomings. This is another case of trying to remove the speck from another's eye without an awareness of the beam in my own eye.

Second, what about *spiritual health?* Sometimes in our pursuit of physical health or simply in our full and busy lives, we neglect our spiritual well-being. Before long, this can impact our physical health.

Orie Miller, long-time executive secretary in MCC, received a wake-up call one day. He had been extremely busy following disasters around the world, administering relief programs, and attending board meetings of organizations such as a college, a mission society, a publishing company, the American Leprosy Mission (as chairman), Goodville Mutual Casualty Company (as president), and much more. He was also running the Miller-Hess Shoe Company.

One morning he went to his office and asked his secretary to take dictation. He began but stopped abruptly and said, "Start over again." He dictated a few sentences and again asked her to scratch it. Then turning to her, he explained that he could not go on because he had neglected to have his quiet time that morning. He asked her to come back in half an hour.

When she returned, his dictation flowed freely. That incident made him realize that he had neglected to nurture his soul and take care of his spiritual health.

Third, what about *exercise?* This is part of sustained good health. Many North Americans have a sedentary lifestyle and are overweight. Long before careful studies were made comparing fitness levels, longevity, and exercise, we knew that mail carriers on average live several years longer than their less-active colleagues in the post offices, sorting the mail and selling stamps.

I love to ride on London's red double-decker buses. Each time I go to the upper deck and walk to the front for a super view of the city. With every new passenger up there, the conductor, usually a woman, has to climb up again to punch the ticket. This "poor" (but blessed) woman walks that bus all day, going up and down the stairs hundreds of times. Studies have shown that she will likely live about two years longer than the driver of that bus, seated comfortably up front in his padded seat.

It doesn't take expensive exercise equipment or a fitness club to break the sedentary habit. We do not have to jog or run. Regular brisk walking will do. In general, to increase fitness and prolong life, women need to walk two miles in half an hour and men two miles in less than 27 minutes three days a week. People 70 and older, may take about 43 minutes to walk those two miles. The important thing is to get up from that easy chair, begin to exercise, and stay with it.

The same is true in our spiritual life. We need to nourish our souls through regular Bible reading, prayer, and church attendance. If we don't pay as much attention to our inner as to our outer person, our spiritual life will shrivel and in turn affect our physical health. Dr. Cooper would say, "I told you so."

Help me, Lord, to overcome the temptation to settle for what is not even second best. Strengthen my will to nurture my body and soul for my own good and your glory.

27

What About Our Prodigals?

But while [the prodigal] was still far off,
his father saw him and was filled with compassion;
he ran and put his arms around him and kissed him.
—Jesus, in a parable, in Luke 15:20

We are familiar with the three parables Jesus told and Luke recorded in chapter 15: the lost sheep, the lost coin, and the lost son. Each has a happy ending.

The story of the prodigal is especially profound. The son wanted to leave home. His father wouldn't stop him and even gave him his inheritance, to do with as he pleased. He squandered it. As long as he had money, he had friends; when the money was gone, his friends were gone. Typical.

Herding swine is no fun anytime, anywhere. Pigs stink. The boy was a Jew, and for Jews, pigs are not just dirty but religiously and ceremonially unclean (Lev. 11:7). How low could a fellow sink with that stink? Having graphically told it all, Jesus added an extra touch of drama: the pigs had food to eat, but the boy was starving. At this point, Jesus introduces a surprise: the boy "came to himself" (Luke 15:17).

I heard "came to himself" illustrated this way: A young fellow was drawn into gambling and lost all his money. He kept gambling and lost his coat. The third time he lost his shirt. He still gambled and lost his shoes, then his pants. With nothing left but his underpants, he "came to himself" and realized his desperate condition. Like the prodigal, he said, "I will get up and go to my father" (15:18).

In *Good News About Prodigals,* Tom Bisset says, "Research shows that at least 85 percent of all prodigals, including the angriest rebels, eventually return to the faith." I want to believe such encouraging news.

Yet before the prodigal returns, parents and grandparents suffer dark days, weeks, months, and years. I can see the prodigal's father going to the gate every day. He shields his eyes against the setting sun, to see if his boy is coming home. Thousands of fathers and mothers go through such trial and torture. One father journaled his prayers during anxious years of waiting:

Lord, why did you let it happen?
Why did you let our son get blind?

If it were a blindness of the eyes,
we could endure it:
but, Lord, you allowed him to fall
into the blindness of the soul.

You are wise and powerful,
You could have prevented it.
You are loving and kind,
Why did you not stop him?

God, our hearts cry out for him.
You gave him a keen mind;
we gave him a good education.
Your Spirit brought him to faith in you!

Why does he now claim no faith?
Embrace another way of life?

Bring him back, O Lord!
Bring him back to us,
bring him back to the people of his faith,
bring him back to the church.
O Lord, bring him back to yourself!

Whatever the reasons for leaving, the result is agony and pain. The parents and the grandparents agonize as they ask themselves, "Where did we fail?" But where are the parents and grandparents who have not failed in some measure? There is a feeling of guilt. They feel helpless. There seems to be nothing they can do.

They may or may not understand that their child left because he felt hemmed in at home and at church. Perhaps he was spiritually confused, bored, or angry. Prodigals may see their leaving as an honest search for truth. Perhaps other attractions crowded out the familiar and displaced the traditional.

Some things the apostle Peter says about false teachers may also apply to certain prodigals. They may think they are free at last, but instead "are slaves of corruption, for people are slaves to whatever masters them." Peter even says, "It would have been better for them never to have known the way of righteousness than, after knowing it, to turn back from the holy commandment that was passed on to them" (2 Pet. 2:19-21).

The Anabaptists put a high value on the spiritual life of their children. In one prayer, they ask the heavenly Father to draw our children "with the tug of your mercy unto the knowledge of your eternal truth. Otherwise, take them from this life in their childhood" (Gross, *Prayer Book for Earnest Christians*, 63).

Parents hurt so much because of their prodigal child; they don't realize that in their suffering, they are as confused as their child. Two parents in Kansas told me about their wayward daughter. The father was angry, and his wife cried during the ordeal of sharing this painful bit of family history. The daughter left home and church and went off with a no-good fellow, a bum.

Several times during that sad tale, the father said: "We didn't raise her that way. She knows better. When she left,

I told her, 'Don't even think about coming home until you've straightened yourself out.'"

In contrast, we have the story of our close friends' only daughter who left home and slammed the door as she left. The father told me that painful and heartrending story as we sat together in an airplane some 40,000 feet above the Atlantic.

She was a good girl, a bright student, curious and venturesome. She felt hemmed in at home and in her conservative church. She felt stifled. One day it all came out like a volcano erupting. She could take no more. She'd had it. She wanted fresh air. With that, she opened the door to leave home.

Her parents hugged her once more, kissed her good-bye, and wished her God's blessing. Then her father told her the most beautiful words he could have said in that traumatic and tense situation: "You are leaving us. Your mother and I would like you to remember how much we love you. Remember this also: no matter where you are and no matter what time of the day or night it is, you can always call us collect."

"Call us collect" would be a good title for a sermon or a book. It speaks volumes of love and forgiveness, of an open door and a warm heart. It is the father in Luke 15, waiting and looking down the dusty road for his son.

The prodigal prepared a speech to make when he reached home: "Father, I have sinned against heaven and before you; I am no longer worthy to be called your son; treat me like one of your hired hands" (15:19). When he met his father, he said the first part but didn't offer to be a hired hand. Once I asked a professor why the prodigal didn't finish his speech. His answer: "It's difficult to talk when someone is kissing you."

How long do some parents have to wait for that day? How long must they suffer the pain? My friend who went through such an experience and recorded his feelings in poetic prayers, has this to say:

Lord, I know that waiting is part of life.

We waited many years for our children.
Then at last John was born.
We waited for him to say the first word,
to take the first step,
repeat the first prayer.

We waited for him to grow up,
to become a young man.
We waited for him to say "yes" to you.
He took his time.
And when he did,
and joined the church,
our cup was running over.

And then he left.
He was restless.

And now we wait.
We wait for him to come back to you, Lord.
We wait for him to come back to the church.
We wait and wait.
We have waited many years,
long and anxious years.
And we will continue to wait.

Lord, this is the hardest of all our waiting.
Help us to wait in hope.
Lord, help us to wait and believe
that he will come back.

As they wait, parents and grandparents can remember that the leaving may not have been as much a rejection of the faith as a conscious or unconscious search for greater truth. Often the leaving is a reaction against stuffy church traditions, tedious sermons, family rules that seem restrictive, and a desire to speak for themselves instead of parroting what parents or pastors say. It is comforting for the rest of the family to see the leaving, not as rejection and rebellion, but rather as a search for truth, even if expressed awkwardly and in hurtful ways.

Sometimes children leave because of outward matters—such as dress, jewelry, or hairstyles—that to them seem marginal to Christian faith. One evening in Ohio, a father told me in great detail how in his former Amish church, the men let their hair grow as a condition for church membership. He thought it was stupid. He went to the local barber and had his hair cut in the way of the world. Then he left the Amish church.

Though he joined a church where hairstyle is not important, he still has strong feelings about hair. That had been his Rubicon, his battle for freedom from rules, his stand for independence. Yet he became quite worked up while telling me that his son came home from college with long hair. It was the hippie era, and the young fellow did what his father had done, but in reverse. The father couldn't take it. His story was so sad and funny that I didn't know whether to laugh or cry.

More often, however, the prodigal leaves home because of more serious misunderstandings and realities. Once more, let our poetic friend speak to this issue:

Lord, you know that John says
that he cannot believe
that you are.

So he left the church,
left the people of faith.

But he has not turned his back on truth.
The search for truth.

He searches it diligently.
He defends what he believes to be truth—
Freedom and dignity for all people;
Food and shelter for everyone.
He is confident that truth is a reality,
Truth is life.

That is so wonderful!
We are so grateful,
because he is bound to discover
that you are the Truth,
the Way and
the Life.

And truth cannot be divided,
All the pieces of truth that he finds
are part of You.

Oh, thank you, Lord,
for your encouragement
and comfort.

Another encouragement and comfort is to know that God does not measure time as we do. We are impatient and find waiting difficult. Our society demands instant gratification. God waits for the right time, as when he sent Jesus to be born as Savior of humankind. Why did he wait thousands of years? Paul says, "When the fullness of time had come, God sent his Son" (Gal. 4:4).

"The fullness of time" is an interesting term. Bible scholars tell us that several events had to take place before the time was "full." There was the Koine or common Greek that people of different nations could speak. That made it possible for news to spread quickly. The Romans had built good roads that made it easier to spread the news. The pagan gods had failed to satisfy the people. There was a spiritual vacuum waiting to be filled. Such events had to happen before the time was "full" for Jesus to come. God's timing was perfect.

While we wait, God is at work in the lives of prodigals, sometimes using people, events, or even disaster to reach them. We can trust that in "the fullness of time," God will touch our son or daughter, our beloved grandchild.

After our daughters graduated from college, they went into voluntary service in Africa. We were experiencing the empty-house syndrome. Someone told us, "You have done what you could. Now they are gone. There is nothing you can do for them anymore."

For a few days, we believed that. One day in the garden, it occurred to me that we could still do at least three things: (1) Pray for them. (2) Remember them with cards, letters, and telephone calls, especially on birthdays and other special occasions. (3) Take care of our own walk, so we would be an encouragement to them, not a stumbling block. We can also do these three things for our prodigal children, confident that God loves them even more than we do.

As parents and grandparents, we need to learn to let go. That is almost as hard as waiting. Putting our prodigal child entirely in the hands of God may be the best for the prodigal as well as for us as parents and grandparents.

Thank you, Lord, for your truth through Paul: "All things work together for good for those who love God." Help us to let go of both our regrets and our prodigal child. We are in your hands, Lord, and that's all that matters.

28
Needed: An Absorbing Interest

Jesus . . . went about doing good.
—Peter, in Acts 10:38

The other day I watched small children at play. They were so absorbed in the game that they didn't hear their mother's call for dinner. They were oblivious to the world around them. That's how my granddaughter is with a book. She's in another world. That's how Jesus was during his ministry: totally absorbed in interacting with people, always concerned about doing good.

How different from so many seniors! They're bored and don't know what to do; some are not physically able to do much. In retirement homes, the staff tries to interest seniors. They bring in entertainment. They sit with residents, cutting things out and pasting them together. They play games and assemble jigsaw puzzles, to stimulate their minds. Yet little is satisfying or lasting. Before long, it's over, and the seniors just sit there and wait for the dinner bell.

For many people, this started long before retirement, as Isaac Watts keenly depicts in this poetic satire:

Horace Paraphrased
There are a number of us creep
Into this world to eat and sleep,
And know no reason why they're born
But merely to consume the corn,
Devour the cattle, fowl, and fish,
And leave behind an empty dish.

The crows and ravens do the same,
Unlucky birds of hateful name;
Ravens or crows might fill their place,
And swallow corn and carcases [carcasses].
Then if their toombstone [tombstone] when they die
Ben't [be not] taught to flatter and to lie,
There's nothing better will be said
Than that "They've up and eat all their bread,
Drank up their dring [drink] and gone to bed."

Old age and the end need not be like that. As Mark Twain said, "Wrinkles should merely indicate where the smiles have been." Yes, life is a task to be accomplished, a task often left unfinished. This can be discouraging. Yet Tennyson is still right: "'Tis better to have loved and lost / Than never to have loved at all."

One evening as I watched TV, Larry King asked Andy Rooney how old he was. "I'm 80, and I hate it." At first, I was shocked, but Andy explained: "I love life so much! And to think that I'm nearing the end is troubling. I just hate it!" Yes, we may face diminishing capacity, but we are right to put up a fight. As Dylan Thomas says,

Do not go gentle into that good night,
Old age should burn and rave at close of day;
Rage, rage against the dying of the light.

Some years ago I was corresponding with my friend Samuel, in Switzerland. He is about my age and a much-sought-after public speaker. We had shared thoughts about retirement and when to stop accepting invitations to speak in churches and schools.

He had the last word on that: "It all depends on the answer to one question: Are you still alive? If the answer is yes, then keep on speaking. Nothing in the Bible says we are to stop witnessing for Christ when we have reached a certain age. Age has nothing to do with it."

I sent him a beautiful coffee-table book. On each right-hand page was the picture of an older man or woman, and on the left were just a few lines giving basic facts: name, age, personal interests, and current projects.

As I studied the book, I noticed the photo of a retired lawyer who spends all his time writing briefs and trying to persuade Washington to pass a law for the benefit of poor people. Flipping the page, I saw a woman artist who had painted scores of pictures in her life. She was working on what she hoped would be her best, a masterpiece. Her concern was to live long enough to finish it. She was in her upper nineties.

One double-page spread featured an author of more than fifty books. He was writing his magnum opus, the greatest achievement of his life. He, too, hoped he would have the time and energy to finish it.

Suddenly I realized something they all had in common: *an absorbing interest.* Each one knew exactly what she or he would do each morning. Each had a task to do, a job to finish. Each job was a choice, something important to that person, something that gave great satisfaction. Each also had enough good health and financial resources to pursue that interest.

Blessed are you when you have an absorbing interest: One more quilt to make for the relief sale. One more day to volunteer for that good cause. One more chance to speak an encouraging word to the woman next door who always seems so sad. One more opportunity to share your spiritual pilgrimage with someone who needs to be assured that we have a caring and loving God.

My energy level is low, and my world has shrunk. I am not complaining, Lord. I simply ask you to help me focus on something useful to others and satisfying for myself.

29
It's Not Too Late—Yet!

Therefore, my beloved, be steadfast, immovable,
always excelling in the work of the Lord, because you
know that in the Lord your labor is not in vain.
—Paul, in 1 Corinthians 15:58

When we see the word *therefore,* it is a good idea to ask, "What is it there for?" "Therefore" is a bridge between something that has gone before and something that follows. In the verse above, 57 verses precede it and one verse follows it. The first 57 verses of 1 Corinthians 15 are about the resurrection. After saying that much, Paul wants to sum it up and answer the question "So what?" It's the bottom line, and the transition is the word "therefore."

Paul is saying, "Now you know what all that long discourse is about. It's not for speculation, not to frighten you, and not to cause arguments. Let's stay connected to the reality of this world and to life here and now. The upshot of knowing about the resurrection is to be steadfast, immovable, and keep on doing good." That's what "therefore" is there for!

Here is a good way to begin thinking about what to do with the rest of your life. Imagine that you have arrived at your last day on earth. You are dying. You have no pain and are fully conscious. You look back on your life. When that last day comes, *how* (in what style) will you wish that you had lived?

Happy day! Good news! This is likely not our last day, so

we still have time to live the way we wish we had lived. It's not too late—yet!

When I do such reflecting, I realize that there is so much in my life that wasn't really my choice. It was not my choice to be born a white male, with blond hair. It was not Elfrieda's choice to be born into a family of fourteen children with genetics leading to heart problems (and already death for eight). It was not her choice to be born with a heart that would eventually need a pacemaker, and with a physical condition that calls for swallowing handfuls of medication.

Elfrieda received her pacemaker in 1989, just as we were preparing to travel to the former Soviet Union. We asked the doctor, "Is the trip risky?" Without wanting to appear flippant, he asked, "Do you care *where* you die?" When Elfrieda said that was not important, he told her to fly away and have a good time. The man was a doctor, a psychiatrist, and a theologian, all in one. Ever since, we have appreciated his response.

We went, but as soon we were in Russia, we were in trouble. At airports, we had to pass through electronic security. The doctor had warned Elfrieda not to do this because of the pacemaker. When we protested, asking for personal frisking, they didn't understand because we didn't know the Russian word for *pacemaker*.

Finally, we were in a doctor's home. We asked him to write the word *pacemaker* in Russian on a piece of paper, for us to show at airports. To our surprise and his embarrassment, he didn't even know the word.

What excitement we brought into their house with that pacemaker. First, the doctor wanted to see it. Then his wife, a nurse, and their daughter went into his study to see it, too. I was left alone at the dinner table. They had so many questions. It was the first pacemaker they had seen.

Back in the States, I wrote a long trip report with a brief paragraph about the pacemaker incident. I used the word several times. When our volunteer MCC secretary placed the typed report on my desk, I saw that instead of *pacemaker* she had consistently written *peacemaker*—which certainly also fits Elfrieda. This shows that we North Americans have trouble with words, too.

Yes, there is so much in life that is not our choice. If we had selected our parents more carefully, we would have been born different people. We live with our genes and our givens.

However, the fact remains that we have much more influence on who we are and what we make of our lives than conceded by some pessimists who dwell on predestination. Take the example of smoking. Did I or didn't I? That will make a great deal of difference in my health during retirement. One Sunday in church, we were asked where we planned to spend eternity: in smoking or nonsmoking? Our choices in this life have eternal consequences.

Other factors totally under our control are drinking, being workaholics, losing our tempers, carrying grudges, and a host of other health-affecting factors. We cannot go back and choose different parents, but we can make changes even at this late stage. It's not too late—yet!

We can stop smoking and drinking, break the compulsive work habit, and control our egos, the cause of our short tempers. We can begin regular exercise programs and do something about our eating patterns. Books abound with testimonies from people who have successfully broken habits that damaged their health.

In his story "Walk in the Light While There Is Light," Leo Tolstoy tells about a man who wants to break his old habits, but is not sure he can do it. He says, "But for an old man, well, let me say it for myself: I am not living with any obligations, and to tell you the truth, simply for my belly. I eat, drink, rest, and am disgusting and revolting even to myself. So it is time for me to give up such a life."

With God's help, we can make changes. It's not too late—yet!

We also need to develop a sense of humor. That is so good for our health—which is not what it used to be. A man went to the doctor and told him all about his ailment. When at last he was finished, the doctor asked, "When did this problem start?" The man responded, "What problem?"

One husband told his friends at the coffee shop how difficult it was for him to communicate with his wife because of her hearing loss. When he came home, his wife was standing by the picture window, looking out into the garden. Remembering what he had just told his buddies, he thought he would find out just how bad his wife's hearing was.

Standing in the doorway behind her, he called out, "Martha, I'm home." There was no response. He walked halfway into the room and tried again: "Martha, I'm home." Still no response. So he walked right up behind her: "Martha, I'm home." She turned around and said, "Yes, George. For the third time, welcome home!"

The money question never goes away. I don't know how my mother did it, but her timing was perfect. During the years when she was a widow, living on a farm, she thoroughly enjoyed supporting missions, relief, and other good causes. She kept writing checks. When she died, the money was all gone! Fantastic! She had done it! She died broke but with treasures in heaven (Matt. 6:19-21; James 2:5).

Mother knew exactly where her money went and for what purpose it was used. She gained a lot of joy from casting her bread upon the waters (Eccles. 11:1, KJV). She was a firm believer in the motto "Do your givin' while you're livin', so you're knowin' where it's goin'."

We do need to keep back enough for unexpected expenses. However, perhaps in this area, too, we can open our wallets and purses a bit wider. We can reach out to the needy in love and support, knowing that God loves a generous giver. It's not too late—yet!

The evening of life has come, and the shadows are lengthening. Every new day is a day of grace. We have had to give up a great deal, but we will not resign from life. It is possible to live intensely even if the body is failing. We have learned that trials and misfortune give as much meaning to life as good fortune, and sometimes they give even more meaning.

We surrender to God more and more, but that does not mean that we turn our backs on the world. Eleanor Roosevelt said, "One must never, for whatever reason, turn his back on life." Paul Tournier counseled, "Acceptance of old age is the best preparation for death, but also, conversely, the acceptance of death is the best preparation for old age."

The apostle Paul affirms, "So we do not lose heart. Even though our outer nature is wasting away, our inner nature is being renewed day by day" (2 Cor. 4:16).

It's not too late—yet! It's not too late to make sure that renewal happens.

How good you are to us, Lord. Always another day, another opportunity, another smile. Help me to understand and accept the fact that being is more important than doing.

30
Caught in the Middle

Do not cast me off in the time of old age;
do not forsake me when my strength is spent.
—An aged worshiper, in Psalm 71:9

The first time I heard the expression "parenting your parents," it sounded strange, like a twisted joke. We had been taught to "honor your father and your mother" (Exod. 20:12). We knew Paul's exhortation, "Children, obey your parents in the Lord, for this is right" (Eph. 6:1). "Parenting your parents" sounded weird.

With 15 million Americans over the age of 75, more than 6 million of them are being parented by their children. These parents can no longer manage their finances, do their shopping, or take care of themselves in the bathrooms. Children in their 60s are taking care of parents in their 80s and 90s, and 75 percent of these caregivers are women.

At the same time, they are caring for their own children (40 percent) and often holding down jobs. They are caught in the middle. According *Newsweek*, "The average American woman will spend 17 years raising children and 18 years helping aged parents" (July 16, 1990). Men are less willing to help aging parents, even when they are his own. Many dependent seniors are desperately afraid of burdening their busy children and are just as afraid of being alone. So we find out how cruel our culture can be to the aged.

In many countries and even in some North American communities, aging parents move in with their children.

According to a 1990 report by the U.S. Department of Health and Human Services, 14 percent of the men and 26 percent of the women over 85 years of age live with one of their children.

This happens for economic, social, or medical reasons or simply by custom. Parents and children usually have the same cultural backgrounds, traditions, values, and religion; they often feel that such a move is right. In other cases, there may be friction about shared living arrangements. Children and parents may no longer hold the same values and faith. Some parents may even prefer to live in a retirement or nursing home.

Will such an extended household work if small children are in the home and their mother has a job? In *Should Mom Live With Us?* Carlin and Greenberg say, "Only those involved in pertinent areas of gerontology or actually practicing this living arrangement know how this mixture of two [or more] generations under the same roof can produce tension and conflict."

A major problem in parenting parents is that roles blur and frequently are reversed. In many ways, the parents are no longer in charge; their children are. That is difficult for both parents and children who need to find new ways of relating to each other.

In some families early relationships were congenial, with a caring, loving, and forgiving atmosphere. The same is likely to happen again when roles are reversed and children parent their parents or parents move in with the children. If early family experiences were not so congenial and the climate less caring and loving, that will likely carry over when roles are reversed.

Some parents move close to the children but not in with them. My parents built a smaller bungalow, separated from the big Saskatchewan farmhouse by trees and a garden. That gave my parents some privacy and independence.

They still had easy contact with my sister and brother-in-law, who took over the farm operation.

Most Amish families provide a retirement cottage or house wing called the *Daadihaus*. Tourists in Holmes County, Ohio, or Lancaster County, Pennsylvania, can spot a *Daadihaus* near the main house on Amish farms.

This seems to be an almost ideal solution, but it is not realistic for most seniors. As parents and their children struggle with what to do or where to go, feelings of frustration, guilt, and helplessness are common. The prospect of moving into a retirement center may alarm some. They have heard nightmarish tales of neglect and loneliness in these institutions.

Elfrieda, a nurse, had the night shift at Fairmount Rest Home, in Ephrata, Pennsylvania. A delegation of Baptists and Mennonites from the former Soviet Union visited us. We swapped stories about caregiving in their country and in ours. They told us that in spite of an acute housing shortage, they still made room for aged parents to live with their children.

They had heard hair-raising stories about Americans pushing parents out of their homes and warehousing them in large isolated centers. They wondered how much of such heartlessness and cruelty was based on fact. When they learned that Elfrieda was working in one of these places, they asked me to show it to them. They wanted to see this outrageous treatment of seniors with their own eyes.

Alerted by telephone that we were coming, Elfrieda was at the door to meet us at eleven that night. She took us to the spacious and spotlessly clean dining room. They looked around and at each other, but said nothing. Then they inspected the modern stainless-steel kitchen. They raised their eyebrows. We walked through the well-stocked library and into the chapel. They just shook their heads. They didn't know whether all this was real or whether they were dreaming. But what about the people? They hadn't seen the people yet.

In subdued lighting, we tiptoed to the rooms where the people were sleeping. With Elfrieda as the escort, we walked the corridors and glanced into dozens of rooms. They couldn't believe that only two people were in a room, and that each room had its own bathroom and telephone. It all was so contrary to tales they had heard.

We ended the tour in the well-lit office. They wondered how many people were working there. With slightly over 100 residents, many of them in the nursing care unit, they thought that 20 staff persons would be maximum. When we told them 60, counting three shifts, they were speechless. Finally, their leader said he had one more question: "Where can my friends and I get applications to move into this human warehouse?"

Not all retirement communities are of that quality, and many seniors have images of them much like those of our Russian friends. Many North Americans want to remain in their own homes. They dread the move and resist it to the utmost.

This makes it so difficult for their children, who feel guilty about having their parents make such a move. They know the parents might feel abandoned and pushed aside, though some are glad not to burden their children. The move may be so necessary, and the children try so hard to reassure parents of their continued love. Nevertheless, this is a crucial period in the lives of the parents and in the lives of the caregivers.

During seniors' first months in a retirement community, the children and parents need to stay in close touch—and then keep that pattern going. The parents need closeness and encouragement as they adjust to the new environment, strange people, rules and regulations, and, frequently, new diets. If friends and neighbors, as well as members of the church, can join the support group, so much the better.

As for feeling guilty, there is no reason for that. Children are not responsible for the parents getting older, becoming helpless, and needing extra care. The caregivers are not responsible for how well the parent adjusts. The only thing caregivers are responsible for is to be as caring, listening, and loving as possible. However, as Barbara Deane points out in *Caring for Your Aging Parents,* just loving them is not enough.

Growing old is inevitable and often painful; it can also be complicated. Take the health question. At first sight, caregivers may feel totally helpless in matters of poor health. We expect the doctors to deal with the parents' health. But the family has a responsibility, too.

Doctors are trained to deal with acute care; they also learn to handle chronic conditions. Some doctors feel uncomfortable with older patients; they know the patient is not going to get well. Others are delighted to see any slight improvement in such a patient.

Whether it is Parkinson's or Alzheimer's disease, strokes or heart attacks, older patients are less likely to get quality care than younger patients. This is partly true because older patients may neglect to tell the doctor about their symptoms and feelings. They often think that their pains are normal for older people and they should not bother the doctor.

Hence, it is necessary for caregivers to be as informed as possible on health issues. If a doctor fails to explain these issues thoroughly, then caregivers must persistently ask the doctor for explanations or find another doctor. In addition, a geriatric nurse, an occupational or physical therapist, a social worker, or a psychologist can help. By attending meetings of appropriate organizations, caregivers can learn a great deal more about taking care of the aging parents than what the doctor might say in a few brief moments.

The money question arises again. Elderly people are often targeted as victims of fraud. How about arranging for a durable power of attorney, a guardianship, or a living trust? Estate planning may be beyond the caregivers' skills, but outside expertise is available. Caregivers can find help so they will not need to assume more responsibility than they can handle.

Caregivers caught in the middle, with responsibilities to children as well as to parents, need to guard against burnout. It is not only their physical strength that is being taxed but their emotional strength as well. What about all those other skills required of them, not merely shopping but filling out endless Medicare forms, watching over diets, medications, and exercise? There also are social and spiritual needs to be met.

When totally drained and exhausted, caregivers themselves need help. They need to know when to recruit spouses and siblings. Some extended families dump an unfair portion of responsibility onto one caregiver. The family physician can help assess the situation and give guidance on when or if the retiree should live in a retirement or nursing home.

There are many other complex problems. I return to the basic function of caregivers: to listen, learn, and love. Aging is not a problem to be solved; it is a stage of life to be lived. If caregivers can contribute to making this stage a little less painful, a bit more hopeful, and add even a small measure of enjoyment, then they have done their part.

Lord, you know that I am caught in the middle: my children need me and my parents need me. I love them all, but I need your help. My energy is low and my nerves are strained. Show me where to cut back and still do your will.

31

The Importance
of Perspective

Give thanks in all circumstances;
for this is the will of God in Christ Jesus for you.
—Paul, in 1 Thessalonians 5:18

As parents, we taught our children to say "thank-you." That was teaching them good manners. Deep down, we hoped they would grow up to be thankful people.

One sixteenth-century Anabaptist tract speaks of "Two Kinds of Obedience," *servile* and *filial*. "The servile [kind] looks to the external and to the prescribed command of [the] Lord; the filial kind is concerned about the inner witness and the Spirit."

The servile, never doing more than what is required, "is Moses and produces Pharisees and scribes; the filial is Christ and makes children of God." As children of God, we have an inner desire to obey, not simply an outward command, but the inner prompting of the Spirit. More than anything else, we want to please God.

Paul told the Thessalonians that "the will of God in Christ Jesus" is for us to be thankful "in all circumstances." Nobody can *make* us be thankful. A calendar date can be a reminder, perhaps even a nudge, but it can never make an ungrateful person thankful.

Gratitude has little or nothing to do with how much we have of this world's goods. Some rich people always want more; some poor people are profoundly grateful for the little they have.

Being thankful is akin to being happy. Everybody likes being around thankful people. Being thankful makes us feel a lot better about ourselves and the world. Being a grouch is bad for our health and harmful to our spirits. If more of us would realize that being thankful is in our best self-interest, perhaps some people could be persuaded to make the switch.

The problem for most of us is being thankful *in all circumstances*. That seems like a tall order. However, the moment we say "order," we're back to servile obedience, obeying an outward command, not a prompting of the heart. If we act this way as adults, we are physically grown-up but emotionally and spiritually children, doing what we are told without reflection or feeling.

Once I was a hobo in the Great Depression. Hoboes are honest men looking for work, not bums, tramps, or vagrants. I traveled with hoboes who "rode the rods," but I preferred to sit on top of the train rather than on the rods under the boxcars. I visited "hobo jungles," small forest clearings near town where we shaved, rested, shared our food, and swapped stories.

I heard stories of men going from one place to another for two years and finding only three months of work. I heard of hunger and cold, of wives and children left at home without provisions, and of loneliness, heartache, and police brutality. It was an education for me unlike anything I learned at university. I experienced firsthand a totally different world from the one in which I had been brought up. In many respects, it was a depressing, sad, and miserable world. It was a world without hope.

It was also a dangerous world. We were constantly in danger of physical accidents: we had to catch the train after it was moving and get off before it stopped. We risked being caught by police. Some of these guardians of the law understood us, but others were as cruel and heartless as the

Depression and unemployment itself. They would catch hoboes, knock them down, beat them, and occasionally even shoot them.

What were the hoboes to do? When there was no work in one town, they had to go to the next, and the freight trains were the only transportation they could afford. I sat on top of a train with about eighty men sitting or lying on the roofs of countless freight cars, all in search of work. Any work, it didn't matter what, just so it was work that would yield some pay.

We were a miserable lot, a pitiful sight. We rubbed smoke and steam out of our eyes, held onto our caps so the wind wouldn't blow them away, ducked bridges and tunnels, and made sure we jumped off when the train slowed down so the police wouldn't catch us. It was important to jump long before the train stopped.

One day I saw a man reading a book on top of a freight car. I crawled along, jumping from one boxcar to another, and sat down beside him. We introduced ourselves: he was a teacher, I was a student. He kept reading. It was a cold, windy day, and the pages were flipping. I asked what he was reading. He showed me the book: *Crime and Punishment*, by Dostoyevsky. Then we had a long talk, possibly several hours.

Most of the hoboes were from the working class, many without skills or training. Yet every now and then, there was someone like that teacher or like me. I never thought we were poor; at that time, we simply had no money. We were immigrants and had just bought the farm, which called for regular payments. Then the Great Depression hit.

I was twenty-one and wanted more education. My parents agreed and were sorry they could not help me financially. I remember our farewell. All nine children stood around the foot-pedal organ and sang hymns for half an hour. My mother quietly wiped tears from her eyes. Father read some Scripture and led in prayer.

Sitting on top of the freight train, all those memories came floating by me like smoke from the steam engine. I had nothing, not even enough money to buy a ticket to Sudbury, Ontario. I didn't know a single person in that nickel-mining town. I had no idea where I would sleep, how I would buy food, or if I would find a job.

All I knew was that I had to have money to go back to the University of Saskatchewan for my third year. I didn't need much, just enough for tuition and books, rent to pay Mrs. Willms for a small attic room, and oatmeal to last me through the nine months. As before, my regular diet would have to be oatmeal. Instead of sugar and milk with it, I would have Shakespeare and Tolstoy. After all, I was an English major.

With those musings, I didn't hear the train rumbling, the wind rushing, or even the engine's shrill whistles. I didn't see the other hoboes, the freight cars, or the ever-changing landscape. Even now, many years later, I remember how I sat there dreaming—and counting my blessings. Just how blessed could a young man be!

There I was, in good health, with a loving family praying for me, my parents' blessing on my further education, and no wife or children to support like so many of the men. I had the prospect of going back to school in the fall, and the firm belief that I was in God's care and keeping. Nothing could happen that God had not planned for me.

I began to recite Scripture, putting myself in the texts: "The LORD is my shepherd; that's all I want!" Then hardly knowing what I was doing, I started to sing. I was so thankful! So happy! So undeservedly blessed!

Thank you, Lord, for letting me see things in perspective, for showing me how blessed I am.

32

How Can We Know God's Will?

*The disagreement became so sharp
that they parted company.*
—Luke, in Acts 15:39

The story of the disagreement between Paul and Barnabas is well known. Barnabas wanted to take John Mark along on a missionary journey. However, Paul firmly refused because Mark had "deserted them in Pamphylia and had not accompanied them in the work" (Acts 15:38). It is both discouraging and encouraging to know that these fine Christian people and servants of the Lord could not agree. We're not the only ones!

Nevertheless, the scene raises a question about knowing the will of God. If both Paul and Barnabas knew God's will, they surely would have done it. Why didn't they know? Did they receive different messages from God? Could it be that one of them or perhaps both were not really tuned in to hear God?

Misunderstandings and tensions arise so easily when seniors with their children and grandchildren must find God's will: Should we move in with the children or not? Stay in our home or move into a retirement community? Is it time to step back a bit and let the children take more responsibility? How shall we discipline the grandchildren when they are with us? There is no end to these dilemmas.

It becomes more problematic when one party claims that God told him or her this or that. How does anyone know the will of God without checking other sources? When I was with MCC, we would occasionally receive an application from a prospective volunteer who would say that God wanted her or him to go to Bolivia, for example. If we had no opening in Bolivia, could we steer that person to serve in Brazil? Would we be going against the will of God?

In 1983, Elfrieda and I received a call to serve a church in Scottdale, Pennsylvania. It was totally unexpected. We discussed it, prayed about it, and decided to let the matter rest for the day. We'd pick it up again later. There was time.

Imagine our surprise when the devotional reading in *Disciplines* the next morning was based on Genesis 12:1-3, God's call to Abraham to leave his country and go to an unknown destination. The writer challenged readers:

> Abraham obeyed God's call without vacillating. He was called to a specific and special mission. . . . Our mission today is to be partners with God in Christ Jesus in redeeming persons from a life of meaninglessness to a life of purpose. With the nudging of the Holy Spirit, we discover specific areas where our ministry can happen. . . . *Forgive us, Lord, for being afraid to follow your call. Change our fear to faith.*

Was that reading a coincidence, or was God trying to tell us something? Can we know the will of God? If so, how does God reveal it to us?

I definitely believe that we can know God's will for us, whether we are teenagers or seniors. Finding God's will is like the captain who always brought his ship safely into a difficult harbor. Asked how he did it, he replied, "I see four blue lights up the river, and I line my ship up with all four of them. Then I know that I'm safe because I'm in the right channel."

Let me suggest that there are four blue lights to reveal the will of God for our lives. It is not safe to go by only one or two of the blue lights. All four must be lined up so they seem like one light. Here are the four lights:

The Bible

We call the Bible a lamp to our feet and a light to our path (Ps. 119:105). When we look into the Word of God for guidance, we need to look for guiding principles rather than detailed instructions.

For example, neither Old or New Testament mentions smoking. Does that mean it's all right to smoke? Literalists might interpret it that way, but in so doing, they would ignore certain basic principles mentioned frequently in the Bible. These principles do relate directly to smoking.

Think about stewardship. We are to spend our money wisely, holding it in trust from God. Paul says, "It is required of stewards that they be found trustworthy" (1 Cor. 4:2). We are not worthy of trust if we burn money instead of buying bread for our children or for other hungry people (Isa. 55:2).

We also believe that our bodies are the temples of the Holy Spirit. Paul also says, "Do you not know that your body is a temple of the Holy Spirit within you, which you have from God, and that you are not your own? For you were bought with a price; therefore glorify God in your body" (1 Cor. 6:19-20). Lawsuits are waged against the tobacco industry because the medical profession has proof that tobacco has destroyed thousands of bodies.

We were having an orientation for Polish youth invited to spend a year in the United States. I was telling them that their smoking would be a problem in the nonsmoking families they would be joining. Nothing I said seemed to impress them. As soon as we had a break, they were outside, lighting their cigarettes.

Then suddenly in a session they all sat up and paid attention. What had them thinking seriously at last about their filthy habit? I told them about slaves in America and how horrible and inhumane slavery had been. They understood that because they had felt like slaves when the Soviet Union occupied their country. They knew what it was like not to be free, not to be able to make their own decisions.

During a break, they had just told me that Russia made the Polish government issue a postage stamp with Stalin's picture on it. There was only one problem with that stamp: it wouldn't stick. The government discovered that the glue was good and so was the paper. The stamp didn't stick because the Poles would spit into the face of Stalin, rather than on the back of the stamp.

They were leaning forward to hear all I might say about slavery. At last I was talking about something close to their experience. I described a slavery even worse than being a slave to another person or nation. This is when we are slaves to ourselves, to habits we cannot break. I felt that I was right on target.

Several of the young people nodded their agreement. Others came to talk to me after the session. Freedom is a great theme in the Bible. Galatians is all about freedom (see Gal. 5:1). Jesus says, "If the Son [Christ] makes you free, you will be free indeed!" (John 8:36).

We need to search the Scriptures for other principles that may apply to a decision we are facing.

Prayer

The second blue light is prayer. Jesus prayed a great deal and taught his disciples to pray. As seniors, we have much to pray about: ourselves, other old people, our families, conditions in the world, and much more. We have time to pray; at last, we are not rushed. Yet we have to confess, in the words of Scriven's hymn, "O what needless pain we bear, all because we do not carry everything to God in prayer."

Prayer is talking to God and listening to God. It is common courtesy to give equal time to conversational partners: you talk and then let me talk as long as you did. We ought to treat God with at least the respect we give each other. We should talk to God in our prayers, and then listen to God's Spirit speaking to us directly and through fellow believers. Sometimes I feel that when we say "Amen," it is like the end of a one-way telephone conversation where we did all the talking and then hung up. Amen!

Most of us are far enough along on our spiritual pilgrimage that we know God sometimes answers prayers in unusual ways. Abraham sent his servant out to find the right wife for Isaac. The servant prayed,

> O LORD, God of my master Abraham, please grant me success today. . . . I am standing here by the spring of water, and the daughters of the townspeople are coming out to draw water. Let the girl to whom I shall say, "Please offer your jar that I may drink," and who shall say, "Drink, and I will water your camels"—let her be the one whom you have appointed for your servant Isaac. (Gen. 24:12-14)

This is like the young pastor looking for a wife among the lovely young ladies in his congregation. Puzzling over a choice and perhaps inspired by Abraham's servant, he prayed that the Lord would show him the one to marry: "Lord, when I visit my parishioners, they offer me tea or coffee. When I ask for half a cup and a young lady fills my cup only half full, let her be the one you have selected for me."

After the pastor submitted his problem to the Lord, he went merrily about his work. One day in a home, the young lady asked whether he would have some more coffee. He said that he had already drunk two cups, but, yes, he would be glad for just half a cup. To his surprise and joy, she poured only half a cup.

After courtship and the wedding, the pair settled down in

the parsonage. One day he told his wife about his prayer and that half cup of coffee. He thought she wouldn't remember it. "Do I remember it?" she responded. "I was never more embarrassed in my life. I wanted to fill your cup, but the pot was empty."

Was that God's doing? Is that how he answers prayer? Why not? We read the Abraham story as biblical truth. Why couldn't God answer a prayer today in an unconventional way?

Reason

The third blue light is reason. Of all God's creatures, we are the only ones who can think, reflect, evaluate, and contemplate. We are to worship God with all our hearts, soul, *minds* (reason), and strength (Mark 12:30). That means that when we ask God for an answer, he expects us to use our heads, to ask ourselves whether what we are planning to do is *reasonable.*

Does it make sense? Is it reasonable that at my age, I plan a trip by car from Pennsylvania to California? Does it make sense that I think about moving in with my daughter's family when their house is already crowded?

More often than not, God's will for us is closely tuned to our gifts and abilities. One good farmer had problems communicating with people. To the surprise of his church, he announced that he wanted to preach because he kept dreaming about it. He said he kept seeing two letters in the sky, *P* and *C*. He felt the Lord was telling him to *Preach Christ.* With discernment and patience, the congregation gently explained that the *PC* he kept seeing in his dreams meant *Plow Corn.*

Conscience

Conscience, the *still small voice* within each us (Rom. 2:14-15), is the fourth blue light. Conscience is the sense of what is good or evil. The conscience can be converted or perverted (Titus 1:15). We need to educate our consciences properly. It is not safe to say, "Let your conscience be your guide." Conscience alone cannot be trusted. It must be lined up with the other "blue lights."

I don't know if Hitler's conscience bothered him when he exterminated the millions of Jews and other "undesirables." He likely thought he was doing the world, and especially Germany, a good turn by getting rid of them so Germany could create a "pure" race of tall, blond, blue-eyed Aryans.

Before conversion, Saul/Paul had a clear conscience as he persecuted fellow Jews who became Christian believers (Acts 23:1). Then he had the Damascus Road experience. No, by itself, conscience is not a safe guide.

However, if you line up the *Bible, prayer, reason,* and *conscience,* while sharing mutual counsel with fellow believers, then I believe you will know God's will. You will be like that ship's pilot who was sure he was in a safe channel when he lined up the four blue lights.

O Lord, our God, you guided the Hebrew people through the wilderness by a cloud during the day and a pillar of fire by night. You guided the wise men to Bethlehem by a star. Guide us too, we pray, now that the evening of our life has come. Let us know your will for us; and when we know it, give us the courage and the joy to do it.

33

Turning Reversals into Victory

We know that all things work together for good for those who love God.
—Paul, in Romans 8:28

We need to make provision for setbacks. That's why hospitals have generators standing by in case of a power failure, and that's why we carry spare tires in our trunks. What provision have we seniors made for failure?

King Saul had a wonderful start in public life but ended in ruin. So did Judas. In a parable on greed, Jesus told of the rich fool. He had barns bulging with grain, but his life was empty and cut short by God (Luke 12:15-21).

These three turned success into failure. What could they have done differently? Let's look at the important and fascinating matter of turning failure into success, or transmuting hard times or persecution into victory.

In the Middle Ages, it was the dream of alchemists to transmute base metals like copper into gold. They tried to extract juices from plants to cure all the ills of humanity. They failed, but their experiments helped achieve today's level of medicine, chemistry, and mineralogy. In the realm of technology, failure and defeat are accepted as part of the discovery process.

Boeing in Wichita, Kansas, would report the crash of an expensive plane as "progress." After a crash, they could find out exactly what was wrong with the test model and correct the mistake. They would transmute the failure into success.

Paul was convinced "that all things work together for good for those who love God." He had the same mind-set that the Boeing people have. Trouble? Failure? Misfortune? Persecution? What's that? How are we going to make progress, in the technological as well as in the spiritual world, without setbacks? That Arab proverb must be true: "All sunshine makes a desert."

We had a dear friend in England who was fond of children. She hoped to have a family of her own. This was denied her. We witnessed first the disappointment and then the transformation or sublimation of her heart and mind. Instead of letting the disappointment ruin her life, she became the "mother" of hundreds of poor children from the slums of Liverpool.

This angel became the heart and soul of the Invalid Children's Aid Association, loving these neglected children more than their own mothers did. It was our privilege to work with her and this organization for some time. She found meaning and purpose in life through transmuting failure into success, defeat into victory. She was very happy.

In the Old Testament, few people experience this transmutation as dramatically as Joseph does. His world collapses when his brothers throw him into a pit and then sell him to merchants who drag him off to Egypt as a slave. The favored son lands in a prison in Egypt. He's in deep trouble.

Notice how the tables are turned when the brothers come to buy grain in Egypt. They don't recognize Joseph. All they know is that this man is next to Pharaoh in authority and power. Then he reveals himself to them. Trembling with fear, they're sure he's going to get even with them.

What happens? Joseph hugs them, kisses them, and they all cry. Then he says, "Even though you intended to do harm to me, God intended it for good" (Gen. 50:20). He gives credit to God for being the great Transformer.

In the New Testament, Paul convincingly illustrates this

same principle as he lists his troubles:

> Five times I received from the Jews the forty lashes minus one. Three times I was beaten with rods. Once I received a stoning. Three times I was shipwrecked; for a night and a day I was adrift at sea; on frequent journeys in danger from rivers, danger from bandits, danger from my own people, danger from Gentiles, danger in the city, danger in the wilderness, danger at sea, danger from false brothers and sisters; in toil and hardship, through many a sleepless night, hungry and thirsty, often without food, cold and naked. (2 Cor. 11:24-28)

Wow! Did Paul ever go through deep waters! Yet this same Paul can say, "We know that all things work together for good." He affirms, "In all these things we are more than conquerors through him who loved us" (Rom. 8:37). These are not pious or empty phrases; these are words spoken out of conviction based on personal experience. At the end of his life, Paul can say, "I have fought the good fight, I have finished the race, I have kept the faith" (2 Tim. 4:7).

Thus Paul took setbacks and wove them into the pattern of his life, making it a beautiful and rich model for us to follow. He transmuted every pain and disappointment, every trial and hardship, into success and victory. Paul knew that when his life was in danger and events raged around him like a tornado, God was there at the center of his life, taking care of him. Edwin Markham expressed this truth beautifully:

> At the heart of the cyclone tearing the sky
> and flinging the clouds and towers by
> is a place of central calm;
>
> So here in the roar of mortal things,
> I have a place where my spirit sings,
> in the hollow of God's palm.

The reformer Martin Luther demonstrated much the same attitude toward failure and difficulties. The man had so many opponents that he thought he saw the devil and threw an inkwell at him. Thousands opposed Luther, the pope opposed him, and his own Roman church opposed him. Then he had the courage to meet his enemies face-to-face.

Friends warned Luther not to go to Worms lest his enemies kill him. He replied, "If every tile on every roof along the way were a devil, I would still go!" Luther went to the great debate.

Luther's final words at the Diet of Worms on April 28, 1521, still echo through the corridors of time: "Hier stehe ich, ich kann nicht anders. Gott helfe mir. Amen (Here I stand; I can do no other. May God help me. Amen)." That stand took more than mere courage; it was possible only after a lifelong practice of using obstacles and difficulties as stepping-stones to greater heights, a way to success.

Helen Keller also shows us how to transmute difficulties into success. The story of her life is so amazing that I can hardly believe it. However, it is documented by trustworthy witnesses. Helen was eighteen months old when an illness left her blind and deaf. Because she could not hear, she did not learn to speak. I cannot imagine myself in a pitch-black, silent world. That was the world of poor little Helen Keller.

Helen's story is well known and worth repeating. Annie Sullivan, a teacher only twenty years old, entered Helen's life when she was seven. At first, Annie tried desperately, but without success, to reach the little girl in her personal prison. Then Annie trickled water on the child's wrist. At the same time, she gave Helen water to drink and traced the word *WATER* on her hand. Then the prison walls began to crack, crumble, and fall down.

Once the barrier was broken, nothing could stop Helen. She went to college, wrote examinations in open competition with other students, and studied Latin, Greek, German, and French. I don't know how she managed to speak in public when she could not hear a word she was saying. It all began on that exciting day in 1887 when she learned the word *water*.

Helen traveled the world to help deaf and blind people, legally classified with idiots and given up as hopeless. "Immured in silence and darkness," she said, "I possess the light which shall give me vision a thousandfold when death sets me free." What a testimony of overcoming obstacles and difficulties not of her own doing, transmuting them into success and victory!

Perhaps we can learn a few lessons from these men and women. First, reversals and defeat are relative and are often seen as such only by people whose yardstick for measuring success is the dollar or a public office. Leo Tolstoy has been considered a failure by some because he gave away all his wealth and died a poor man in a lonely railroad station. But today all over the world, his books inspire and teach people.

Second, suffering and pain are a natural part of life. In 1 Peter we read, "Beloved, do not be surprised at the fiery ordeal that is taking place among you to test you, as though something strange were happening to you" (4:12). Peter is saying that suffering and pain are normal in life, but defeat is not. Christians are meant to conquer. "Rejoice insofar as you are sharing Christ's sufferings, so that you may also be glad and shout for joy when his glory is revealed" (1 Pet. 4:13).

Third, transforming setbacks into victory is the way God works. At Creation, "God saw everything that he had made and indeed, it was very good" (Gen. 1:31). However, it didn't stay that way. Sin came into the world (Gen. 3). What did God do about it? He sent Jesus, "not . . . to condemn the world, but in order that the world might be saved through him" (John 3:17). Instead of failure, there is success, as Paul says: "Death has been swallowed up in victory!" (1 Cor. 15:54).

Finally, this victory is available to all of us if we are in Christ and he in us. We already know that apart from Christ, we can do nothing. If we give Christ first place in our lives, we can affirm with Paul, "I can do all things through [Christ,] who strengthens me" (Phil. 4:13).

The center of a hurricane is calm and quiet. Likewise, our turbulent and chaotic lives will be transformed when Christ is at the center, leading us from disappointment and failure into triumphant victory. That's how God works, and that's how we also can do all things with his help.

I do believe, Lord, that all things work together for good for those who love you. When the next difficulty comes my way, help me to see it as an opportunity and turn it into a positive experience.

34
Walking by Faith

Now the LORD *said to Abram, "Go from your country and your kindred and your father's house to the land that I will show you."* . . . *So Abram went, as the* LORD *had told him.*
—Genesis 12:1, 4

Abram ("exalted father") was a man of faith and was renamed Abraham ("father of a multitude," Gen. 17:5). We wonder why Terah migrated with his son Abram and Abram's wife, Sarai, and his grandson Lot. They left Ur, headed for Canaan, but settled a few miles away at Haran, by a tributary of the Euphrates (11:31; this Ur was likely in northwest Mesopotamia, near Haran).

Why did they leave Ur? Was Ur crowded or corrupt? Did the family want to escape pagan worship? Was war threatening? Did Terah have trouble with his clan? Were they part of a general migration from Mesopotamia to Canaan? Did God's call come to Terah and to Abram? All we know is that when Abram was seventy-five years old, God told him to leave his country. "So Abram went, as the LORD told him" (12:4).

At our age, our faith has also been tested many times. We, too, have taken smaller or larger steps in obedience, not always knowing where they would lead. While I was a student at Goshen (Ind.) College, we received a call to serve the Eden Church in Moundridge, Kansas. After an exchange of letters, a telephone call, and a personal interview with members of the board, we accepted.

There was only one snag: Elfrieda and I were Canadian citizens in the United States on student visas. We could not accept a salary. The Immigration and Naturalization Service (INS) office in Chicago made that clear: "Not one dollar or out you go!"

No problem. We had served eight years as volunteers with MCC in Europe, so we knew how to get by on little. We also had learned that we never have problems; we only have challenges. All we had to do was apply for immigration visas to the United States. As legal immigrants, we would be allowed to accept a salary.

We filled out the forms and handed them to the American consul in Winnipeg, Canada. He smiled and said everything was in order. When our visas had been approved, we would be notified. We asked, "Do you have any idea how long we might have to wait?"

The consul studied our forms again and noticed that Elfrieda and I were born in Russia and were naturalized Canadian citizens. He reached for a document listing countries and their annual quotas of immigrants allowed to settle in the United States. The consul found Russia and put his finger on it. He looked at us, then at the paper, pushed it aside, and sat back in his chair.

The news was not good. It was the beginning of the Cold War. We expected that, as Russian-born applicants, our wait might be a few months. We were not prepared for his answer: "The Russian quota is very small. There are many applicants." He reluctantly told us the facts: "If my calculations are correct, your number will come up about 120 years from now." He wasn't joking.

Did we have a problem or a challenge? We had already accepted the call to serve the church. What should we do? Abram had accepted the call, not knowing where he was to go. We knew where we were going, but 120 years is a long time to wait for government permission and our first paycheck.

We went to Kansas, moved into the parsonage, started our pastoral work, and made sure that not a dollar was paid to us by the church. Meanwhile, we discovered that there was a loophole in the law: rabbis, priests, and ministers were not subject to the immigration quota. Happy day! Nevertheless, we still had to wait some months before our papers came through and we were finally legal immigrants.

That was an unforgettable time for us in Kansas. We had no income, no reserves, and the INS was watching like a hawk to make sure the church did not pay us. In MCC, we had received full maintenance plus $10 monthly pocket money. A year at college had eaten up what little we had saved. Yet the Lord provided.

In the morning, we would open the parsonage door and find a bottle of milk and a loaf of bread. While we were still at breakfast, the telephone would ring: another invitation to dinner. As we left dinner, our hosts would pack up a chicken or some ham for us. A neighbor had a cornfield ready for the picking and told us to help ourselves anytime. When I pulled up to a filling station, a member of the church saw me and paid for the gas, without saying a word.

All this was legal—and exciting. We had never lived like that, literally from hand to mouth. It was fun, too. We felt a bit like Elijah when the ravens brought him "bread and meat in the morning, and . . . in the evening" (1 Kings 17:6). He made it, and so did we. It was a wonderful experience in faith and trusting God.

Lord, sometimes you challenge us to follow you and obey you when we know so little about the future. We thank you that our experiences of the past have taught us to put our hands in yours and thus be always safe.

35
Recipe for Happiness

*Let each of you look not to your own interests,
but to the interests of others.*
—Paul, in Philippians 2:4

I heard of an old woman who was so lonely that she sent herself letters. The next time I heard that story, it was a college student who wrote to herself. Could that be true? Can a person get that lonely?

I've heard of prisoners in solitary confinement being so lonely that they came away with a new definition of hell: loneliness. But to write letters to yourself? Stick postage stamps on them and have the mail carrier bring them back to you? That's nonsense. A lot of us get fooled by other people, but we don't deliberately set out to fool ourselves. If you were sad to the point of crying, would you tickle yourself to make yourself laugh? Of course not.

Yet maybe this is not nonsense, and maybe it has happened. In fact, I did something almost like that last spring. The summer is gone, and it is November and getting colder. Today I put my short-sleeved shirts into storage bags and hung the long-sleeved shirts in the closet for winter.

During this annual ritual, one shirt rustled when I put it on the hanger. It sounded as if there was paper in the pocket, but that couldn't be: I always wash them before I put them in storage. When I looked I found two crisp ten-dollar bills! Wow!

It was my money. I had put it into that shirt pocket about

six months ago and forgot about it. But I remember thinking that it would be a surprise when I found it later, and it would make me happy. It did!

We know that the best recipe for happiness is to make *other* people happy. The Bible is full of such parables and teachings. "Let each of you look not to your own interests, but to the interests of others" (Phil. 2:4). Jesus says we are to die to self, like a grain of wheat in the earth, so our lives will be fruitful (John 12:24).

I have frequently been asked for a definition of "Christian service," and I respond, "Christian service is living for others." Like Jesus, who "went about doing good" (Acts 10:38). That's beautiful and really quite simple: living a day at a time and doing good to others as we have the opportunity.

However, it's not easy, especially in North America. This "doing good" lifestyle is so opposite from what the media and our current culture press onto us. We live in a society that is youth oriented and self-centered. The commercials tell us, "You deserve the best. If it feels right, do it. Take care of number one. Everybody else is doing it. If others are lacking food, clothing, and housing, that's their fault."

So the arguments go until even we at our age are sometimes tempted to believe those selfish lines, at least just a bit. Meanwhile, many of our young people have totally swallowed that hedonistic philosophy.

We want to make sure we don't fall into that trap. Living for others is still the road to happiness. The angels may smile kindly on us if once in a while we treat ourselves to some happiness. Never at the expense of others, of course, but just fooling ourselves, like putting twenty dollars in a pocket to find it later. Or maybe, just maybe, even writing letters to ourselves.

36

Why Not Confess?

Confess your sins to one another,
and pray for one another,
so that you may be healed.
—James 5:16

Why is it so difficult to confess when we have done wrong? It seems to start in kindergarten and plagues us all through life. "He pushed me!" "No, I did not!" The company car was returned from the airport with a dent in the fender. Who did it? Nobody would confess or even report that it was hit while parked.

On Sunday we hear Psalm 32 read from the pulpit and have no intention of following David's example: "I acknowledged my sin to you, and I did not hide my iniquity; I said, 'I will confess my transgressions to the LORD,' and you forgave the guilt of my sin" (Ps. 32:5).

Okay, maybe we do confess to the Lord, but we certainly are slow to confess to each other. It is interesting that we confess to God but not to another human, and certainly not to our spouse. Catholics at least confess to a priest, but Protestants don't even do that. As a result, the wrong we do hounds us the rest of our lives. We desperately want peace but can't get it.

A refugee woman came to our camp in Gronau, Germany. While waiting to emigrate, she worked in the camp kitchen, and then we took her to Paraguay. There she pioneered with other women who didn't know if their husbands were dead or alive. Life was hard, very hard.

On top of the struggle for survival, she had an uneasy conscience. A little voice kept telling her she had done a wrong that needed to be straightened out. She put it off, thinking she might confess later. Years passed while she had no peace. She had so much trouble and a nagging conscience in her life of pioneering in that cruel Chaco. How sad! Then one day a letter from her came to my desk. At last she confessed.

While working in the refugee kitchen before emigrating, she told me, she took a meat grinder belonging to MCC, packed it with her meager belongings, and took it to Paraguay. Recently she had recommitted her life to Christ, but she still had no peace because of the stolen kitchen utensil. Now that she had confessed, she asked what she should do with the meat grinder. I didn't know whether to laugh or cry when she added that the meat grinder was already broken when she swiped it.

How long had she gone around with a guilty conscience? *Thirty years!* Thirty years because of a stupid broken meat grinder. Thank God that she had a sensitive conscience. The still small voice finally did get through to her.

I received another letter:

> Enclosed please find a check for the amount of thirty dollars, which according to my reckoning is the amount that I still owe you from my personal allowance which I overdrew when I served under you in Morocco in 1960. Having recently recommitted my life to Christ, I know I cannot effectively go on in the faith without making right past mistakes. Along with the check, please accept my humblest apologies for letting this thing go so long. I am truly sorry.

This February 4, 1975, letter was written *fifteen years* after the event.

The unsettling part about delayed confessions is that

they are not forgotten and suddenly remembered many years later. If that were the case, one might consider it one redeeming factor in the sad episode. However, from conversations and letters about confessions, including my own experience, it is clear that the wrong committed keeps popping up in one's memory. It gives the offender no peace.

Here's another confession:

> Dear Peter Dyck: Greetings. I will come straight to the point. I have a confession to make. The Lord has made me conscious of a sin in my life that is not cleared up. In 1947 to 1949 when I was a refugee in Germany, I needed dentures. When the dentist asked for payment, I told him to charge it to MCC. And he did. Now I am 82 years old, hard of hearing, and almost totally blind. I have to dictate this letter to another person. But I want peace. And that is why I am writing and enclosing a check for $120 to pay for the dentures. MCC has done so much for us. The Lord bless you and your good work.

This lady waited *twenty-four years*. One wonders how often she thought about her transgression. Every time she took a bite? Every time she took the dentures out for the night? Did it ever spoil her appetite while eating a delicious apple pie? When she was eighty-two, she was thinking of her end, so she quickly made it right before meeting her Maker. One cannot fault her for that. However, why could she not have had the peace that she longed for many years earlier?

> Greetings in the name of Jesus. I was reminded today of something which I desire to have cleared, so I will not need to doubt or have a troubled conscience. I served in PAX from 1958 to 1960. On our Palestine tour, I bought a small pocket watch in Amman, Jordan. I believe I paid around $12 for it. As I remember, I wasn't sure whether customs were to be paid on it or not. And I have wondered ever since whether I should have declared it and paid cus-

toms for it. Could you answer this for me? And if I owe something, how can I possibly pay my debt? I would appreciate it if you could help me. Thank you.

This letter was written *fifteen years* after the event. The irony is that there was no duty to be paid on the watch. However, for fifteen years, his conscience bothered him, not once or twice, but as he says, "ever since" he bought the watch, all because he didn't clear it up right away. The last sentence of my response to him was this: "I hope that straightens out the matter and you can sleep with a good conscience."

Why is it so difficult to confess our mistakes or wrong-doings? What can we seniors do about it? It seems to me that there are three things:

First, we need to clear up anything in our lives that may be troubling us. Don't delay; do it today. Pick up the telephone or the pen and do it.

Second, talking about it is the first step, but in many situations, that is not enough. The talking may be too general if every other sentence begins with an *if:* "If I have hurt you," or "If what I did was wrong," and so on. There needs to be honest confession. Lacking that is like walking around with a splinter in your foot; it keeps bothering you. Conscience is like a splinter, like a smoke alarm screaming until we do something about it.

Many situations require restitution or payment. We may need to perform a service or some tangible deed to make things right and clear our conscience.

Third, while admitting that it is difficult, make sure our young people understand that confession shows strength of character, not weakness. In kindergarten, we might deny that we pushed the other guy so that he fell and hurt himself. As grownups, we don't do that anymore. Paul put it so aptly, "When I was a child, I spoke like a child, I thought like a child, I reasoned like a child: when I became an adult, I put an end to childish ways" (1 Cor. 13:11). We need to make a choice to act as adults and stick with it.

The letters of confession in my file all talk about needing to clear the matter up for their own sake, to regain peace of mind. Not one of them mentions a principle. None of them says that it is for the sake of the other person or organization that was wronged. All of them want cleansing and relief for themselves.

Martin Luther was right when he said: "It is a dangerous thing to go against your conscience." We could add to or modify that: it is a dangerous thing to *ignore* your conscience.

> For as the heavens are high above the earth,
>   so great is [God's] steadfast love
>   toward those who fear him;
> as far as the east is from the west,
>   so far he removes our transgressions from us.
>   (Ps. 103:11-12)

If we confess!

Lord, I need you. I can't go on like this. You know all things, so you know what I have done that wasn't right. You know how restless I've been ever since. I'm weary and tired. I want to forget it, but I can't. I want peace of mind, but it eludes me. Lord, I don't want to go on like this, not one more day. Enough is enough. You must help me do what I have to do. I can't do it alone. If you go with me, Lord, I'm ready.

37
Caring Enough to Share

The point is this: the one who sows sparingly will
also reap sparingly, and the one who sows
bountifully will also reap bountifully.
—Paul, in 2 Corinthians 9:6

There is so much need in the world. The world needs "the bread that perishes" *and* "the bread of life" (John 6:27, 35). The world needs compassion and caring. Those needs are as great here in North America as in Asia and Africa.

We, too, are among the needy. We don't need bread and blankets, but just the opposite: unless we share with others, our inner needs will go unmet. It is a shock to some when they realize this truth for the first time: we are so constituted that we need to share with others if we want to live satisfying and meaningful lives.

Here are three reasons for sharing our possessions and ourselves with other people:

• for the sake of other people, the lonely, the marginalized, and the poor.

• for the sake of God, who created us and gave us salvation through his Son.

• for the sake of ourselves.

It has been said that unless we share, we will go to the dogs. The truth is that unless we share, we will probably go to hell! That's strong language, but do we remember what happened to Scrooge? Unless we care and share, our lives will shrivel up; we will be dead before our hearts stop beating.

On the other hand, here is good news: if we do share, it will come back to us! In Ecclesiastes 11:1, we read, "Send your bread upon the waters, for after many days you will get it back." God rewards faithful giving. We all love to hear Malachi 3:10:

> Bring the full tithe into the storehouse, so that there may be food in my house, and thus put me to the test, says the LORD of hosts; see if I will not open the windows of heaven for you and pour down for you an overflowing blessing.

Isn't that wonderful! It's like the farmer in Kansas who said that the Lord was shoveling it in faster than he could shovel it out—provided that he shared first.

> There is a destiny that makes us brothers,
>   None goes his way alone;
> All that we send into the lives of others
>   Comes back into our own. (Edwin Markham)

There is one catch in all this. It doesn't work if I say to myself, "Aha, now I know what will make me happy. Now I know the secret of a joyful life. I will share my goods and myself with other people. And, presto, it all comes back to me, multiplied!"

Not so fast, my friend. Sharing with others doesn't work if I "use" other people to make myself happy.

It is true that we must share if we want to be happy, and that we will find the bread again that we shared with others. It is true that God will open the windows of heaven and shower blessings upon us. It is true that "there is a destiny that makes us brothers [and sisters]."

However, if the motivation for sharing is to satisfy ourselves, if it is scheming, then it is nothing more than camouflaged selfishness. The result is not life but death.

Sharing without caring degrades both the recipient and the giver. There is a great deal of that kind of cold and heartless sharing. Tolstoy said that if we really cared for that beggar in the street, we wouldn't just give a quarter or a dollar: "We would either do more, or we would do less!"

If we give the beggar that dollar, it will not change his miserable lot; he will still be begging tomorrow, next week, and next year. If we do more, we might need to take him home, clean him up, and get him a job. Who knows how much more trouble that would be for us!

Tolstoy is right; if we really care, we will either do less or do more. Do we give the dollar because we care, it's needed, and/or that's all we have (the widow's mite)? Or do we give merely to ease our conscience, when we could give much more? Do we withhold the dollar because we are callous, or because we are working on another way of helping?

Here are seven suggestions. We can become caring persons—

1. By accepting God's love for us. When we do that, the Holy Spirit can change us into loving and caring persons.

2. By making caring homes where parents provide object lessons of caring and sharing for children and grandchildren to see and emulate.

3. By standing in the place of those who are hurting, the lonely, the marginal, and the poor.

4. By making a beginning, no matter how small it may be, even if only a dollar.

Willy Brandt, the former chancellor of Germany, knew he could not do much to change the climate of the Cold War between the Soviet Union and the United States. Nevertheless, he reached out to Poland and other countries bordering Germany on the east and signed peace treaties with them. This became known as the "politics of small steps." We can learn from Brandt to have the courage to take the first small steps for peace, caring, and sharing.

5. By recognizing the difference between giving service and being a servant.

The motives for giving are varied, ranging from altruism to self-interest. After the war, the Marshall Plan was imaginative and wonderful, helping Germany get back on its feet. Yet the United States did this not so much because Germany was cold, hungry, and humiliated from losing the war.

Its main purposes were (1) to keep Germany from turning to the Communist bloc and against the United States and (2) to stabilize international order by promoting democracies and free-market economies. Politicians and historians say that the Marshall Plan was in our own best interest, politically and economically.

Similarly, individuals often calculate what is in their own best interest and perform a service with that in mind. This ulterior motivation for service is in stark contrast to the spirit of a true servant, who acts only because it is in the best interest of someone else. In the first case, the motive is self-interest; in the second, it is caring love. The first is merely doing; the second is authentic being.

6. By acknowledging that Jesus is Lord. God is at work in history. Someone said, "There's God and there's you; sooner or later, you're going to settle down on one or the other."

7. By recognizing and joyfully accepting the fact that we are not alone in this venture, this task. We are a part of a new community of believers, the church.

Search me and try me, O Lord, and help me discern my own motives for any service I perform for others. Thank you for your own example of going about and doing good.

38
Shoot to Kill?

> *You shall not murder/kill!*
> —God, in Exodus 20:13 (NRSV, note)

We were sitting at the dinner table. He told me he had been a policeman before his retirement. I asked, "Did you always carry a gun, or were you ever like a bobby in England, just carrying a cudgel?" He laughed and replied, "A policeman without a gun might as well stay home and rock the baby."

I wanted to learn from him. "Did you ever have to use your gun?" He gave more than a one-word answer: "We were trained not to be trigger happy, not to shoot too soon. But, yes, I have used my gun."

I hesitated with the next question, but I needed to know: "Have you ever killed someone?"

This time he looked at me quizzically, then emphatically declared, "If you have to shoot, you always shoot to kill!" I wondered, "Why not shoot at the legs, or shoot the other fellow's gun out of his hand?" He just laughed: "Where do you come from?"

I have verified that with other police officers: they do some constructive things, but when they shoot, they "shoot to kill!" Soldiers keep order in desperate circumstances, rescue people, and do cleanup. Yet they are trained and methodically conditioned to kill people.

While recycling newspapers, I found the strangest cartoon in the "Beetle Bailey" series. A soldier is practicing target shooting. His superior says, "Rocky, I didn't give the order to fire!" Rocky explains, "I saw a rabbit running across the range and shot it." "That's cruel," says the officer. "Shooting animals is a misuse of your weapon. Remember, that gun is to kill PEOPLE!"

That became personal and clear to me when a judge ordered me to put on a military uniform, get training, and help win a war. In 1944, I was in England with MCC, trying to prevent deaths from nightly bombings. As a Canadian, I was counted as a British subject. My induction order came as I was about to take some older people out of Birmingham to safety in the countryside.

What should I do? My British friends shrugged: "An order is an order!" There I was, a young man, away from family and church, facing a major dilemma with major consequences. Three years earlier, I had come to England as a volunteer; the law had caught up with me.

I refused to join the army. Facing Judge Burgess in Manchester at my second trial, I held out my arms for him to handcuff me and send me to jail. If he wanted to ship me back to Canada, he could do so, but I would not obey his order to become a killer. It was my moment of truth, my Rubicon that I have never regretted.

Since then, I have thought a great deal about what it means to be a peacemaker. As a young man I loved to run races, 100-yard dashes. One lesson I have learned is that peacemaking is not a sprint but a marathon. You just keep on and on! Saying no to war and violence, though morally and biblically right, was only my start on the long road to becoming a peacemaker. Peacemaking is an art that has to be learned. My family and church had taught me the way of peace, and now I was claiming that way for my own.

My friend Nick and I were watching fifty children playing on the school lawn. Nick was in the air force and ready to go on a bombing mission over Germany that night. We talked about the lovely sight of innocent children romping on the grass. I turned to Nick: "Are you capable of gathering up all those children and throwing them into a burning furnace?"

He looked as if I had gone mad: "Peter, I thought we were friends. Who do you think I am?" My answer was also a question: "Of course, we're friends; that's why I'm blunt with you. Tell me, Nick, what's the difference between taking these children and throwing them into a burning furnace and taking the furnace, the bomb, and throwing it onto the children to incinerate them?"

He couldn't answer. I had cornered him. For a while, I talked like that to other people. Today I am ashamed of that tactic. It may have been logical, but it wasn't peacemaking. Gandhi said we must never paint opponents into a corner; we should take their hands and together search for a new and better way. I had painted Nick into a corner. Years later, I am still learning how to become a more effective peacemaker.

Here are some lessons I have learned:

1. The first casualty of any war is *truth*. It is unthinkable to wage a war and be truthful. The ways of sacrificing truth are so deceptive and insidious.

Before going into combat in WW I, soldiers were gathered for a worship service. They always sang Julia W. Howe's "Battle Hymn of the Republic": "As he died to make men holy, let us die to make men free." What a wonderful thought, to identify with Jesus as you go out to meet the enemy! Nevertheless, it's a lie; soldiers are not sent out merely to die, though many will do so; they are sent out to kill. That's what they are trained to do. Their tools and equipment are for one purpose—to kill the enemy while protecting themselves.

What if the army chaplain had suggested they sing it truthfully: "As he died to make men holy, let us kill to make men free." One officer in the Vietnam War even said they had to bomb a village to save it. What kind of salvation is that? Truth is the first casualty of every war.

2. The second casualty is *love and respect for others.* During WW I, soldiers on the German and Allied sides of the Maginot and Siegfried lines were ordered to stop shooting one Christmas Day. Soldiers crawled out of foxholes and shook hands with the enemy. They began to see each other as human beings. As husbands and fathers, they chatted and showed family photos. When this was reported to the generals, they called off the cease-fire and ordered the soldiers to resume shooting!

3. The third casualty is *ecological fallout.* It is common knowledge that the military is the most ecologically destructive organization. From Vietnam to Bosnia and Rwanda, from the Middle East to the former Yugoslavia, armies destroyed houses, schools, and hospitals, leaving the poor people homeless. They also killed trees and poisoned the atmosphere. In Kosovo, military action left rivers toxic from destroyed chemical plants.

4. Finally, a fourth casualty is the *mission of the church.* In war, professing Christians kill their own brothers and sisters in the Lord. They do much of this from a distance. But suppose a Christian soldier meets a non-Christian soldier? What is he to do?

Jesus says, "Go therefore and make disciples of all nations, baptizing them in the name of the Father and of the Son and of the Holy Spirit, and teaching them to obey everything that I have commanded you" (Matt. 28:19-20). If the Christian kills the non-Christian instead of bringing the good news of salvation to him, then he has blasted him into eternity, where nobody can reach him with the gospel.

War is contrary to the will of God. There is no violent way to peace; *peace is the way,* in all human relations. Those working for a greater measure of justice and doing it in a peaceful even though confrontive style, are working for peace. First justice, then peace, never the other way around. The psalmist said: "Steadfast love and faithfulness will meet; righteousness [justice] and peace will kiss each other" (Ps. 85:10).

As seniors, we must share the message of peacemaking with our young people. They are exposed to so much violence on the screen, in schools, in homes, and on the streets. They think this is the normal way of life. Sad to say, in some situations, it is true.

Our children and grandchildren must understand that peacemaking has to be learned just as killing has been learned. We can remind them of their own learning experiences from potty training to driving cars, from baking apple pies to becoming doctors. Everybody has to be trained, whether they are nurses, teachers, farmers, carpenters, astronauts, peacemakers, or killers.

We are not born with a natural instinct to kill. David Grossman, a military expert on the psychology of killing, reported findings in his article "Trained to Kill" (*Christianity Today*, Aug. 10, 1998): In the Civil War, most soldiers refused to pull the trigger or fired over the enemy's head. So the military has systematically trained soldiers and conditioned their responses to overcome this natural inhibition. They want to make at least 75 percent of the soldiers willing to shoot.

Grossman confesses, "I spent almost a quarter of a century as an army infantry officer and a psychologist, learning and studying how to enable people to kill. Believe me, we are very good at it. But it does not come naturally; you have to be taught to kill."

In a TV program (Mar. 27, 1997), a WW II pilot was interviewed. He had been trained for low-flying attacks over Germany, the most dangerous kind of flying. "We were trained to be efficient killers. I was proud and I was happy. It was wonderful. I felt so good and so proud!"

It is a sobering and unsettling fact that our children learn violence and are systematically conditioned to kill, from

TV, movies, and video games. When children play interactive video games, their reflex skills are systematically conditioned just as those of a soldier or police officer in training. After a while, they will be able to kill instantly, by reflex, without thinking what they are doing and without later having a bad conscience about what they have done.

In the same way, peacemaking has to be learned. It has to begin in the family, and the sooner the better. Proverbs 22:6 says, "Train children in the right way, and when old, they will not stray." This peace training can take many forms: We can supply our children and grandchildren with appropriate literature and supervise their TV viewing. We can invite peacemaking people into our homes and churches. We can encourage the children to make the right kind of friends.

One of the most effective ways of teaching peacemaking is by example. Just watching our own words and actions will do more than many words of advice. Our children and grandchildren will absorb and copy us without knowing it. As the proverb says, "An apple doesn't fall far from the tree."

Two things are of utmost importance in becoming peacemakers. We give due respect to the many non-Christians working for peace, personally, through legislation, and by other means. But we won't go far unless we have the peace of God in our hearts.

Second, we need to be clear on the difference between method and motive in peacemaking. Be wary if peace is merely a method, something to try: if it "works," fine; if not, discard peace in favor of another method. On the contrary, our peacemaking is based on a motive rooted in the deep conviction that peace is the only way and that peace is the will of God. Then, no matter what the consequences, peace is the way to go.

Lord, make me an instrument of your peace!
(Francis of Assisi)

39

Love Is Never Lost

For this is the message you have heard
from the beginning,
that we should love one another.
—1 John 3:11

Mention *love* and you are right in the heart of the gospel: "God so loved the world that he gave his only Son" (John 3:16). Anabaptists in the sixteenth century put love into the center of their life and teaching. They said this love must extend to all people, even to the enemy (Matt. 5:44).

In 1569 the authorities were closing in on Dirk Willems of Asperen, Holland, to execute him for his faith in Jesus Christ. He escaped over the newly frozen canal. His pursuer fell through the thin ice and was about to drown when Dirk Willems returned and pulled him out of the freezing water. The pursuer wanted to let him go, but the town mayor would not allow it. Dirk was burned at the stake.

Another Anabaptist was tied to the stake to be burned when he called out in a loud voice, "Stop!" The magistrate and clergy standing nearby thought he was about to recant. They were surprised to hear him say, "I see a man in the crowd without shoes. I have good shoes on; why burn them? Please take them off and give them to that man."

Margaret Hellwart of southern Germany, near Stuttgart, loved Jesus and enjoyed telling about her joy in the Lord and instructing women. However, the church and civic authorities were not happy with her and were determined to silence her. The earlier practice was to kill Anabaptists or lock them up in prison. Around 1620, when they were dealing with Margaret, they had stopped such drastic measures in this part of Germany. What could they do to silence her?

They repeatedly chained her to the floor of her house. She was like a dog tied in a kennel, able to run around a limited area. Margaret could take care of her husband and children, prepare their food, and wash their clothing. At last, the authorities thought they had rendered her "speechless."

Nevertheless, women visited her at home, and some became Anabaptists. Margaret often managed to get free, visit neighbors, and attend Anabaptist meetings.

Love is never lost. A seed may fall into the ground and be buried, but if you wait a while, a new plant will grow up from it. Four hundred years after Dirk Willems and Margaret Hellwart, we tell their stories and are inspired to follow their example of loving Jesus and living for him. Their witness and love for the Lord was not lost.

It's like trees and shrubs that grew on earth millions of years ago. They absorbed the sunlight, grew, and died. In swampy areas, trees grew to giant proportions. When they fell over, they formed layers of peat sometimes twenty feet thick. When the earth convulsed and folded, this mass of peat was buried deep under the earth. It was compressed to the thickness of just a foot or so. In that process, it was fossilized and changed its composition.

In modern times, clever men dug down into the earth and found this hard, black rocklike substance. They brought it up. To their surprise and joy, they discovered that it would burn. They called it "coal." Now we use coal mostly for generating electric power.

The scientists have accounted for the heat released from the coal in power stations and in the living room fireplace, and the light that flickers on the walls; they are the same heat and light that came from the sun millions of years ago. It was stored in those trees that became peat and finally coal. The light and the heat originated in the sun.

The sun's rays, bringing heat and light to earth in eight minutes and twenty seconds, had been stored for millions of years and then released; they were never lost. So also love is never lost, although for a while we may not feel it or see it.

This lesson from nature is of utmost importance for seniors. We are impatient; we want to see our children and grandchildren respond quickly, certainly in our lifetime, to the love we have shown them. In that sense, we are still like children who stick a seed into the ground and are disappointed when the plant doesn't come up right away.

We need to cultivate patience and trust. We need to trust in the goodness of God. Trust in the Lord: in his own good time, the love we sowed will bear fruit. We need faith, in faith believing that love is never lost. We need to remember that truth the next time we sit in front of our fireplace, warm ourselves by the glow of the coal fire, and watch the light flicker on the walls.

Lord, you gave me the life that I am now living. You created the world in which I live. Forgive me when I forget that and when I take too much for granted. When there is so much going on around me, I sometimes get the feeling that we are making things happen. Teach me to remember that the world and all that is in it is yours; we can only move within the limits of your eternal laws. I thank you for one of these eternal laws, that love is never lost.

40

Incarnation as Identification

The Word became flesh and lived among us;
and we have seen his glory,
 the glory as of a father's only son,
 full of grace and truth.
—John 1:14

People around us are lonely. Some are discouraged, others are confused. We would like to help them, cheer them up, and give them hope. But how?

There are many ways, but let's try God's way of identifying with others. The Indians used to say, "Walk a mile in their moccasins." What people need is not sympathy but empathy.

Look at it this way: When God created the world, it was perfect. Then sin spoiled it. God had to decide whether to scrap what he had made and start over, or fix it. The Bible says that he opted for fixing it.

First, God thought he would save just a few good people, Noah and his family, and drown all the bad guys. It didn't work; pride and evil still hung around. Then God thought he would select one nation, the Hebrews, and through them bring order and peace to all the other nations, but that also didn't work.

God sent prophets who pounded their pulpits and shouted, "Thus says the LORD! Shape up or ship out!" The Israelites paid no attention to them; they even killed some prophets. As the Old Testament drew to a close, God made one last effort to save his beautiful world by calling the "remnant" (Isa. 10–11). They were just a handful of left-overs, but those few faithful people, the remnant, would be the means through which God would save his world. "Then they shall know that I am the LORD" (Ezek. 6:10).

At the close of the Old Testament, the problem was not fixed or solved. Then God had another idea. He always does. He would go down to earth himself. Then people would believe that he loved them and wanted only the best for them. How could he do that? How could the Creator of the universe, the omnipotent one, go and live among the people he had made?

Didn't we just say he always has another idea? Many years later, clever theologians studied what he had done and tried to explain it, but they couldn't. They did what they often do in such situations; they made up a big new word to describe the mystery. They called it the *incarnation*. The Germans called it *die Menschwerdung Gottes:* God became a human being, a *Mensch.*

It staggers the imagination. We can't understand it. Some say it's a scandal; others call it a stumbling block or say it's foolish. The harshest critics call it blasphemy. But the Gospel of John says, "In the beginning was the Word, and Word was with God, and the Word was God. . . . And the Word became flesh and lived among us, and we have seen his glory, the glory as of a father's only son, full of grace and truth" (John 1:1, 14).

That is how God finally "fixed" it. In his Son, he came to earth himself as a baby, who grew up like any other person. Then he went about teaching, healing, feeding, and saying, "The Father and I are one!" (John 10:30). "I am in the Father and the Father is in me" (John 14:10).

Two things greatly troubled the religious leaders of that time. One was the fact that Jesus made himself equal with God: the *incarnation*. The other was that he socialized with people whom they considered unworthy, riffraff, the scum of the earth. The leaders simply called them "sinners."

Jesus *identified* with these seekers. He talked with them, touched them, ate with them, healed them, and loved them. The leaders could not understand that the *incarnation* was in fact *identification*.

Someone asked a missionary couple whether they liked their work in Africa. They replied,

> No, my wife and I do not like dirt. We have reasonably refined sensibilities. We do not like crawling into huts through goat refuse. We do not like association with ignorant, filthy, even brutish people. But is a person to do nothing for Christ he does not like? We have orders to go!

If these missionaries went only by their feelings, they would stand at a distance from the people, shouting the good news to them: "Jesus loves you!" However, they would always be careful not to get too close. They would never dream of putting their arms around them and hugging them. But with no identification, there would be no harvest. However, the love of Christ urged them on (2 Cor. 5:14). Let's hope they made friends with "even brutish people."

The incarnation as identification is a powerful lesson, not only at Christmas when we worship the baby in a manger, but every time we encounter our own children and grandchildren. We need to ask ourselves whether we identify with them, whether we truly put our arms around them. Do we really empathize with them and not just sympathize and pity them?

When a problem needs to be fixed, we try all the conventional ways from scolding to ignoring. But how about trying to identify with them the way God did?

We sometimes hear people say that God wouldn't understand. After all, he is God, and I'm just a little person. Think again. Have we had any experience that Jesus did not have?

He was lonely and misunderstood, tempted and contradicted, falsely accused and ridiculed. People twisted his words and twisted cords to make a whip for scourging him.

Jesus cried. He prayed and wondered why God didn't answer. His closest friends deserted him. He was tortured and killed. We had better think again before we say Jesus doesn't understand. He understands us because he came to identify with us! There is no experience we might encounter that Jesus did not also experience (Heb. 4:15).

A young American volunteer was assigned to Camel's Neck, an isolated village in Algeria near the Sahara Desert. He lived with the people and helped them improve their gardens, fields, herds, houses, and much more. In the evenings, the men sat for long hours with him, debating and comparing the teachings of their Koran with the teachings of the Bible. He told me that these discussions were a lot more interesting and fruitful than some of our Sunday school discussions back home.

When I visited Camel's Neck, a number of people at different times stepped out of the crowd on our tour of the village. They quietly came up behind me and whispered, "You're not going to take Johnny away from us, are you?" They loved him.

During the two-hour inspection tour, Johnny carried a filthy little girl in his arms or on his shoulders. She had come running up to him when we arrived, and he had scooped her up in his arms. They were obviously good friends.

At last we were alone in the jeep again, plowing sand and going back to "civilization." Not thinking what I was saying, I blurted out, "That girl was dirty!" My comment upset Johnny so much that he almost lost control of the jeep. "She's a lovely girl!" he said several times. I agreed and apologized. Then there was silence.

After a long time, he asked, "Peter, was she really dirty?" I said I didn't want to rub it in, but, yes, she was filthy dirty from head to foot. Then he commented, "Isn't it interesting? When I came here two years ago, I thought all the people were dirty. Now I don't see that anymore!"

Instantly the penny dropped. I knew why the people loved Johnny and why they did not want me to take him away. He identified with them. Because of that, more things were happening in that community than improved animal husbandry and new varieties of vegetables in their gardens. They were comparing the Koran with the Bible, Mohammed with Jesus, and together searching for more meaningful lives.

God's incarnation was identification with us. In the incarnation, God gave everything; he gave himself. Suppose we as Christians, no matter how loudly or eloquently we proclaim the good news, do not identify with our fellow human beings as God did. Then the incarnation is nothing more for us than a fancy theological word without meaning.

Lord, you say that when we minister to people who are hungry, thirsty, strangers, naked, sick, and in prison, then we serve you. Help us now, in the evening of our lives, to also minister to the lonely, the confused, the angry, and those who have so little hope. Lord, give us the grace to serve by identifying with them. Help us to love as you loved.

41

The Opposite
of Stealing

*Thieves must give up stealing; rather let them labor
and work honestly with their own hands, so as to
have something to share with the needy.*
—Paul, in Ephesians 4:28

We came home and found the door open, with the door-
knob ripped off and lying on the ground nearby. A thief had
broken into our house. The thief found no money but had
made off with some household items and a valuable quilt.

We wondered why anyone would do such a thing and
concluded that it could be the lack of proper home training. It may have started early in that person's life. Actions,
however small and insignificant, have a way of becoming
habits that shape our character and determine our life.

A friend showed us his little vegetable garden, located
under a mammoth tree. Surely he knew that the tree's root
system robbed the vegetables of vital nourishment, and the
leaves kept the sun out. I asked him why he had placed his
garden in this strange place.

He said he hadn't done that. When he planted the garden years ago, no tree was there. Then one day he noticed
a little volunteer plant growing up among the cabbages. He
meant to pull it out but never got around to it. Standing
there with his arms stretched out like the branches of the
tree and looking up to its height, he said, "It just got away
from me!"

I thought, *How funny.* How apt a picture of little sins like stealing. They start small and then just get away from us. His habit of ignoring the tree caught up with him. Likewise, someone who starts in with small thefts may develop a big problem with stealing, perhaps from greed, or from a mental disorder, kleptomania.

Sometimes stealing seems necessary for survival. In Africa, a man knocked on the door of an MCC couple's house one morning and asked if they had found a pair of glasses in their home. They asked him if he had been there the previous night and stolen their radio and tape recorder. He confessed that he had done so, but he pleaded with them for the glasses. Without them, he couldn't see, and he was too poor to buy another pair. He likely had trouble finding an honest job.

People in the developing world have said that we North Americans and Europeans are rich at their expense. They are poor because we determine the price of coffee, bananas, and other products they sell us. They claim we do not give them a fair price.

There are many kinds of thievery. Breaking in and stealing is one kind, but there are more sophisticated ways of doing it, like underpaying employees, cheating on income tax, paying kickbacks or graft, or beating telephone companies out of millions of dollars by electronic scams. Our ancestors (and eventually us) benefited from land often wrested unfairly from Native Americans.

A newspaper reported that thieves took mink coats from ladies playing bingo in a church in New York City. The writer hinted that perhaps those mink-coated ladies were rich at the expense of the poor. There is more than one kind of thievery.

Obviously, there is also more than one response. In the case of direct stealing, most North Americans first think of punishment. That is why our jails are overcrowded. More and more people are seeing the futility of this system based on revenge. They advocate for a redemptive way of dealing with criminals. Some call it *restorative justice.*

This is where you and I can help. It's something like this: Suppose you have an orchard and a thief steals your apples. It's the duty of the police to apprehend the thief, but it's the responsibility of the Christian and the church to turn the thief around so he doesn't want to steal anymore.

The eighth commandment says, "You shall not steal!" That's in the Old Testament (Exod. 20:15). When we get to the New Testament, that commandment still stands. But we are to do even better. This is the sense of what Paul tells the Ephesians:

"Before you became Christians, you used to steal from other people. A lot of your stealing was done at the public baths. Now that you are Christians, you have stopped stealing. You are working with your own hands to make an honest living. That's two good steps, but it's not enough. Now you must take a third step: you must give away and share with the poor."

One can almost hear some of those early Christians complaining, "But, Brother Paul, isn't that going a bit too far? Aren't you preaching an upside-down kingdom?"

Yes, he was (Acts 17:6). The opposite of stealing is not just to stop stealing and to earn your own living; the opposite of stealing is to work and save so that you can share with the needy. Before we were believers, we stole; now as Christians, we give.

I have never heard a sermon on Ephesians 4:28 nor have I preached one. We simply assume that the people in our churches were not thieves at one time. It often was different in the early church, as people of various backgrounds and lifestyles were converted.

Still, I find it fascinating that Paul turns their experience around from taking to giving, from thinking of self to concern for others. No wonder the early Christians were seen as radicals, thought to be a bit out of touch with reality.

Can seniors learn something from this? We can search our souls about the stealing part. I hope we have earned our money honestly, fairly, and by the sweat of our brows. However, some of us have somewhat more than we need. Should we be more generous? Can we say that we worked hard and saved our money so that we would "have something to share with the needy"?

You have blessed us, Lord, so that we can pay our bills and have some left over. We want to be good stewards, but we also are concerned that we not become a burden to others. Show us, Lord, how much we need to keep and how much we can give to the poor. Thank you!

42

Living in the As-If Mode

He has rescued us from the power of darkness and transferred us into the kingdom of his beloved Son.
—Paul, in Colossians 1:13

Suppose a king and queen were to adopt a deserted orphan child found in the street, take the child to their royal palace, give the child a bath, shampoo, and clean clothes, and sign all the legal adoption papers. The child would then be a prince or princess. The child would have a lot to learn, from proper table manners to correct speech, but would always have the status of royalty.

Some Germans say, "Werde was du bist (become what you are)." The child might use street language and have bad table manners until the royal training took place. Yet nothing would change the fact that the child had been transferred from the status of a deserted orphan to that of being royalty, in the family of a king and queen. This child would be living *as if* born into the royal family.

To live in the *as-if* mode suggests that the kingdom of God has already come and that we are in it. We are already transferred, as Paul puts it, from the kingdom of darkness into the kingdom of God's beloved Son. Our status is no longer the same. We may still have to change a lot and become what we are, but nothing can alter the fact that we are already in the kingdom of God.

We are called to live in the as-if mode. This means to be compassionate, to love, to be peaceful, to always be ready to share, to forgive, to serve, and to live by other virtues of God's kingdom.

The response of the world is that this is crazy. In his book *The Success Fantasy,* Tony Campolo tells about eating in a restaurant in Haiti, the poorest country in the Western hemisphere. The waiter brought the food, and Tony was about to start eating. Suddenly eight children had their noses pressed against the window near his table. They all looked hungry and stared at his food. The moment the waiter saw them, he pulled down the shade and told Tony, "Enjoy your meal! Don't let them bother you!"

Tony comments, "Isn't that what we all do? We pull down the blinds so we don't have to look at the poor and hungry of the world." We excuse ourselves: "It's crazy to think we could feed all those hungry people."

While the world says it is crazy to attempt to live in the as-if mode, many Christians say it is impossible. Nevertheless, whether crazy or impossible is not our concern because we have no choice. The Bible commands us to live in the as-if mode. This is binding for the followers of Jesus. Furthermore, it is the only sane and sensible alternative to the destructive and futile lifestyle of our society.

We know that living in the as-if mode can have serious consequences: Jesus, Gandhi, King, the Anabaptists, and many others have gotten themselves killed trying to do it. Peter said:

> Beloved, do not be surprised at the fiery ordeal that is taking place among you to test you, as though something strange were happening to you. . . . If you are reviled for the name of Christ, you are blessed. (1 Pet. 4:12, 14)

When we said yes to Jesus in baptism, something wonderful and drastic happened. Paul explains, "When you were buried with him in baptism, you were also raised with him through faith" (Col. 2:12). This is clear in the symbolic drowning through baptism, especially dramatized by immersion. Believers go under the water, showing that they die to the old life of sin. By God's grace in Christ, they come up a new person.

Peter makes the same point from a different perspective: "You are a chosen race, a royal priesthood, a holy nation, God's own people. . . . Once you were not a people, but now you are God's people" (1 Pet. 2:9-10).

At this point, we connect with young people again. Popular culture has told them that the big divide is death, and they believe it. Everything changes when we die. That's the big watershed. Now we are on this side, and then we are on the other side of the grave. That is the big change awaiting all of us.

Kindly but firmly, we must tell the youth that is not true. In some ways, death changes little. If we have lived without God on this side of the grave, we will be without God on the other side, and the Bible has a name for that place. If we have lived with Jesus before death, we will see him and rejoice after death.

The big divide is not death but when we say YES to Jesus. Paul says it most emphatically: "So if anyone is in Christ, there is a new creation: everything old has passed away; see, everything has become new!" (2 Cor. 5:17). That is when everything changes. We are transferred from darkness into light, from being orphans in the gutter to being welcomed into the king's palace.

In this new creation, our goals in life change, our values change, and our purpose for living changes. We start living in the as-if mode, living as if the kingdom of God has already come because it *has* come. It has not come in its fullness, but it is already here. Theologians talk about the kingdom being here "already but not yet" completely fulfilled. The child has been adopted by royalty but still has to learn to live and behave like a prince or princess.

The world cannot understand our as-if faith and lifestyle. That is why the world is trying so hard to lure and push us into its mold, to get us to live by its standards and values. The church also has trouble with as-if faith and lifestyle. That is why some teach that the Sermon on the Mount is not for us except to make us feel guilty or for a future "dispensation." But Jesus surely wanted his disciples to live that way then and wants us to live that way now, regardless of consequences.

We are to be the salt of the earth, the light of the world, a city built on a hill for everyone to see (Matt. 5:13-14). We are to turn the other cheek, go the second mile, and forgive those who offend us (5:39, 41; 6:12). We are to love the enemy (5:44). This is radical.

Most Anabaptists believed all this and tried to practice it in the sixteenth century. That's why they are called the "radical left wing of the Reformation." They actually tried to live in the as-if mode: they believed that the kingdom of God had come and that they were in it. The kingdom was already here but was not yet in its fullness. They were children of God, yet they were still in this world, trying to become what they were.

This is the message for our young people. Share it with them. Make sure they understand that death is simply a door through which we must all pass to the other side, but passing through that door will change little. As we are here, so we will be over there. The big divide is when we commit ourselves to Jesus Christ as Savior and Lord and start living in the as-if mode.

Eternal God, you have planted in us the yearning for a fuller and more satisfying life. You have given us a glimpse, just a taste of the life that will be ours one day, provided that we live now in the as-if mode. Thank you for that foretaste and the assurance that the rest will follow.

43

The Taste of New Wine

Neither is new wine put into old wineskins;
otherwise, the skins burst, and the wine is spilled,
and the skins are destroyed; but new wine is put
into fresh wineskins, and so both are preserved.
—Jesus, in Matthew 9:17

Perhaps this is a message for us seniors. Jesus is replying to people who have asked why John's disciples and the Pharisees fast, but Jesus' disciples do not (Mark 2:18). He is challenging these status-quo people to take another look at tradition and consider breaking into new life with new forms of expression.

I know nothing about wine, but I think I know what Jesus was talking about in the Matthew text. In typical picture language, he is saying something like this:

"You people all know at least two things about wine. First, new wine ferments and produces gas. The gas puts pressure on the container, the wineskin. Second, new wineskins are elastic, but old wineskins get hard and brittle. They won't expand with the pressure of the fermenting wine, so they split. A third and obvious point is that when they break, there is a double loss: both the wineskin and the wine are gone."

The people understood the implication. Jesus was saying that their traditions and laws were like the old wineskins; they couldn't contain anything new. They resented that. They were furious. They defended their old ways, like Tevye in *Fiddler on the Roof* saying repeatedly, "Tradition, tradition!"

Tradition is not all bad. Without tradition, we would have to invent the wheel again with every new generation. There are excellent personal and family traditions, as well as church and national ones. Many traditions should be preserved. The secret is to know which are worth keeping and which have served their purpose and should be discarded. That's a tough one for seniors, who usually tend to hang onto their old wineskins longer than their children and grandchildren do.

Some people always resist the new. They were against the railroad, the automobile, the radio, and television. If Copernicus were living today, they would shout him down just as people did in the early sixteenth century. He announced that the earth rotates daily on its axis and goes around the sun each year. Even the pope said that wasn't true. The idea of the earth moving was absurd; anybody could see that the sun moves around the earth.

When Jonas Hanway invented an umbrella in England, the people shouted obscenities at him and pelted him with stones. Another new thing came from England: the Sunday school. When it arrived in North America, many people resisted it. One Mennonite preacher wrote a pamphlet entitled "35 Biblical Reasons Why the Sunday School Is of the Devil."

One look at this phenomenon of resisting change, and we know that we are not dealing with something trivial or academic. This is real and of crucial importance. The Pharisees knew it was important when Jesus mentioned the new wine and the old wineskins, and we know it today. The problem of resisting change, of opposing the new, is compounded by the fact that just as the natural world abhors a vacuum, so does the spiritual world.

The apostle Paul knew that empty heads and hearts don't stay empty; they fill up with something. That is why he urged the Ephesians, "Do not get drunk with wine, . . . but be filled with the Spirit" (5:18). They understood Paul: "Make your choice, it's either one or the other, the spirit of the world or the Spirit of God."

Elfrieda and I tasted "new wine" during and after the war in voluntary service: We were rescuing old people and children from bombed cities in England, feeding and clothing war victims in Holland, and moving refugees from Russia to South America. With joy and new vitality, we sang, "I feel the winds of God today; Today my sail I spread!" God's "wind [Spirit] blows where it chooses" (John 3:8).

Now as octogenarians, our challenge is to have our wineskins ready so that God can once more pour new wine into them. God gives the new wine. It is our responsibility to see that we have new wineskins. We will need them, because—

1. Moving into retirement is a totally different ball game from the ordered routine of life in the family and at the workplace. Unless we are mentally and physically prepared for change, our old wineskins are going to crack and break.

2. We are entering the final phase of our lives when our relationships with our children and grandchildren need to be reevaluated and adjusted to meet current needs.

3. We will suddenly find ourselves with lots of time on our hands, drastically reduced responsibilities, and the frightening prospect of being bored.

4. Now we have the freedom and wonderful opportunities to pass on the lessons we have learned about life, other people, and ourselves.

5. The old-wineskin mentality and status-quo people are easy prey for extremes, splintering, and the spirit of the world.

6. We have experienced numerous transformations within ourselves that have been road signs to a fuller and richer life. Now is the time to move out in that direction.

7. We are close enough to the final edge of life to sense

the great mystery of passing into the beyond.

8. We need to get new wineskins for ourselves because God is not yet finished with us.

Almighty God, I thank you that even now, in the evening of my life, you challenge me to take a careful look at things that might need changing. You know how I tend to resist change. Forgive me, Lord. Open my eyes to see new truth, open my mind to recognize and accept good changes, and open my heart to receive you in a new way. Spare me, Lord, from spiritual blindness, from being content with things just as they are. I am getting old, but I don't want to be an old wineskin.

44

Why Not Travel?

*Come now, you who say, "Today or tomorrow we
will go to such and such a town. . . ." Yet you do not
even know what tomorrow will bring. . . . Instead
you ought to say, "If the Lord wishes, we will live
and do this or that."*
—James 4:13-15

Many people look forward to travel in their retirement
years. And why not? Elderhostel, for example, combines
travel with education or volunteer opportunities. If one can
afford it and health permits it, travel can be fun and certainly educational.

We learn about food, for example. In Russia, I found out
that they make five kinds of borscht, not just the recipe we
used at home. In India, I learned to eat rice with my fingers;
in Morocco, I discovered the delicious taste of couscous.

I also discovered that when you are served a sheep's eye,
you can't bite it. It's not firm enough to be cracked, it's too
slippery, and it won't squash. It'll glitch around in your
mouth like a candy, from one side to the other.

You must also remember that while a sheep produces lots
of mutton, it contributes only two eyes, so they are special.
If the host gives you a sheep's eye, accept it gratefully. It's
his way of saying that you're his honored guest. Then say a
silent prayer, "Lord, help me," and do it right. Everybody at
the table, especially the host, will be watching you. They
want to be sure you enjoy that specialty.

Don't just gulp it down. That would be rude. Have you no manners at all? Roll it around over your tongue. Smile as you do it. Look at the other people around the table and nod several times to your host. You get the idea. After a while, you can swallow it. *Guten Appetit!*

On the other hand, maybe you want to be like the woman from Los Angeles at the table next to ours in a Moscow restaurant. She heard us talking English and asked where we were from and whether we were eating Russian food. When we told her we were and that it was quite good, she told us to be more careful.

She said she never touches local food. When traveling in foreign countries, she only asks for hot water to dissolve her little package of concentrate brought from California. Then she knows she won't get sick. How exciting!

You can avoid contact with the local people by staying at the International Hilton and listening to what "professional" tour guides tell you. One such traveler told me with excitement how good it felt that in Geneva, Switzerland, right in the heart of the city, he had found a McDonald's restaurant.

There is another way. A woman in Algeria offered us buttermilk. We were walking along, my colleague and I, after a typical couscous dinner, exploring the yard of our host. There were sheep and shacks, dirt and weeds, and suddenly I heard the familiar ugh-ugh sounds of a butter churn!

Looking over the wall, we saw a woman making butter. She was one of the host's three wives, obviously not his favorite or she wouldn't be out there. She was sitting on the ground, in the dirt and dust, with sheep and dung all around her. She had a simple tripod made of three sticks. Hanging from the top of the tripod was a sheepskin, belly up, filled with cream.

With a jerk, she pushed it away from herself, and the contents inside made an ugh sound as it left her and an ugh sound as it swung back again. Ugh-ugh, ugh-ugh, as she pushed it away and it came right back, ugh-ugh. I could tell by the sound of the ughs that it was almost finished; the butter was separating from the buttermilk.

Just then she saw us. Instantly she got up, gave us a big smile, and went looking for something in the dirt and weeds among the sheep. She found it: a rusty old tin can. She wiped it out with the edge of her long skirt, and for extra cleanliness, she blew on it. Next, she opened one end of the sheepskin to drain out some buttermilk for us. I wished she had opened it at the neck instead of the other end, but never mind.

Then she brought us the buttermilk treat, in a rusty tin, with threads of sheep's wool, and all. In keeping with her culture and upbringing, the Algerian woman did exactly what Elflrieda does when unexpected guests arrive at our house in Pennsylvania: she served the guests a drink.

Oh, yes, travel can be interesting and educational—unless you are like the man from Kansas who visited us in Germany. He was traveling around the world. He had been to Africa, India, Japan, China, and Russia. Europe was his last stop. Our girls were excited, wanting to hear his stories. Elfrieda served a delicious dinner. As we were enjoying the dessert, we asked him about his travels. This is how the conversation went:

"So you're traveling around the world. How exciting! Could you tell us about some of your experiences in India?" We waited. He looked at each of us as if he wanted to say, "Why are you doing this to me?" At last he spoke: "Oh, my! India! That's sure different! Sure is different!" More silence. We waited. Elfrieda poured another cup of coffee.

After a while I asked, "Could you perhaps tell us something about Japan? I believe that's very different from India?" Again a long silence. Then at last he said, "Sure is; you can say that again. You're right, Japan is very different from India." We waited. The girls began to look at each other and then tried to read our faces. Nothing happened.

Eventually I continued prodding: "Elfrieda and I were both born in Russia. I've been back there six times. What can you tell us about the places you visited in the Soviet Union?" By this time, we didn't expect him to tell us anything, and he didn't. He just said several times, "My, oh, my, what a country! What a country! Sure is different!"

When he was gone, we looked at each other as if to say, "Can you believe it? He has traveled around the world and has nothing to say!" Then we all burst out laughing. It must have been more than thirty years ago. Our girls were small then, but they still remember it to this day. Whenever that evening with the world traveler is mentioned, we don't quite know whether we should laugh or cry.

Travel can teach us several valuable lessons:

1. The world is big and beautiful and interesting. God gave us legs so we can wander, eyes so we can see his marvelous creation, and ears so we can hear strange and lovely sounds. I have a nose so I can tell when I'm in the *souk*, the Arabic market; and I have taste buds so I know the difference between apple pie and couscous. What a waste of God's creation and neglect of our five senses if we don't experience some of the variety in the world!

2. When we travel, we discover who we are and why we were made with the capacity to dream dreams. We discover a degree of sameness in all people in spite of striking and sometimes startling differences. We pick up ideas and find handles for making this world a bit more sane, loving, and peaceful. We more fully realize that we are not the center of the universe. In the eyes of others, we are just as odd and funny as they appear to us, and sometimes we are just as exasperatingly difficult.

3. When we travel, we have the opportunity to share the good news of Jesus with people who do not know him. We

can fellowship with those who do know and love Jesus Christ; we can learn from each other and encourage each other.

4. Suppose we've seen exotic places, eaten the strangest foods, and heard the most musical languages. We've been on the mountains, in the deserts, and on the high seas. We've flown the skies and seen the wonders of the world. Nevertheless, we know in our hearts that we are going to be the happiest people in the world when we get home. As the popular song says, "Highways are happy ways, when they lead the way to home. Highways bring happy days, to the waiting hearts at home!"

5. Finally, we know that back home we are the most blessed of all people because we have loving families and friends who want to hear about our experiences. They may prod us to tell them just one more story. They ask questions when they see our pictures or videos. They are dreaming about the day when they, too, will retire and can go and see God's beautiful world.

O Lord, how beautiful you have made your world! The people are so strange and funny, and yet so much like myself. How did you do all that? How did you create the animals and birds, the mountains and oceans? Thank you for letting me experience it all with my five senses. Thank you for the hints you have given us that this is only a foretaste of what is waiting for us in glory.

45

Never Too Old to Play or Pray

There is nothing better for them than to be happy and enjoy themselves as long as they live.
—The Teacher, in Ecclesiastes 3:12

Pray without ceasing.
—Paul, in 1 Thessalonians 5:17

Playing comes naturally; praying has to be learned. Children love to play. They play with their toes when they are still in the crib and with almost anything as soon as they are out of it. I have seen poor children in Africa play with a stick and a little wheel on the end of it. They would take turns endlessly amusing themselves by holding the stick in their hand and running that little wheel as fast as they could along the dusty road.

When do seniors stop playing and why? From conversations with older people, I gather that some stopped playing early in life, when they were married or entered business. They didn't have time for such foolish things. Little did they know that they were taking one of their first giant steps into premature aging. There are other reasons for not playing. In my background, it was a cultural phenomenon.

My father never played with me, at least not that I remember. He was a grown-up, head of the household, provider, leader, and model; for him to get down on the floor with a little child was unbecoming. It just wasn't done. Fathers did not play ball with their older children. Mothers would play with their babies but let the rest of the children to their own games—unless they squabbled and needed her to settle matters. What a pity! Today we are more enlightened on that matter.

When we were visiting the famous Rijksmuseum in Amsterdam, we stopped in front of Rembrandt's imposing painting, *The Nightwatch*. It is huge and there is so much to see. Elfrieda and I were studying it and whispering quietly to each other when a man beside us said in a loud voice, "That's not so special. Anyone could paint that!" We were stunned, as were the other visitors. Nobody said a word. The crowd scattered.

In discussing the incident later, we realized that the man had not made a comment about the picture as much as about himself. If he had known anything about art, he would not have said what he did.

When it comes to aging, many people know more about it than they admit. That may be worse than not knowing that one does not know, like that man in Amsterdam. They are in denial and present themselves as escaping the aging process. They still play the old games of being "thirty and holding," instead of accepting their age and thanking God for it. Society especially pressures women to deny their age.

Some say that age is a matter of the mind: if you don't mind, it doesn't matter. That seems to be the motto of many seniors who are avid players of one kind of game or another. A retired friend, Gordon Sprunger, in Berne, Indiana, was playing shuffleboard when he noticed that a nurse was recording their shots. His immediate reaction was that they didn't need a nurse to keep score for some old duffers pushing disks around.

Gordon didn't know that she was from a nearby hospital and interested in gerontology. When he found out that she was serious about what she was doing, he wrote her this poem:

To a Geriatric Nurse
The nurse said her name was Kim, when we met,
she'd come to observe the geriatric set,
to watch them at work, to watch them at play,
to see how they spend a typical day.
They have games and crafts and exercise
and reading and study to make them wise.
Some are into serious walking,
others prefer just sitting and talking.
Then there are those who spend their time
in writing verses and making rhyme.
Still others enjoy afternoon naps.
Some struggle with bottles with childproof caps.
Some may like flowers or a vegetable garden.
All these they can do as their arteries harden.
Then there's Geritol, Tylenol, and also Ben Gay,
these too are a part of an oldster's day.
After seeing all this and thinking it through,
is there any conclusion apparent to you?
Or do you, at last, surprisingly find
that aging is mainly a state of the mind?

(In *Rhyme Doesn't Pay*, © Gordon Sprunger, used by permission)

What physical exercise does for the body, mental exercise does for the mind. To keep their minds sharp, many seniors play table games. The list of good games is long: checkers, Chinese checkers, Yahtzee, Mancala, Monopoly, Rummicube, card games of all kinds, and chess.

Chess needs to be in a separate category. I admit that I am prejudiced. So is the excellent *Encyclopedia Britannica*, with four pages telling about the Baptists, for example, and fourteen pages on chess. There is evidence that it originated in China before the second century B.C., then spread to India much later.

Elfrieda and I count chess as our favorite game. The world would be a better place if everyone would "play chess, not war." We used to keep score with pencil and paper. Then we simply took two cups with ten pennies in each. The loser would surrender one penny to the winner. Over a period of ten years, we have never succeeded in emptying all the pennies from one cup into the other. We are that even in our chess skills.

If we are not too old to play, we are not too old to pray. Praying has to be learned. We teach children to pray before meals and at bedtime. The disciples went to Jesus and said, "Lord, teach us to pray" (Luke 11:1). Prayer includes thanksgiving for blessings and intercession for others. The two major components are praise and petition.

I praise God for being the Creator and Sustainer of the universe and all life on earth. I petition God because I am weak and God is strong. I need God's sustaining power and guidance. My family and friends also need God's sustaining power and guidance.

These feelings of need are universal and experienced by people everywhere and at all times. In ignorance, people from ancient times turned to worshiping false gods of stone or wood. In America today, astrology, fortune telling, and other psychic tricks have become a substitute religion for millions of people. Twenty years ago there were about 1,000 professional astrologers in the United States; today there are more than 5,000. Each year, people buy more than 20 million astrological books. Many people surf for horoscopes on the Internet.

So what shall it be, prayer or astrology? Since nature abhors a vacuum, it could easily be the horoscope if it is not prayer. However, to pray without ceasing does not mean to be on our knees all the time. There are some people who take that literally and do nothing but pray all day.

When we were visiting our daughter, Rebecca, in Lesotho, we frequently passed a Catholic convent where nuns seemed to be doing nothing but praying. They would recite thousands of Ave Marias or Hail Marys in endless succession. Praying was their life's mission.

We probably don't pray enough or we pray too mechanically. Jesus was talking about such people when he said, "When you are praying, do not heap up empty phrases as the Gentiles do; for they think that they will be heard because of their many words" (Matt. 6:7).

A young man from Germany came to the United States as an exchange visitor for a year. He had the good fortune to be placed in a family where morning devotions were something that everyone participated in, looked forward to, and enjoyed. The experience was so unlike in his family. This is how he described it:

> Ever since I can remember, my father would sit at the head of the table. After breakfast he would tear off the day's sheet from a Scripture calendar, read the designated Bible verse and the comments, and then recite the Lord's Prayer. I am now 23 years old. With 365 days in the year, I suppose I have heard my dad say the Lord's Prayer about 8,395 times.
>
> When I returned after my year in the States, where I had experienced such a wonderful spiritual renewal, I just about screamed that first morning back home at the breakfast table. You can't imagine how it feels to hear the same prayer droned out mechanically day after day all your life. I just knew something had to be done about it.

He knew better than to confront his father, who was unaware that his recitations were meaningless. So the son spoke to his sister about his wonderful experience in the States and about his concern to change things at home without bringing down the roof. The sister, using good psychology and diplomacy, did not confront her father but spoke to her mother. The mother spoke to her husband.

I asked what happened. His face lit up and he smiled. "Everything is changed. Now all four of us, my parents, my sister, and I, take part in the devotions. We take turns reading and praying." With a bit of a grin, he added, "I don't think the angels in heaven are unhappy that we have not said the Lord's Prayer for months."

Alta Mae Erb of Scottdale, Pennsylvania, had a similar and yet different problem. She came to me one day with an unusual request. I knew her as a retired teacher and a devout Christian who read her Bible, prayed, and attended church regularly. I was surprised that she asked me to help her with her prayer life. This is how she explained her situation.

> I want to pray for the missionaries and for the hundreds of volunteers serving around the world with MCC, but I don't know their names or where they are serving. I don't know anything about their programs or their problems. How can I pray intelligently for them when I am so ignorant?

Then she said something that really made me smile. She confessed that she was so tired of just lumping it all together and praying, "Dear God, bless all those missionaries and MCC workers." She added quite seriously, "I think God is tired of it, too."

I decided to present her with the *MCC Annual Workbook* of almost a hundred pages. It listed some fifty countries, hundreds of projects, budget figures and problems or, as we in MCC prefer to say, challenges galore. In addition, I gave her a list of almost a thousand volunteers and promised that I would get a similar list of the missionaries.

I was sure she would throw up her arms and protest that this was too much. To my surprise, she accepted the documents gratefully, saying that they would be a great help to her in her prayer life.

From time to time, I wondered what she was doing with all that information. When I visited Alta again, she told me with a radiant smile that her prayer life had changed since she had those documents. She could make specific petitions for the workers and thank and praise God for them and their service. I asked her to explain, to give me a feel for the change. What she said was both a surprise and a lesson for me.

"No more of those generic prayers. No more lumping everything together and just asking God to bless the whole lot. First, I spend about half an hour reading the Bible. Then I take the *MCC Workbook*."

She picked it up and showed me where the bookmark was placed. "Now I am in South America. This morning after I read the Bible, I read the report on Brazil. Some parts I had to read several times to really understand them. When I know what the workers are doing there, when I understand their assignments and their problems, their hopes and their dreams, and when I know their names—then I start praying for them, naming them one at a time.

When she thanked me again for the two documents, I felt a bit guilty, but at the same time I felt inspired and profoundly humbled. I had never prayed like that myself, and I was her pastor. Alta was ninety-three years old. Then she told me that after spending about an hour reading the Bible and the reports, meditating, and praying, she would pick up her needle and go to work making quilts for MCC to distribute to poor people. What a woman! What an inspiration to me!

O Lord, where would I be if I couldn't play and pray anymore? Thank you from the depths of my soul.

46

The Death of a Spouse

The LORD is near to all who call on him,
to all who call on him in truth.
He fulfills the desire of all who fear him;
he also hears their cry, and saves them.
—David, in Psalm 145:18-19

It is almost twelve o'clock, and I expect to hear Elfrieda call from the kitchen that dinner will be ready in a few minutes. I cannot imagine it otherwise. We have been married fifty-five years. Oh, I do remember coming home one time and wondering why she was nowhere to be seen—only to realize with a shock that I had left her at church. Frequently, we have been separated for days or even weeks, during our service with MCC.

One time, for example, she escorted a shipload of refugees to South America while I stayed in Europe to prepare another load. Her ship, the ill-fated *Charlton Monarch,* foundered, and they drifted on the Atlantic without power or enough food. Eventually they were towed into a distant port. Instead of the usual two or three weeks, that journey lasted five weeks.

During all that time, we had no communication from her because of the ship's power failure. We were separated for a couple of months, then we met again. What a rejoicing that was! To be separated from your spouse for a few months is one thing; to be separated permanently is something we have not yet experienced. We are not looking forward to it.

In his book, *The Death of a Wife,* Robert L. Vogt says,

"Nothing in marriage or in family life prepares you for that first time you enter an empty house after the death of a spouse." His house and his life seemed empty. He was more alone than he had ever imagined possible.

Vogt has a powerful message for the husband and wife who live together, not quite happy and not too unhappy, either. They were not really together as one in love but not unhappy enough to separate. He confesses, "Each of us had honest religious feelings. Yet we often prayed as two, seldom as one. Our religion was mostly 'me-and-God,' when it should have been 'we-and-God.'"

Then came Vogt's belated realization:

> We now pray together always. Death creates unity in our prayer. Now I spend time in church with you, in fact I am with you all the time. The separation of death paradoxically brings many things together.

How wonderful and how sad! Why do married couples not experience this kind of unity and togetherness more during their lifetime?

Ralph Waldo Emerson well describes a successful life:

> To laugh often and much,
> to win respect of intelligent people
> and the affection of children;
> to earn the appreciation of honest critics
> and endure the betrayal of false friends;
> to appreciate beauty;
> to find the best in others;
> to leave the world a bit better,
> whether by a healthy child,
> a garden patch, or a
> redeemed social condition;
> to know even one life
> has breathed easier
> because you have lived.
> This is to have succeeded.

There is a lot of speculation about death, an afterlife or resurrection, and the return of the Lord. Notwithstanding all the predictions, no one knows the time of the End. Jesus said it would come like a thief in the night, at an unexpected hour (Luke 12:40). So it could be soon, this year, or a thousand years from now. We don't know.

I surprised one audience when I said it would be within the next twenty years. My explanation was simple. At 85, I do not expect to live longer than that. When I go to be with the Lord, or when the Lord returns to earth, that is all the same as far as my life is concerned. For me, it will be the end of life on earth and the beginning of life elsewhere.

I can safely say that as far as I am concerned, the Lord will return *for me* within the next twenty years, likely the next ten years. Whether twenty, ten, or one year, the fact remains: many of us will either leave a spouse mourning or we will be left to mourn.

When a life ends, loved ones grieve. Some pretend to go on as before, yet none of us will be exempt from grief. Men often deny and delay grieving—not a healthy way of dealing with it. In *Grief Observed,* C. S. Lewis says, "Bereavement is a universal and integral part of our experience of love. It follows death as normally as marriage follows courtship."

The authors of *Getting to the Other Side of Grief* say, "Don't avoid pain—attack it. Don't endure the grief—manage it." They also discredit the common notion that time will heal grief. Either you work through it, with God's help, or the grieving process extends. With God's help, we can do something about our loneliness; we can do something about interrupted family relationships. We can gather new strength from friends and churches.

Johann Christoph Arnold wrote one of the best books on death and grieving: *I Tell You a Mystery.* He tells stories of people he has known and counseled, how they went through suffering and grief to continue living in hope and even in joy. The death of a spouse is not and should not be the end of our positive and purposeful living.

As leader of the Bruderhof Communities, he has been close to many suffering and dying people. In the book's introduction, Arnold says,

> The people in this book lived life to the full—not for themselves, but for others. In serving a cause greater than themselves, they found the pearl of great price and sold all they had for it. In return, they received a sense of purpose and inner direction, courage, and even joy in the face of suffering and death. They lived and strived for the love that, as John says, "casts out fear," and because of this they were able to meet their Maker with peace of heart and mind.

Only God knows which spouse will die first. If both spouses are truly living for the love that casts out fear, then "parting is such sweet sorrow" (Shakespeare); we both are wrapped in the arms of God. If I am left, I expect the death of my spouse to be extremely difficult and the grief to be heartrending.

I am confident, however, that the God who has sustained me this far will also help me in overcoming pain, loneliness, and grief. I base this assurance on God's promises and my experiences. God declares, "I will never leave you or forsake you" (Heb. 13:5). He means it, and I believe him.

For our life together in marriage, we thank you, Lord. When that hour of separation comes, give strength and courage for one of us to carry on alone, awaiting eternal bliss with you.

47

Woes and Joys
of Grandparenting

*Like good stewards of the manifold grace of God,
serve one another with whatever gift each of you
has received.*
—1 Peter 4:10

There is no substitute for the quiet pleasures and deep satisfaction derived from being a member of a family. The Bible starts by saying that in the beginning God, the Creator and Sustainer of all life, established the human race in families. Long passages in the Old Testament do nothing but list members of families.

For example, Genesis 10:1, 5 introduces such a list: "These are the descendants of Noah's sons, Shem, Ham, and Japheth, . . . by their families." In Leviticus 25 we see detailed instructions to Israel about keeping the year of Jubilee. Verse 10 declares, "It shall be a jubilee for you: you shall return, every one of you, to your property, and every one of you to your family."

In many parts of the world, the family still is the basic structure of society. That no longer fits much of North America, where 45 percent of new mothers in the past decade were unmarried, under the age of 20, or without a full high-school education. Where are the fathers? The children of these unmarried people often do not have a secure family life. About half the people who marry get divorced.

When divorced people remarry, the relationships of their children to the grandparents can become strained. Grandparents assume they have a natural right to a continued relationship with their grandchildren. But the new husband (more often than the wife) may not see it that way. When he sees the grandparents coming to his house, he regards the visit as interference in their lives. Yet the parties could find neutral meeting places for grandparents and grandchildren. Conflicts frequently arise between the custodial parent and the parents of the noncustodial parent (former spouse).

Today between five and seven million children in the United States are being raised by their grandparents. This has become relatively common in the postwar years. Parents and grandparents survived the Great Depression in the 1930s and WW II in the 1940s, then welcomed the relatively quiet Eisenhower years in the 1950s. They went to church, frowned on divorce, and only whispered the word *abortion*. The family unit seemed to be intact.

With the turbulent 1960s came the "God is dead" hype, "free love," revolts against authority, and a breakdown of morality.

Dr. Spock in his popular book *Baby and Child Care* called for common sense instead of rigid schedules. He said that "good-hearted parents who aren't afraid to be firm when it is necessary can get good results with either moderate strictness or moderate permissiveness. On the other hand, a strictness that comes from harsh feelings or a permissiveness that is timid or vacillating can each lead to poor results."

Nevertheless, out of reaction to earlier harsh parental discipline, many young parents leaned rather far toward permissiveness.

Some forty years later, Scott Peck reflected on the possible relationship between guilt feelings and neurosis. Parents were trying to raise guilt-free children. In *Further Along the Road Less Traveled,* Peck said, "What an awful thing to try to do to a child. . . . Our jails are filled with people who are there precisely because they do not have any guilt."

The 1970s and 1980s brought drug and gun abuse, family violence, and a general breakdown of traditional family values.

There is another obstacle to a healthy grandparent-grandchild relationship: our society has mostly relegated the aged to sideline roles. Media portray them as people in rocking chairs, feeble or infirm, detached and uninterested in the real world, unemployed and unoccupied. Though some may fit this image, it is an unfair caricature.

Even the government, in defining unemployment, classifies a retired but healthy person who volunteers to work 36 hours a week as "unemployed." In a society driven by money and the possession of material goods, such a person is not "gainfully employed."

The issue of communication is another factor in a healthy grandparent-grandchild relationship. I was anxious about communication as our five grandchildren grew older. When they were small, playing with them was easy and came naturally. When they were of school age, we could talk about their friends and experiences in school. Sometimes we reached back into our own memories and told how it was in our day.

As they were growing up, I began to wonder if the time would come when we would have nothing to talk about. Would our worlds be so far apart that they would not want to come to our house anymore? I thought the day would come when they would protest, "Oh, no! Not Opa and Oma's place again!"

Our grandchildren became teenagers and started moving into their twenties; they still come to visit. They telephone and send e-mails, and our hearts overflow with thanksgiving. This is unmerited grace. It is a source of deep satisfaction and joy that we do not take for granted.

In some families, it is a foregone conclusion that the grandparent-grandchild relationship is going to be rocky. That relationship might not even exist because of the inherited family climate. People do influence each other. At our seniors' dinner table, I told a Tolstoy story I had just read. He describes how two families lived in tension beside each other. It all started over one egg.

Ivan's hen flew over the fence and laid an egg in Gabriel's garden. When Ivan's wife knocked on Gabriel's door and asked for permission to gather the egg, he told her to go home and mind her own business. She was not to go tramping through their garden looking for a stupid egg.

Soon this ugly mood spread to the children. Instead of playing together as before, they began to avoid each other. Sometimes they fought over nothing. Then the ugly mood that started with Gabriel spread to Ivan. After the men quarreled, they faced each other in court.

The judge sentenced Ivan to thirty lashes. Ivan mumbled outside the courthouse that the lashing would burn his back, but just let Gabriel wait—he would see some real burning. That's exactly what happened. Ivan set Gabriel's barn on fire, but the wind blew in the wrong direction. The fire also burned down all of Ivan's buildings and half the village. It all started with one egg.

Leo Tolstoy's stories are certainly true to life. A resident at my table, an old lady in her eighties, responded to the egg story by telling us that her grandmother had a quarrel with her sister over twenty-five cents. Because of that strained relationship, they never talked to each other for the rest of their lives, for forty or fifty years. When family relationships are poisoned like that, it is difficult for grandparents to enjoy their grandchildren.

Enough of the woes. Happily, these situations are the exception, not the rule. I think of how our children and grandchildren arranged for the celebration of our fiftieth wedding anniversary. They invited the people, reserved the church, had the food prepared, and put on a program of unparalleled beauty and richness, skillfully balancing the humorous with the serious, the worshipful with the reminiscing.

Similar things are happening in many families all over the country, and my heart sings for joy. There are about 65 million of us grandparents in North America today—that's a lot of celebrations!

A wise Greek philosopher said that every man in his lifetime ought to build a house. When I announced that the time had come for me to build a house, my family talked me out of it. Perhaps that was just as well. However, being a recycler by nature, I could not resist picking up boards and two-by-fours here and there.

A house burned down, leaving the door intact: the owners said it would go to the scrap heap. I took it home. Neighbor Larry was about to leave with a load of junk when I flagged him down. I salvaged several windows from that load. Never mind that they came from the back of a pickup truck.

My mother, who had nine children and did a lot of mending, saved every scrap of cloth, explaining that every seventh year a patch fits. As my pile of building material grew, so did Elfrieda's curiosity, not to say anxiety: "Peter, what are you going to do with all that stuff?" I responded, "Build a playhouse."

Finally the day came when our grandchildren, Peter and Debby, came to help me build the playhouse. First, we decided to name our structure *Little House*. Then we looked over the building material and planned the size and location. I had dreams of making it look like a Swiss chalet, but it turned out looking like a Canadian grain elevator. The proportions weren't quite right.

What fun we had! Peter, only seven years old, learned to use the saw, and Debby, five, used the hammer. They handed me nails, helped carry materials around, and were busy all the time. Oma would come with drinks and cookies, and we would all sit down and enjoy a snack, talk about the progress, and plan what to do next.

*Elfrieda and Peter at the Little House, with grandchildren Cory,
Debby, and Peter Scott*

When *Little House* was finished, it was clear to all of us
that we had done much more than just build a playhouse
out of recycled material. To be sure, we had a structure with
windows, curtains, and a flower box under the window that
actually did make it look a bit Swiss! It had a solid hard-
wood floor and a high ceiling. In addition to building a
playhouse, other things had happened in the process that
could not be photographed—things that were of more value
than the house itself.

The grandchildren had developed new skills. Peter learned
that when you hit the wrong nail, it hurts. There was a lot
of talking and listening, sharing and laughter. It was perhaps the first of many more times to follow when I felt that
real bonding between us had taken place. It took us about
a week to complete the project; it cost us next to nothing
and was done right in our backyard. *Little House* served our
grandchildren and local children for many years to come.

Often on Saturdays, we would hear an ever-so-gentle

knock on the door. We knew it would be neighborhood children, coming to ask whether they could play in *Little House*. What a privilege and joy to join them for a little while, tell them a story, and serve milk and cookies.

One summer we all piled into a rented RV and went off to a conference in Canada. When three generations travel together in close quarters day after day, it can be nerve-wracking. However, our experience was delightful. There was never a dull moment. Eventually the visiting and singing, the devotions and reading, the laughing and joking tapered off. When things got a bit quiet, we all knew it was time for the blue-light special.

Every day for a week going and a week returning, that blue night-light would be turned on as a signal to open another surprise gift package for someone in the RV. When we arrived back home, only one question was on all our minds: When can we do this again?

Picking cherries was a three-generation family activity for us each year. For a decade, around the Fourth of July we would call our friends Earl and Joyce Schutt, near Gettysburg, Pennsylvania, to inquire about the best time to come and be gleaners. The mechanical pickers shake those hundreds of cherry trees, causing about 95 percent of the cherries to drop off. There were always enough left for us to pick for ourselves and to share back home with ten or fifteen other families.

For a decade, we had cherries to eat all year round and couldn't imagine ever being without them. The fond memories, the long days of picking, the lunch breaks under the cherry trees, and the grandchildren romping around until it again was time to pick—these are unforgettable memories.

It would take too long to tell about the birthday celebrations; the joyful Christmases spent together; the trips to Fallingwater, the Bruderhof community, Sea World, museums, and heritage centers. Ten of us gathered in the workshop here at the retirement center to decorate glass plates with colorful pieces of cloth. The boys made wooden Boy Scout cars. We played mini-golf together, bowled, and swam.

How we did enjoy our trips to Canada to see farmers gathering maple sap and boiling it down into maple syrup, to ride in dog sleds, to skate, and to ski. We went to church together, becoming one in worship and praise of the God who has blessed us so abundantly. We did this with our children and grandchildren.

There are few joys in life that compare to a family experiencing togetherness. That could be togetherness in terms of our proximity one to the other, like all of us crowding into one RV or gathering around the Christmas tree, but even more it is the togetherness of minds and spirits, of hearts and souls. This has to be the pinnacle of joyous grandparenting.

The woes and joys of grandparenting are part of life, alternating like rain and sunshine. As grandparents, we need to remember that on woeful days, it is more important to be than to do, to be loving and patient than to give advice or try to take things into our own hands. When the clouds have passed and the thunder has stopped, grandparents should not hesitate to suggest constructive fun activities in which all can participate.

These can range from a picnic to a fishing expedition, from cooking to quilting, from volunteering to participating in repairing houses damaged in a disaster, and whatever strikes the fancy of grandparents and their grandchildren. It can be a great educational and bonding experience to brainstorm together and test various proposals for such joint activities. Then everyone can feel ownership in the intergenerational events.

Lord, by your example, you have shown us patience and courage, a time to remain silent, and a time to speak out. Help us to be like that as grandparents.

48
Ten Thoughts on Aging

Are not two sparrows sold for a penny? Yet not one
of them will fall to the ground apart from your
Father. . . . So do not be afraid; you are of more
value than many sparrows.
—Jesus, in Matthew 10:29, 31

Now I live among older people and have read manys books
on aging. Here are a few thoughts that have crystallized in
my mind about living the last years of life:

1. Life is a precious gift. We should live it to the full. Celebrate it.

2. Aging is a natural process. We should not fight it but accept it with thanksgiving. When asked how old I am, I can smile, give my age, and say, "Praise the Lord!"

3. At 85, I am much the same as at 35, only more so.

4. The key to a meaningful and satisfying old age is to live for others.

5. We will never know real peace in our lives unless we have forgiven everyone.

6. To laugh often is good for body and soul.

7. We must get rid of regrets by confessing to others and to God. Then we can go on no longer burdened by guilt.

8. We need to take time to dream, to have a garden or a workshop, and to spend time alone.

9. We should devote attention to our grandchildren, for their sake and for ours.

10. Staying close to God is the best way to survive aging and to be prepared for dying.

> Grow old along with me!
> The best is yet to be,
> The last of life, for which the first was made. . . .
> Youth shows but half; trust God; see all, nor be afraid!
> (Robert Browning)

Lord God, where did the years go? Yesterday I was a child, now I'm an old man. It seems as though I have accomplished so little and made so many mistakes. I'm sorry. But you have been patient and forgiving. Elfrieda has been patient and forgiving also. Thank you.

Thank you for my parents.
Thank you for my children and grandchildren.
Thank you for the church.
Thank you for troubles and pain.
Thank you for all those who challenged and encouraged me.
Thank you for giving me another chance after the accident.
Thank you for books and the computer.

Most of all, I thank you, God, for giving me life, for sustaining me all these years, for your love through Jesus Christ, and for the promise of life after death.

Soon, Lord, soon I'll leave this earth and see you. I can't even begin to imagine it; but I believe it! Wow!

I have so many questions I want to ask:
> *Why doesn't the sun cool off?*
> *How did you make everything so incredibly wonderful?*
> *How are you going to give me a new body?*

O Lord, my Lord! How I love you and long to be with you!

49

Lengthening Shadows

Who will separate us from the love of Christ? Will hardship, or distress, or persecution, or famine, or nakedness, or peril, or sword? . . . No, in all these things we are more than conquerors through him who loved us. For I am convinced that neither death, nor life, nor angels, nor rulers, nor things present, nor things to come, nor powers, nor height, nor depth, nor anything else in all creation, will be able to separate us from the love of God in Christ Jesus our Lord.
—Paul, in Romans 8:35, 37-39

Cornelius Isaak died while visiting primitive Paraguayan Indians. He had gone into the bush to find the Moro tribe and bring them the good news about Jesus. He was handing them gifts when a man stabbed him from behind with a crude wooden spear. Cornelius lay in the hospital dying. After he had said good-bye to his wife and children, he asked to be left alone.

The attending physician, our friend Dr. Rakko, told us later that though he had seen many people die, he had never seen anyone die like Cornelius Isaak. He told us about the calm and peace so evident in Cornelius during his last moments on earth.

The doctor could hear him pray and was struck by the fact that repeatedly he heard the word "Moro." Cornelius was asking God to bring the Moro Indians to himself, to lead them out of darkness into light, out of ignorance into the Truth. He was praying for the man who had killed him and for his people.

To reach that stage is evidence of God's grace; it also shows that Cornelius had prepared for the end long before it came. In his book *Learning to Die,* Samuel Gerber talks about learning to live in such a way that when that moment of departure comes, we are ready. We need to be prepared whether death sneaks up on us with slow stalking steps or falls on us suddenly, as in the case of Cornelius Isaak.

One reviewer of Gerber's book recommended it as "eminently deserving of the widest possible readership." Many agreed that it was of "consistently excellent caliber." However, one reader claimed it was the worst book on the market. My hunch is that this man reacted so negatively against the title that he didn't see the positive value of the book.

In our society, we do not talk about learning to die. Many people of retirement age have never seen another person die. It is a moot question with a mute answer, though we all know how inevitable death is for each of us.

Nowadays people rarely die in their homes, surrounded by loved ones. They die in hospitals, tended by supportive white-gowned professionals trained to prolong life as long as possible. Family representatives often are hovering nearby, ready to visit as possible.

Learning to die is entirely and 100 percent a matter of learning how to live. To do that, the following ten hints may be helpful:

1. Take care of relationships with others and with God. The greatest regret at the end of life will not be that we didn't make more money, see more of the world, finish a certain task, or accomplish some great deed. The greatest regret will be that we

fell out with someone and never made that relationship right, were not patient enough with our children, spoke or acted thoughtlessly and rudely to a friend, or were not considerate and loving enough with our spouse.

2. Avoid flirting with mammon. Money and the things we can get for money have a powerful attraction. Fed by a constant stream of commercials, we easily come to believe that certain products are essential for us, things that in former days were and in other countries are considered luxuries. The Bible often uses the word "beware" in warning us not to let the world push and pressure us into its mold.

3. Use time wisely. In this area of life, we are all equal. Whether black or white, rich or poor, educated or uneducated, we all have the same amount of time each day, though some need more of the time to gather enough to live on. Training in the right use of our time needs to begin as early as the ability to tell the time of day or spell the word *time*. Time is a precious gift, not to be wasted or killed. Time coming toward us is opportunity with hair in front but baldness behind. We can grab the opportunity as it approaches us, but once it has passed, there is no way to retrieve it.

4. Learn to control your tongue. What a gift of God that we can communicate with words and songs. How wonderful to hear someone say, "You are special" or "I love you." But the same tongue can also hurt and destroy another person. Jesus' brother James says, "The tongue is a fire!" (3:6).

The tongue also bites like a deadly snake:

> Every species of beast and bird, of reptile and sea creature, can be tamed and has been tamed by the human species, but no one can tame the tongue—a restless evil, full of deadly poison. (James 3:7-8)

That is strong language! Yet James is right: the tongue can spread poison or put the torch to everything around it.

Happily, the opposite is also true: the tongue can be a tremendous comfort and encouragement, a blessing to us and to others. Let's use it in a caring way.

5. Practice saying "I'm sorry." When death comes, it may be too late to say that. Peter asked whether seven times was enough forgiving, and Jesus told him to make it seventy times seven. Just keep saying you're sorry until confession and apology become second nature.

For some people, that is hard on the ego. In their own insecurity, they always need to be right. However, honest apologizing is one of the most liberating habits we can cultivate. We can tell our spouses and family members that we are sorry. We can tell our friends and co-workers. We can tell God. Make sure the slate is wiped clean.

6. Take care of practical details. One day Isaiah came to King Hezekiah with a message from the LORD: "Set your house in order, for you shall die" (Isa. 38:1).

While still in good health, we need to attend to practical details: living will, last will and testament, funeral arrangements, people and organizations to be notified, and so on. We talk about our "loved ones." What kind of love do we show them if we don't make such preparations? They wouldn't know what subscriptions to cancel or what insurance agencies to notify. They wouldn't know what bank to contact or where the car keys are. That would frustrate them!

If they really are your loved ones, then "set your house in order" and show that love.

7. Learn to die by degrees. When we are emotionally attached to objects and have to part with them, it is like a bit of dying. Some people cannot part with anything. An eighty-year-old grandmother still has her childhood doll. A man in his nineties still has his college textbooks even though space is limited.

In his booklet *Die Kunst des Sterbens* (The art of dying), Albert Mauder says, "Learning to die starts with tossing away and recycling, with getting rid of all that stuff." He suggests that "it is a good and spiritual exercise every five years to have a massive raid in your house to get rid of everything that you don't need anymore." Albert admits that this requires discipline and courage, but it is an excellent way to prepare for the final step, when we have to let go of everything.

8. Accept the unfinished and the unfulfilled. This may be a special project, a worthy cause, or caring for your children and grandchildren. The more we love them, the harder it will be to leave them when they are small or immature. Reinhold Niebuhr has addressed this question in a sympathetic and creative way:

> Nothing that is worth doing is completed in our lifetime;
>   therefore we must be saved by hope.
> Nothing which is true or beautiful or good makes
>   complete sense in any immediate context of history;
>   therefore we must be saved by faith.
> Nothing we do, however virtuous,
>   can be accomplished alone;
>   therefore we must be saved by love.
> No virtuous act is quite as virtuous from the standpoint
>   of our friends or foe as it is from our standpoint.
> Therefore we must be saved by the final form of love
>   which is forgiveness.
>
> (*The Irony of American History* [Scribner's, 1952], 63)

9. Be at peace and in harmony with yourself. This is one of the most basic and one of the deepest desires of all of us. Some people play games, pretending to be something they are not. This can be annoying to others and is a constant deterrent to our peace and spiritual growth. Paul Tournier says, "There is in the human heart a need for truth which one can indeed betray, but cannot get rid of."

This need for truth can make us afraid, but it can also make us free. Jesus said, "I am the way and the truth" (John

14:6). "You will know the truth, and the truth will make you free" (John 8:32). When at last we are honest with ourselves, we accept our age, our increasing infirmities, and our physical and spiritual limitations. We have made things right with people and with God. Then we can experience the inner peace that the world cannot give nor take away.

10. Be ready for the final surrender. We have finally reached the stage where we are ready to move on. President John Quincy Adams was walking along the street in Boston one day when a friend stopped him and asked how he was. He replied,

> John Quincy Adams is well, sir, quite well. But the house in which he lives at present is dilapidated. It is tottering upon the foundations. Time and the seasons have nearly destroyed it. Its roof is pretty well worn out, its walls are shattered, and it trembles with every wind. The old tenement is becoming almost uninhabitable, and I think John Quincy Adams will have to move out of it soon; but he himself is quite well, sir, quite well.

This is the blessed stage, when at last we let go of everything and find Everything! It is total surrender to God. I hope we have experienced such surrender earlier in life, in varying degrees, and more than once. When we are on the edge of the eternal, when we look back on our life and know it is like reading the last page of a book, and when we have the confidence that "underneath are the everlasting arms" (Deut. 33:27, NIV) carrying us safely to the other side—then all is well.

All is well!

I ask no more, Lord, than
> *Calm at sunset,*
> *Peace in the evening,*
> *And the assurance that all is well.*

50
When Death Comes

What is your life? For you are a mist that appears
for a little while and then vanishes.
—James 4:14

Death is certain for all of us. We all know it. Then why is
there so little open and honest discussion about it? The
subject of death is almost as closed as the topic of personal
finances.

Fear is certainly one of the reasons. It is not so much the
fear of death as fearing the process of dying. From stories or
the experiences of family and friends, we know how painful death can be, especially when it is a drawn-out affair. To
be ready, it is healthy and helpful if husband, wife, and
children, as they are capable, discuss death-and-dying matters. A close-call accident, a bout with cancer, major sur-
gery—such things make us aware of the need to talk.

We can begin with such practical matters as reviewing
and updating the will. We could read the living will. I want
to make sure that I will be kept alive as long as reasonably
possible, but that there be no "heroic measures." I do not
want intravenous feeding for months or years after it has
been firmly established that I am brain dead.

There are financial matters to handle, such as notifying
Medicare, Social Security or Social Insurance, other agencies, and periodicals. We could prepare a list of persons to
be informed when I die.

Such topics are not so sad and certainly not morbid or

threatening to talk about. They can open the door to discussion of deeper and more personal matters. For example, relationships may need to be cleared up. Perhaps there is some lingering bad feeling or resentment, something that happened a long time ago, created tension, and was not settled.

Tina Warkentin, longtime MCC worker and missionary, tells a moving story about her parents and how they confirmed their relationship in preparation for death. Tina had come home from Africa to visit her aging parents in a personal care home in Saskatchewan. They were both bedfast and in the same room but some distance apart. Communication between them was difficult because both were hard of hearing.

One day the father called Tina to his bed, then he sent her to her mother's bed to ask her whether there was anything between them. Tina carried the message and came back with her mother's word: "No, there is nothing between us. Everything has been cleared up."

After some silence the father told Tina, "Go back to your mother once more and ask whether it would be all right if I would die now." Tina went as told and returned with his wife's reply: "Yes, that would be all right; you may die now."

Another long silence. Then the father asked Tina to return a third time, this time with the message that his wife should not be sad when he was gone. She still had the children and grandchildren, and they all loved her dearly. Furthermore, it wouldn't be long before they would meet again in heaven. He died soon after that.

This delightful story was even richer because Tina relayed it in Plautdietsch (Low German), as the parents had spoken: "Nuscht tweschen onns? (nothing between us? High German: Nichts zwischen uns?)."

Elfrieda and I began using that phrase occasionally, such as when one of us is going on a long trip. Accidents happen so easily. We may or may not see each other again. So we say good-bye, we hug and kiss, and more likely than not, after a little silence, one or the other will whisper, "Nothing between us?" It's such a good feeling to know that things are cleared up, that we have an open and honest relationship, and that there is absolutely nothing between us.

The car accident I had two years ago reminded me of the uncertainty of life. I was driving along Route 30 in nearby Greensburg, keeping well within the speed limit. Suddenly there was a loud BANG. Then all my mental lights went out. I didn't know what had happened, and I don't know how long I was unconscious. I remember at last hearing dull and distant voices.

The people were not far away; they were inside my car, trying to get me out. That was not easy because our new Dodge was a total wreck. At last they managed to unbuckle me and slide a wide board under me. They lifted me up to the height of the seat backs and pushed me out through the broken back window.

In the ambulance, I tried so hard to think of what happened. I remembered the open road ahead of me and the three-lane highway with no traffic left or right. In great pain and in my feeble state of mind, I could only conclude that the engine had exploded. Hence, the loud bang. I did remember the bang.

In the hospital a young man, tall, smiling, and wearing white, bent over my stretcher and said, "Hi there! My name is Gabriel." I studied his face, looked at his white uniform, saw him smile at me again, and thought, *So I didn't make it after all.* On second thought, I wasn't sure because I saw electric lights on the ceiling, I heard voices and saw people, and there were other signs telling me that I was still on earth.

With all the courage and strength I could muster, I replied, "Oh, no, you're not! You're not Gabriel!"

Still smiling, he insisted, "But I am Gabriel. You see, my parents and my grandparents are all devout Catholics, and when I was born they named me Gabriel."

The police officer repeatedly told me that the accident had not been my fault; I could have done nothing to prevent it. A large truck had hit my car from behind and thrown it into the center guardrail. My car had spun off, turned around 180 degrees, and hit the guardrail again a hundred feet up the road. The loud bang I had heard probably came from the air bags and the car smashing against the guardrail.

While lying in the hospital in pain and with broken bones, it was wonderful to know that there was nothing between me and my spouse: Whatever happens next, one thing is taken care of: there's nothing between us. It's all cleared up. And I'm glad the other Gabriel has to wait a bit before he can welcome me.

When we have talked about death and dying in the family, or at least with our spouse, have taken care of practical details, and made sure that all human relationships have been cleared up, there is still one all-important matter: our relationship with God.

This is a private and personal matter, but the family or the church family can be of assistance. They come to visit. They pray for and with us. They are there in silence, just putting their arms around us. All of that can be most comforting and reassuring.

We can follow the counsel of James: "Are any among you sick? They should call for the elders of the church and have them pray over them, anointing them with oil in the name of the Lord" (5:14). This is not a last rite but a petition to the Lord over life and death, to spare the patient. We put ourselves in God's hands and trust in his mercy.

A Christian prepares for death by taking care of horizontal and vertical relationships and working through the fear of death. Then there is still one thing that can unsettle us and rob us of the peace we covet for this last step—the question of life after death. Make no mistake about it: belief in the resurrection is the crucial point of our whole faith system.

Many people have no problem accepting Jesus Christ as the Messiah, the anointed one, who delivers us from enemies, bad habits, and sin. They accept him as a great teacher, prophet, and even miracle worker. That is on this side of the grave. Where is the assurance that we will actually pass through "Jordan," land safely on "Canaan's side" *alive,* in what Paul calls our "spiritual body" of the resurrection? (1 Cor. 15:44).

There is no proof other than our faith in the risen Lord. Nobody has come back from the dead to tell us about life on the other side. This is a matter of faith, something we either believe or don't believe. Sometimes we believe, and then again we aren't so sure. Many Christians are sincere disciples of Jesus, good people, wonderful parents and models for their children, always engaged in doing good, always walking the second mile, forgiving and encouraging, reading the Bible and praying. Yet they still resonate with the man who called out, "I believe; help my unbelief!" (Mark 9:24).

In *Life After 50,* edited by Katie Funk Wiebe, Richard Gerbrandt writes an excellent essay, "Toward Death: The Journey We All Travel." However, there is one slip as he says, "The New Testament writers offer Christians a hope that is sure." There is no such thing as *sure hope;* that is an oxymoron, a contradiction of terms.

Paul writes to the Romans, "For this reason it depends on faith" (4:16). "Hoping against hope, [Abraham] believed that he would become 'the father of many nations'" (4:18). "Now hope that is seen is not hope. For who hopes for what is seen [or is sure]? But if we hope for what we do not see, we wait for it with patience" (8:24-25). Paul begins his letter to Titus by mentioning "the hope of eternal life"(1:2).

Michael Martin tells about the day his wife's grandfather Adam was dying and thirsty, and no drink was allowed. Adam said it was okay: "My Master is touching me this moment and giving me streams of living water, and my thirst is quenched; I have peace."

Michael meditates on this "beautiful moment." "Here are our lives—here is our faith, stripped to the bone and naked for all to see. All the theology, all of the tradition falls away like a dead man's flesh, and under it all, at the very bottom of everything, there is only this—that death has no sting" ("Education of a Dreamer," *Christian Living*, Sum. 1997).

Believing in the resurrection is crucial and central to our faith; it cannot be overemphasized. This leads to the expression a "leap of faith," by the Danish theologian Søren Kierkegaard. We either take that leap of faith or we don't. We do have a firm launching pad: First, we believe that Jesus was resurrected after his crucifixion. Second, we accept Jesus' word: "Those who believe in me, even though they die, will live, and everyone who lives and believes in me will never die" (John 11:25-26).

If we take the leap of faith, we are of all people the most blessed. Then we can sincerely sing, "Blessed assurance, Jesus is mine! Oh, what a foretaste of glory divine!" This becomes our message to a hopeless, sick, and dying world: "This is my story, this is my song, praising my Savior all the day long" (Crosby).

After handling practical matters, restoring relationships, and taking the leap of faith—we are ready to die. What happens after that is in God's hand.

Lord, we pray that when we reach the end of our pilgrimage, you will open the gates of heaven wide and receive us unto yourself. In your mercy, Lord, let the transition be swift and painless.

51

Victory Through Christ

Thanks be to God, who gives us the victory through our Lord Jesus Christ.
—Paul, in 1 Corinthians 15:57

Easter is the most joyous holiday on our calendar. Nature decorates the landscape with colorful flowers, birds sing, and women display their new dresses. The cynics say it is only an annual spring fashion show.

Churches have ringing bells and open doors. We hear the faithful sing, "Christ the Lord is ris'n today! Alleluia!" (Charles Wesley). From another church come words of assurance and victory: "Thine is the glory, risen, conquering Son! Endless is the victory thou o'er death hast won" (Edmond L. Budry).

Even children, who understand less than the adults, laugh and run for joy. It's special! It's Easter! Jesus was dead and now he is alive! We can't understand it, but we believe it. It's another mystery of life, so we celebrate.

We celebrate the victory God gives us through Christ and the Spirit. This is already a victory over sin. We proclaim that Christ was raised from the dead. Thus we "who belong to Christ" also anticipate victory over death. Believers "will be made alive in Christ" (Rom. 8; 1 Cor. 15).

I have sometimes wondered why I believe in the resurrection of the dead. Is it because others have taught me so? If that is the only reason, then that is not good enough. Is it because it is written in an ancient book? For some, that is enough, but for me, that isn't good enough. Is it because the belief is so widespread? That is not a good-enough reason for me to believe it.

Perhaps it is because of all of these together, plus something else inside of me. Something inside of me tells me that a wise and loving God wouldn't make a fabulous world, a marvelous universe, and absolutely fantastic creatures, like people, for no purpose. I am not quite sure why I believe that when I die I will be raised again to continue life in another sphere. Nevertheless, I do believe that with all my being.

Some years ago, I was on an administrative trip to Poland over Easter. My friends and I went to a large Catholic church. As we entered, we saw the life-sized papier-mâché Jesus lying in a coffin in the vestibule. Parents lifted up their children to see him. We also stopped for a brief moment. My Polish friends crossed themselves, and then we made our way into the overcrowded sanctuary.

At last, we found standing room in the balcony near the huge organ. We had a good view of the front of the church, where several priests were leading the worship.

After about half an hour, my friends wanted to leave. I was reluctant because the service was not over. Whispering, they explained that we would be coming back. Then I was even more sure we should not leave because we would never get back in; the people were standing wall-to-wall. My friends smiled and asked me to look down into the main sanctuary. I saw that many people were leaving.

Outside, I had more surprises. My friends had no intention of going home. Instead, they took me to the back of the church and asked me to keep looking. They were looking this way and that, around corners of several buildings, behind trees and bushes, even under the cars in the parking lot. I trailed them for about ten minutes of this strange activity until it dawned on me what we were doing.

I remembered that when we left the church and walked through the vestibule, the coffin was empty. Jesus was gone! We and all the other people milling around out there were looking for the risen Jesus.

Back in the church, the mood had changed. The lights were brighter, the priests were jubilant, the organ was louder, and the people began to sing the familiar resurrection hymns of the church universal. My friends looked at me and smiled. Then we all shook hands. Moments later, they laughed and we embraced.

That papier-mâché drama, a human invention, is no reason to believe in the resurrection—though I did think we ought to try that sometime in our church as an object lesson. It was, nevertheless, a fantastic and imaginative way of demonstrating a truth held for two centuries by millions of people: Jesus is alive! The Lord is risen! He is risen indeed!

No more we doubt Thee,
*   glorious Prince of life!*
Life is nought without Thee;
*   aid us in our strife.*
Make us more than conquerors,
*   through Thy deathless love.*
Bring us safe through Jordan
*   to Thy home above.*
        (Edmond Budry, "Thine Is the Glory")

52

Death Swallowed Up

When this perishable body puts on imperishability,
and this mortal body puts on immortality, then
the saying that is written will be fulfilled:
"Death has been swallowed up in victory."
—Paul, in 1 Corinthians 15:54

I have explored some thirty books on retirement and the final years of life. I often found the claim that we all fear old age and death. I question that claim. Many people do have such fears. Yet there are also many authentic accounts of people who lived to a ripe old age, enjoying earthly life and looking forward to resurrection life, of which we know practically nothing.

In *I Don't Know What Old Is,* Wirt says: "So much nonsense has been written on the subject of the hereafter that I wonder why I spend time refuting it, and yet something intelligent about Heaven does seem to be called for in a book on aging." Not surprisingly, his only source of "intelligent" information is the Bible.

Richard Gerbrandt says, "All that can be known about life after death is a revelation from God" (*Life After 50*). In other words, no one has been to the other side and come back to tell about it. So we are back to square one: Do we or do we not believe the Bible is true?

In the Old Testament are occasional hints of belief in resurrection, as in Isaiah 26:19: "Your dead shall live, their corpses shall rise." The otherwise rather pessimistic Teacher, who claims that "all is vanity," also says, "The dust returns to the earth as it was, and the breath [Spirit] returns to God who gave it" (Eccles. 12:7).

In preexilic writings, the dead are in a shadowy existence, in Sheol. On the whole, however, neither the resurrection nor the afterlife are clear in the Old Testament until Daniel 12:2: "Many of those who sleep in the dust of the earth shall awake, some to everlasting life, and some to shame and everlasting contempt." Some of the Jews, especially the Sadducees, did not believe in resurrection at all (Mark 12:18).

All this uncertainty changes when we turn to the New Testament. Here we have the words of Jesus: "For when they rise from the dead, they neither marry nor are given in marriage, but are like angels in heaven" (Mark 12:25). We also have witnesses attesting to Jesus' own resurrection after his crucifixion and death (John 20:19; Col. 1:18; and so on).

Paul wrote to the Thessalonians, "Since we believe that Jesus died and rose again, even so, through Jesus, God will bring with him those who have died" (1 Thess. 4:14). Salvation history can only be understood in the light of Jesus' birth, death, and resurrection. According to John, the resurrection of Jesus is the final proof that "God did not send the Son into the world to condemn the world, but in order that the world might be saved through him" (John 3:17).

That brings us to the dramatic meeting of Jesus and Martha outside the village of Bethany, the home of Mary, Martha, and their brother Lazarus (John 11). Martha says to Jesus, "Lord, if you had been here, my brother would not have died" (v. 21). That is both a compliment and an accusation. She is saying, "You could have saved his life, but you didn't." Jesus replies, "Your brother will rise again."

Martha believes that. She says, "I know that he will rise again in the resurrection of the last day." However, such a distant hope doesn't change the fact that now he is dead

and has been dead for four days. Then comes that enig-
matic statement of Jesus that must have been as hard for
Martha to understand as it is for us: "I am the resurrection and the life. Those who believe in me,
even though they die, will live, and everyone who
lives and believes in me will never die" (John 11:26).

What mind-boggling words! Belief in Jesus is the key to
life everlasting. But we know that when John used the word
believe, he didn't just mean head belief, intellectual assent;
he meant total surrender, trust, and obedience. He meant
belief that would be reflected in our lifestyle, our values,
and our language.

This is the key to understanding John. At the end of his
Gospel, he clearly stresses this key to explain how and why
he writes. *How* he writes is by selecting certain "signs" (mir-
acles) that point to Jesus as the Messiah; *why* he writes is to
evoke belief. Here again John says that believing in Jesus is
to have life:

> Now Jesus did many other signs in the presence of his dis-
> ciples, which are not written in this book. But these are
> written so that you may come to believe that Jesus is the
> Messiah, the Son of God, and that through believing you
> may have life in his name. (20:30-31)

Nothing can be clearer. First, Jesus says, "Believe in me,
and you will live. Always!" Second, he has died and been
raised to be seen by many witnesses. Third, Jesus assures believers that he is not deserting them; instead, he goes ahead
to prepare a place for them:

> Do not let your hearts be troubled. *Believe* in God, *believe*
> also in me. In my Father's house there are many dwelling
> places. If it were not so, would I have told you that I go to
> prepare a place for you? (John 14:1-2)

So Jesus turns to Martha and asks, "Do you believe this?" (John 11:26). Each of us faces this question. Do we really believe that Jesus was raised after he was dead? Do we believe that we, too, will rise again? When that key question is settled in our minds and reflected in our everyday activities, then the time may have come to talk about it with others, especially the children.

Easter is a good time to do that. I did it with a story I called "The Happy Raindrop" (abridged here):

It was a lovely day, and the raindrop had just formed. It had come together in an interesting and mysterious way. It floated along, chatting happily with other raindrops in the cloud. After some time it noticed that it was getting bigger, plumper, and heavier, and also a bit slippery on the edges. Soon it had trouble hanging onto the cloud.

"What is happening to me?" asked the raindrop.

"Why, you are getting ready to fall down to earth," explained her neighbor raindrop cheerfully. "Nothing to be afraid of. You'll enjoy it. Have a good splash!"

With that, the happy raindrop let go and started falling down. As it came closer to earth, it noticed houses and roads, fields and forests. It didn't want to fall on the road and be run over by a truck. Down it went, faster and faster. Then it saw a little boy on the lawn in front of his house. It so happened that the raindrop fell right on the nose of that boy. He laughed and called into the house, "Mom, it's starting to rain."

The raindrop bounced off the nose and splashed to earth. There it joined other raindrops gathering in a little stream that flowed into a river. Floating down the river was fun and exciting. There was so much to see: the boats and the shore, the bridges and the fish. On and on the raindrop drifted with the river. How long this journey was, it didn't know, but it seemed like a lifetime.

Finally, the river emptied into a lake. The raindrop began to float much slower and became tired. Some days it would just lie there on its back for hours, looking into the sky and wondering what was going to happen next.

Then one day the happy raindrop noticed that when the sun was shining on its tummy, warming it all over, it began to feel a bit strange, just the opposite from what it had felt in the cloud when it got heavier. Now it seemed to get lighter. It asked a neighbor drop what that meant.

"Don't you know?" replied the other drop kindly. "You're going to go back into a cloud. You came from up there, and you're going back there. Don't worry; you will hardly notice it. It will happen almost by itself."

That is exactly what happened to the happy raindrop. One day when it was feeling so tired, just lying there and letting the sun warm its tummy, it was slowly lifted up and taken all the way back into the cloud again.

If you tell this story to the children, they will soon catch on that the happy raindrop represents a person, and that you are talking about the cycle of life from birth to death, leading to resurrection. You may want to inject a conversation with a man who doesn't believe a word of it, who says we come from nowhere and go nowhere; out of darkness and back into darkness. Then quote or sing with the children those rousing words, "Lift your glad voices in triumph on high, for Jesus hath risen, and we shall not die" (Henry Ware Jr.).

Watch their faces and hear them shout that the doubting man is wrong. They believe that just as the happy raindrop returned to the cloud, so we will return to God. And why not? Do we not have a wise and loving God? Is anything impossible for God?

While we share with the children, we also minister to ourselves. A still small voice may be whispering, "Unless you change and become like children, you will never enter the kingdom of heaven" (Matt. 18:3).

O Lord, this mystery is too great for me. I only know that you who can make water fall out of the sky and then lift it back up can also take me up when my journey on earth is over.

53

The Trumpet Will Sound

Listen, I tell you a mystery. We will not all die,
but we will all be changed, in a moment, in
the twinkling of an eye, at the last trumpet.
For the trumpet will sound, and the dead
will be raised imperishable.
—Paul, in 1 Corinthians 15:51-52

We have all heard good and bad reading. Reading out loud to a large group is an art that has to be learned. Even ministers sometimes place the emphasis on the wrong word and thus distort or cloud the meaning of a passage. Look at the four words of this title. Where should the accent fall? Obviously, on the key word, but which word is that?

Is it *trumpet?* "The TRUMPET will sound." Why is the trumpet important? Could it not be a bugle? A drum? Even a shout?

Perhaps the word *sound* is where the emphasis should be. A child or youth might read, "The trumpet will SOUND." When you blow the trumpet, there has to be a sound, of course. Again we ask, Is that placing the accent on the right word? If not, then reading it that way obscures the meaning Paul intended.

What meaning does Paul urgently want to communicate to the reader? The chapter of 58 verses makes one point: "The trumpet **WILL** sound!" He wants to communicate that with certainty. He is not saying, "I hope" the trumpet will sound. He is not saying, "I think" it will sound or "maybe" it will sound. In that four-word statement is found all of Paul's theology and the meaning of life. He is saying, "Death is not the end!"

Death is only a transition, a passing from this life into the next. That's how it WILL be. You and I WILL rise from the grave. We WILL continue to live in another world. Life WILL go on. "The trumpet WILL sound!" The dead WILL be raised.

Paul knows that for many people, this is a difficult statement, a hard-to-believe doctrine. He has heard them express their doubts: "But someone will ask, 'How are the dead raised? With what kind of body do they come?'" (1 Cor. 15:35). Paul says that is a foolish question, but I think it's a good question.

Paul knows and we all know that this question cannot be answered. He doesn't know and we don't know. Still, Paul tries to express the impossible in the best way he can. In so doing, he makes an important point: we should not get hung up on details and miss the central truth. Paul tackles the question by citing three basic principles. Like a good teacher, he goes from the known to the unknown.

First, he takes the seed as an example (15:35-38). We sow a grain of wheat, and up comes a plant. The kernel is different from the stalk. Paul is showing that the seed is dissolved, and what has come up is different, but there is continuity. So it will also be with our mortal bodies: dissolution, difference, but continuity.

Second, Paul shows that if we just look around, we recognize that already here in this world, different creatures are created to live in different environments (15:39-41). Birds in the air, fish in water, and so on. Hence, God gave to each creature a body fit to live in a certain environment. So isn't it reasonable to expect that God will also give us a resurrection body, fit for living in the place where we are going after death?

Third, in the history of the human race, there has been change and significant development. With Adam (15:45), we all began as physical bodies, made from the dust of the earth (Gen. 2:7), then in death returning to dust (3:19). But God sent Jesus to redeem us.

With Adam was the old way of life; with Jesus is a new way of life. "So if anyone is in Christ, there is a new creation: everything old has passed away; see, everything has become new!" (2 Cor. 5:17). With this argument, Paul shows that we have a physical body to begin with, but one day we will have a body from the Spirit, "a spiritual body," and be with Christ (1 Cor. 15:44; 2 Cor. 5:5).

Paul is careful not to become specific, not yielding to the temptation of supplying details to satisfy curiosity. He lists these three basic principles and then returns again to the one fact that he is sure about: "The trumpet WILL sound!" "The dead WILL be raised!" "We WILL all be changed!"

O Lord, what a glorious promise! What a future! To be me but in a new body! I am ready, Lord. I am reaching out to you. I am not afraid—only make the transition fast. Please, Lord, let me get home before dark. Amen.

Appendix

Let Me Get Home Before Dark

J. Robertson McQuilkin

It's sundown, Lord.
The shadows of my life stretch back
Into the dimness of the years long spent.
I fear not death, for that grim foe betrays
himself at last, thrusting me forever into life:
Life with you, unsoiled and free.

But I do fear.
I fear the Dark Specter may come too soon—
or do I mean too late?
That I should end before I finish or finish, but not well.
That I should stain your honor, shame your name,
grieve your loving heart.
Few, they tell me, finish well. . . .
Lord, let me get home before dark.

The darkness of a spirit
grown mean and small,
fruit shriveled on the vine,
bitter to the taste of my companions,
burden to be borne by those brave few who love me still.
No, Lord. Let the fruit grow lush and sweet,
a joy to all who taste;
Spirit-sign of God at work,
stronger, fuller, brighter at the end.

Lord, let me get home before dark.
The darkness of tattered gifts,
rust-locked, half-spent or ill-spent;
A life that once was used of God now set aside.
Grief for glories gone or
Fretting for a task God never gave.
Mourning in the hollow chambers of memory,
Gazing on the faded banners of victories long gone.
Cannot I run well unto the end?
Lord, let me get home before dark.

The outer me decays—
I do not fret or ask reprieve.
The ebbing strength but weans me from
mother earth and grows me up for heaven.
I do not cling to shadows cast by immortality.
I do not patch the scaffold lent to build
the real, eternal me.
I do not clutch about me my cocoon,
vainly struggling to hold hostage
a free spirit pressing to be born.

But will I reach the gate
In lingering pain, body distorted, grotesque?
Or will it be a mind
wandering untethered among light fantasies or
grim terrors?
Of your grace, Father, I humbly ask . . .
Let me get home before dark.

(Used by permission of the author)

Bibliography

Arnold, Johann Chr. *I Tell You a Mystery*. Plough, 1996.

Baldwin, S. C. *When Death Means Life*. Multnomah Pubs., 1986.

Benson, Herbert. *Timeless Healing*. Simon & Schuster, 1997.

Berrigan, Daniel. *To Dwell in Peace*. Harper San F., 1987.

Bisset, T. *Good News About Prodigals*. Discovery House Pubs., 1997.

Boucher, Therese M. *Spiritual Grandparenting*. Crossroad, NY, 1991.

Carl, William C. *Graying Gracefully*. Westminster John Knox, 1997.

Carlin, Vivian F., and V. E. Greenberg. *Should Mom Live with Us?* Lexington Bks./Maxwell Macmillan Canada, 1992.

Carson, Lillian. *The Essential Grandparent*. Health Communications, 1996.

Chearney, Lee Ann. *Visits: Caring for an Aging Parent*. Three Rivers Pr., 1998.

Collins, Cary R. *Breathless*. Tyndale House Pubs., 1998.

Cooper, Kenneth H. *It's Better to Believe*. Thomas Nelson, 1995.

Deane, Barbara. *Caring for Your Aging Parents*. NavPress, 1989.

Detweiler, Lowell. *The Hammer Rings Hope*. Herald Pr., 2000.

DeYoung, Curtiss P. *Reconciliation*. Judson Pr., 1997.

Doherty, D. A., and M. C. McNamara. *Out of the Skin into the Soul: The Art of Aging*. LuraMedia, 1993.

Dunnan, Maxie. *Dancing at My Funeral*. Atlanta: Forum Hse., 1973.

Endicott, Irene M. *Grandparenting by Grace*. Broadman, 1998.

Fowler, Ruth. *As We Grow Old*. Judson Pr., 1998.

Fromm, Erich. *The Art of Loving*. HarperCollins, 1989.

Gerber, Samuel. *Learning to Die*. Herald Pr., 1984.

Gross, Leonard, trans., ed. *Prayer Book for Earnest Christians*. Trans. of *Die ernsthafte Christenpflicht*. Herald Pr., 1997.

Guroan, Vigen. *Life's Living Toward Dying*. Eerdmans, 1996.

Hein, Marvin. *Like a Shock of Wheat*. Herald Pr., 1981.

Horne, Jo. *A Survival Guide for Family Caregivers*. CompCare Pubs., 1991.

Jeffress, Robert J. *Say Goodbye to Regret*. Multnomah Pubs., 1998.

Kidder, Tracy. *Old Friends*. Houghton Mifflin Co., 1993.

Kilner, John F., et al., eds. *Dignity and Dying*. Eerdmans, 1996.

Lam, Gwen. *Meditations for Mondays*. Broadman, 1996.

Lin Utang. *The Importance of Living*. Wm. Morrow, 1998.

Macarthur, John F. *Forgiveness*. Crossway Bks., 1998.

Mace, David and Vera. *Letters to a Retired Couple*. Judson Pr., 1985.

McClafferty, Carla K. *Forgiving God*. Discovery House Pubs., 1995.

McQuilkin, J. Robertson. "Let Me Get Home Before Dark." Used by author's permission. In *A Promise Kept*. Tyndale House, 1998.

Meninger, William A. *The Process of Forgiveness*. Continuum, 1996.

Miller, James E. *The Caregiver's Book*. Augsburg Fortress, 1996.

Morgan, R. L. *No Wrinkles on the Soul*. Upper Room Bks., 1990.

Moser, Leslie E. *Older and Growing: Your Eternal Life Beginning Now*. Multi-Media Prodns., 1990.

Nouwen, Henri J. M. *Our Greatest Gift*. Harper San F., 1994.

_____. *The Return of the Prodigal Son*. Doubleday, 1992.

O'Shea, Donagh, et al. *I Remember Your Name in the Night*. 23d. Pubns., 1997.

Peck, M. Scott. *Further Along the Road Less Traveled*. 2d ed. Touchstone Bks, 1998.

Rushford, Patricia H. *Caring for Your Elderly Parents*. Fleming H. Revell, 1985.

Saussy, Carroll. *The Art of Growing Old*. Augsburg Fortress, 1998.

Sayler, Mary H. *First Days of Retirement*. Broadman, 1995.

Schlehofer, Jo. *Celebrate the Older You*. Ave Maria Pr., 1993.

Sheehy, Gail. *Passages*. Bantam Bks., 1984.

Sisk, Ginny. *This Too Shall Pass*. Broadman, 1992.

Smedes, Lewis B. *The Art of Forgiving*. Moorings, 1996.

Smith, Tilman R. *In Favor of Growing Older*. Herald Pr., 1981.

Sanders, J. Oswald. *Enjoying Your Best Years*. Discovery House Pubs., 1993.

Tengbom, Mildred. *Moving into a New Now*. Augsburg F., 1997.

Tournier, Paul *Learn to Grow Old*. Westminster John Knox, 1972.

Tolstoy, Leo. *Walk in the Light and Twenty-Three Tales*. Trans. Louise and Aylmer Maude. Plough, 1998.

Turner, Dale. *Grateful Living*. High Tide Pr., 1998.

Vaux, Kenneth and Sara. *Dying Well*. Abingdon, 1996.

Vogt, Robert L. *The Death of a Wife*. ACTA Pubns., 1996.

Waters, Brent. *Dying and Death*. Pilgrim Pr., 1996.

Weaver, Andrew J., ed. *Reflections on Aging and Spiritual Growth.* Abingdon, 1998.

Welliver, Dotsey. *Laughing Together.* Brethren Pr., 1986.

Wenger, J. C., trans., ed. "Two Kinds of Obedience." *Mennonite Quarterly Review* 21 (1947): 18-22.

Wiebe, Katie Funk, ed. *Life After 50.* Faith & Life Pr., 1993.

Wirt, Sherwood E. *I Don't Know What Old Is, but Old Is Older Than Me.* Thomas Nelson, 1992.

Zonnebelt-Smeenge, Susan J., et al. *Getting to the Other Side of Grief: Overcoming the Loss of a Spouse.* Baker Bks., 1998.

Finished reading
Sept. 3, 2001
Daniel Diener

The Author

Peter J. Dyck was born in Lysanderhöh, Am Trakt, Russia, and was a child there when revolution swept the country and forged the Soviet Union. At the age of twelve, he moved with his family to Canada.

Peter attended Rosthern (Sask.) Junior College and the University of Saskatchewan. He also studied at Goshen (Ind.) College, Bethel College (North Newton, Kan.), and Mennonite Biblical and Bethany Theological seminaries (Chicago).

While pastoring at Sudbury, Ontario, in 1941, Peter was called to Mennonite Central Committee (MCC) service in England. While there, he met Elfrieda Klassen, also a volunteer for MCC. They were married in 1944 and continued working together for MCC in England until the war ended.

In June 1945, they started the MCC relief program in the Netherlands, then helped Mennonite refugees in Germany migrate to South America. The Dycks itinerated extensively in North America to tell about MCC relief programs, the refugees, and their resettlement. Peter was ordained in 1947 to minister to the refugees.

Peter pastored and served with Elfrieda at the Eden Mennonite Church, Moundridge, Kansas, 1950-57; and Kingview Mennonite Church, Scottdale, Pennsylvania, 1983-85.

Most of their lives, however, Peter and Elfrieda have worked with MCC. The Dycks returned to Europe under MCC in 1957 and lived in Frankfurt for ten years. Peter was MCC director for Europe and North Africa. He was responsible for East-West relations and helped with the Bienenberg Bible School near Liestal, Switzerland.

Back in the United States, the Dycks lived at Akron, Pennsylvania, where Peter served MCC at the headquarters and through traveling and speaking. He made repeated visits to the Soviet Union, encouraging believers and building goodwill between East and West.

In 1950, Queen Juliana of the Netherlands knighted Peter. In 1974, he received an honorary doctorate from the University of Waterloo in Ontario.

Peter is the author of other Herald Press books: *A Leap of Faith;* and with Elfrieda, *Up from the Rubble,* telling about the epic rescue of thousands of war-ravaged Mennonite refugees. He has written several delightful storybooks especially for children: *The Great Shalom, Shalom at Last,* and *Storytime Jamboree.*

He is an avid reader and reviewer of books. For many years, he has contributed to *Mennonite Weekly Review, Gospel Herald, The Mennonite, Provident Book Finder,* and other periodicals. For a decade, he wrote a column called "Borders" for *Festival Quarterly.*

Peter J. Dyck is in active retirement in Scottdale, Pennsylvania—still in demand as an inspiring speaker and storyteller. The Dycks have two daughters and five grandchildren. They are members of the Kingview Mennonite Church.

When Peter and Elfrieda die, their bodies will be donated for medical studies and research. They explain that this will be the last service they can perform for others.